THE *souls of people, on their way to Earth-life, pass through a room full of lights; each takes a taper—often only a spark—to guide it in the dim country of this world. But some souls, by rare fortune, are detained longer—have time to grasp a handful of tapers, which they weave into a torch.*

These are the torch-bearers of humanity—its poets, seers and saints, who lead and lift the race out of darkness, toward the light. They are the law-givers and saviours, the light-bringers, way-showers and truth-tellers, and without them, humanity would lose its way in the dark.

—PLATO

VOICES OF SURVIVAL

IN THE NUCLEAR AGE

Conceived and Edited by
Dennis Paulson

Introduction by
Carl Sagan

Capra Press
SANTA BARBARA
1986

Acknowledgments: "To Preserve A World Graced by Life" by Carl Sagan, by permission of the author and his agent, Scott Meredith Literary Agency, Inc. Adaptation from "The Danger of Thermonuclear War" by Andrei Sakharov, by permission of the author and his representative, Efrem Yankelevich, who retains copyright. Adaptation from "A Psychologist Looks at Nuclear War" by Carl Rogers, by permission of the author. Adaptation from "Universal Compassion and Global Crises" by His Holiness the Dalai Lama, by permission of the author. Excerpt from *1984: Spring* by Arthur C. Clarke, copyright ©1984, by Serendib BV, by permission of Ballantine Books, a division of Random House, Inc., adapted for this audience by permission of the author. Adaptation of "On Accidental Nuclear War" by James E. Muller, by permission of the author, and *Newsweek*. Adaptation of "The Deterrence Myth" by Bernard Lown and James E. Muller, by permission of the authors and *The Boston Globe*. Excerpts from *Race to Oblivion* by Herbert F. York, by permission of the author and Clarion Books, a division of Simon & Schuster. Adaptation from "Beyond Psychic Numbing: A Call to Awareness" by Robert Jay Lifton, by permission of the author. Excerpts from *Facing the Threat of Nuclear Weapons* by Sidney D. Drell, by permission of the author and The University of Washington Press.

Cover design by Francine Rudesill.
Design and typography by Jim Cook.

LIBRARY OF CONGRESS CATALOGING IN PUBLICATION DATA:
Voices of survival in the nuclear age.
1. Nuclear warfare. I. Paulson, Dennis, 1941-
U263.V65 1986   355'.0217   86-9688
ISBN 0-88496-249-0 (pbk.)

Published by:
CAPRA PRESS,
Post Office Box 2068,
Santa Barbara, CA 93120 USA.

Dedication

...in general, to *all* of our world's children, who naively believe we adults are holding their future together, yet presently are given no voice whatsoever in their planned annihilation, despite the fact—yet unknown to them—they may not survive this terrifying century, poised as we all are atop the razor's edge between nuclear arms-control and nuclear holocaust.

...in particular, to my own beautiful children—Atisha, 11, and Mallika, 10—who inspired this entire project in July of 1982, atop Half Dome in California's vast, calm, measureless High Sierras, where Mallika, then 5½, stated the most profound hope in the nuclear age...with affection:

"It's nice you get a life before you die."

Contents

3. The Prognosis

4. The Solution

INTRODUCTION

W<small>HEN</small> we get to the point, as we one day will, that both sides know that in any outbreak of general hostilities, regardless of the element of surprise, destruction will be both reciprocal and complete, possibly we will have sense enough to meet at the conference table with the understanding that the era of armaments has ended, and the human race must conform its actions to this truth, or die. . . .

Some day, the demand for disarmament by hundreds of millions will, I hope, become so universal and so insistent, that no man, no men, can withstand it. We have to mobilize the hundreds of millions; we have to make them understand the choice is theirs. We have to make the young people see to it that they need not be the victims of the Third World War.

—PRES. DWIGHT D. EISENHOWER, 1956

Carl Sagan

THERE IS NO issue more important than the avoidance of nuclear war. Whatever your interests, passions or goals, they and you are threatened fundamentally by the prospect of nuclear war. We have achieved the capability for the certain destruction of our civilization, and perhaps of our species, as well. I find it incredible that any thinking person would not be concerned in the deepest way about this issue.

It's commonly said that we don't appreciate a thing until it's gone; that we generally lack the power to imagine the world without this or that characteristic. I speak to you in favor of life. By profession, I'm a planetary astronomer. My job is to examine other worlds. It's invigorating, exciting, even magical work for me. And in the last 20 years, the United States and the Soviet Union have accomplished something stunning and historic—the close-up examination of all those points of light, from Mercury to Saturn, that moved our ancestors to wonder and to science. Just think of what we are doing. We have sent a machine 1.8 billion miles to inspect the planet Uranus. We have four spacecraft that are leaving the solar system bound for the stars. We have landed on Mars. It is astonishing!

We have studied broiling, cratered Mercury; and Venus, a hellhole of

CARL SAGAN, *U.S. astronomer, is the most popular science writer in the world today. Professor of astronomy and space sciences, and director, Laboratory for Planetary Studies at the Center for Radiophysics and Space Research, Cornell University, his classic* Cosmos *(1980) is the best-selling science book ever published in the English language; the accompanying Peabody and Emmy Award-winning television series was seen in 60 countries.* Contact *(1986),* Comet *(with A. Druyan, 1985),* Broca's Brain *(1979) and* The Dragons of Eden *(1977, Pulitzer Prize) are among his other works.*

Deeply involved in spacecraft exploration of the planets and in the radio search for extraterrestrial intelligence, Sagan's awards include NASA Medals, 1972, 1977, 1981; Priestly Award, 1975; Seaborg Prize, 1981, and most recently, he co-received (for discovering nuclear winter) the Leo Szilard Award for Physics in the Public Interest, from the American Physical Society.

a planet that has a temperature greater than that in the hottest household oven, and an atmosphere that contains hydrochloric acid, hydrofluoric acid and sulfuric acid. The nearest planet is amazingly unpleasant. We have scrutinized the stunning rings of Saturn. We have looked at the moons of Jupiter and Saturn. Every one of these worlds is lovely and instructive. But, so far as we know, they are also desolate and lifeless. During the Viking mission to Mars, beginning in July, 1976, in a certain sense, I spent a year on that planet. I lovingly examined the boulders and sand dunes, the reddish sky, the ancient river valleys, the soaring volcanic eminences, the steppes in the polar terrain. But there was no life on that planet—not a blade of grass, not a mouse, or a beetle, or even, so far as we can tell, a microbe. For one reason or another, these worlds have apparently not been graced as our world has with life. Life is a comparative rarity. You can have 20 or 30 or 40 worlds, and on only one of them does life appear and sustain itself.

The Earth is an anomaly; in all the solar system, it is, so far as we know, the only inhabited planet. I look at the fossil record and I see that after flourishing for 180 million years, the dinosaurs were extinguished. Every last one. There are none left. No species is guaranteed its tenure on this planet. And we've been here for only about a million years, we, the first species that has devised the means for its self-destruction. We are rare and precious, because we are alive, because we can think. We are privileged to live, to influence and control our future. I believe we have an obligation to fight for that life, to struggle not just for ourselves, but for all these creatures who came before us and to whom we are beholden, and for all those who, if we are wise enough, will come after us. There is no cause more urgent, no dedication more fitting for us than to strive to eliminate the threat of nuclear war. No social convention, no political system, no economic hypothesis, no religious dogma is more important.

A WORLD WAR TWO EVERY SECOND

Every thinking person fears nuclear war. And every technological state plans for it. Everyone knows it's madness. And every nation has an excuse. There's a dreary chain of causality. The Germans were working on the bomb at the beginning of the Second World War. So the Americans had to make one. If the Americans had one, the Soviets had to have one. And then the British, the French, the Chinese, the Indians, the Pakistanis, and so on. By the end of this century, many more nations will have collected nuclear weapons. They're easy to devise. Fissionable material can be stolen from nuclear reactors. Nuclear weapons have become almost a home handicraft industry. And because of technological miniaturization, nuclear weapons also can be sent in diplomatic pouches. For all we know, right now there may be a dozen nuclear weapons in Washington—or Moscow—in embassy basements.

The conventional bombs of World War II were called blockbusters. Filled with 20 tons of TNT or so, they could destroy a city block. All the bombs dropped on all the cities in World War II amounted to some two million tons of TNT, two megatons. Coventry and Rotterdam, Dresden and Tokyo, all the death that rained from the skies between 1939 and 1945. . .a hundred-thousand blockbusters: two megatons. Now, two megatons is the energy released in the explosion of a single more or less humdrum thermonuclear weapon, one bomb with the destruction force of the entire Second World War. But there are tens of thousands of nuclear weapons. The strategic missile and bomber forces of the Soviet Union and the United States are—at this moment—aiming warheads at more than 15,000 designated targets. No place on the planet is safe. The energy contained in these weapons, genies of death patiently awaiting the rubbing of the lamps, is far more than 10,000 megatons—but with their destructive capability concentrated efficiently, not over six years, but over a few hours, a blockbuster for every family on the planet, a World War II every second, for the length of a lazy afternoon.

The yield—the explosion equivalent—of the Hiroshima bomb was only 13 kilotons, the equivalent of 13,000 tons of TNT. In a full nuclear exchange, in the paroxysm of thermonuclear war, the equivalent of a million Hiroshima bombs would be dropped all over the world. At the Hiroshima death rate of some hundred-thousand people killed per equivalent 13-kiloton weapon, this would be enough to kill a hundred billion people. But there are only 5 billion people on the planet. This disparity is given the conventional term 'over-kill,' which falls far short of conveying the horror implied by the steady hoarding of these instruments of death. In a full nuclear exchange, not everybody would be killed by the blast and the firestorm, the radiation and the fallout. The survivors would witness more subtle consequences of the war. Many possible, full nuclear exchanges would burn the nitrogen in the upper air, converting it to oxides of nitrogen which would, in turn, destroy a significant fraction of the ozone in the ozonosphere, which would then let in solar ultraviolet light, which would have as a minor consequence skin cancer for light-skinned people who are the ones who built the weapons in the first place, but as a more serious consequence, the destruction of large numbers of microbes in a vast ecological pyramid that we understand very poorly, but at the top of which we sit.

THE NUCLEAR WINTER

Ultraviolet light also destroys crops. The dust put up into the air in a full nuclear exchange would reflect sunlight and cool the Earth—no one yet knows by how much. Even a little cooling could have disastrous, agricultural consequences. Birds are more easily killed by radiation than insects. Plagues of insects, and consequent further agricultural disorders, are a likely consequence of nuclear war. And there's another kind of plague to worry about. The plague bacillus is endemic all over the Earth. At the moment, not many humans die of it, not so much because it's absent, but because our resistance is high and our sanitation is generally adequate. However, the radiation produced in a nuclear war, among its many other effects, debilitates the body's immunological systems, causing a deterioration in our ability to resist disease;

and sanitation services would be primitive, at best, in the post-holocaust environment. In the longer term, there would be mutations—new varieties of microbes and insects that might cause still further problems for any human survivors of a nuclear war, and perhaps, after a while, when there's been enough time for the recessive mutations to recombine and be expressed, new and horrifying varieties of humans. Most of these mutations, when expressed, would be lethal. A few would not. And then there would be other agonies: the loss of loved ones; the legions of the burned, the blind and the mutilated; disease; long-lived radioactive poisons in the air and the water; the threat of tumors and stillbirths and malformed children; the virtually complete absence of medical care; the hopeless sense of a civilization destroyed for nothing, and the knowledge that we could have prevented it and did not.

This is an unpleasant, but I do not think, an alarmist picture. It is, I believe, a conservative estimate of what would happen in and after a full-scale nuclear war, because the effects are synergistic and nonlinear, gathering force in unimagined combinations.

The dangers of nuclear war are, in a way, well-known. But in a way, they are not well-known, because of the psychological factor—psychiatrists call it denial—that makes us feel it's so horrible that we might as well not think about it. This element of denial is, I believe, one of the most serious problems we face. If everyone had a profound and immediate sense of the actual consequences of nuclear war, we would be much more willing to confront and challenge national leaders, of all nations, when they present narrow and self-serving arguments for the continuation of mutual, nuclear terror.

Denial is remarkably strong, and there are many cases in human history where, faced with the clearest signs of extreme danger, people refused to take simple corrective measures. To give one of many examples, there was, some 25 years ago, a tsunami, a so-called tidal wave, in the Pacific, which was approaching the coast of the Hawaiian Islands. The people who lived there were given many hours' warning to flee the lowlands and run to safety. But the idea of a great, crashing wave of water 30 feet high, surging inland, inundating and washing houses out to sea, was so unbelievable, so unpleasant, that many people simply ignored the warning and were killed. One schoolteacher thought the report to be so interesting that she gathered up her children and took them down to the water's edge to watch. I believe that one of the most important jobs that scientists have in this dialogue, this polylogue on the dangers of nuclear war, is to state very clearly what the dangers are.

THE SPECIAL U.S. OBLIGATION

Increases in the number of nuclear weapons by one nation have never deterred any other nation from stockpiling its own nuclear arsenal. Rather, the evidence is much more compelling that such proliferation leads to a substantial, indeed to an exponential, growth of nuclear weapons, worldwide. No nation is ever satisfied that it has enough weapons. And 'improvements' by the other side force us to 'improve' our weapons system. Now, if that's true, it has an interesting implication, because exponentials not only go up, they also go down. It suggests that a concerted effort to *increase* the nuclear weapons and delivery systems stockpiled by one nation will result in a corresponding increase by other nations. But likewise, a concerted effort by any one nuclear power to *decrease* its stockpile of nuclear weapons and delivery systems, might very well have, as a consequence, a decline in the nuclear weapons and delivery systems of other nations, and, at least up to a point, the process can be self-sustaining. I therefore raise the question whether there is some special obligation that the United States has, as the nation that first developed nuclear weapons and the nation that first used nuclear weapons on human populations, to decelerate the nuclear arms race. There is a wide range of possible options, including small and safe unilateral steps, to test the responses of other nations, and major bilateral and multilateral efforts, to negotiated, substantial, verifiable force reductions.

There are clear, economic disabilities in maintaining the warfare state. It's apparent that the enormous, economic growth of the German Federal Republic and Japan since the Second World War is due, in part, to the fact that they did not have to maintain major military establishments. In general, nations with smaller fractions of their budgets devoted to armaments and armies, exhibit greater industrial productivity and economic growth. Mutual arms reductions, done in such a way as to preserve deterrence against a nuclear attack, are in everybody's interest. Disarmament would be in the interest of the United States, where we obviously cannot simultaneously maintain humane, social programs, an enormous military establishment, and a balanced budget. (It is not even clear that we can maintain any two of the three.) It is at least equally in the interest of the Soviet Union, where grim, economic problems are looming. If the USSR were able to relieve some of the pressure for weapons developments, it would be able to put that money into consumer products, housing, better medical care, and other activities which would help its people. A comparable conclusion applies here. It's only a matter of getting started. Of course there's some risk. It takes courage. But as Einstein asked, in precisely this context, "What is the alternative?"

WHAT ABOUT THE RUSSIANS?

There are hawks and doves on both sides, although there is a tendency for the official propaganda of Nation A to tell us only about the hawks of Nation B, and vice versa. I would like to remind us that there are serious debates in both nations, whose outcomes are by no means certain. As early as 1981, there was an important meeting held in the United States near Washington, called the Airlie House Conference. Physicians from the USSR, the USA, and a number of other nations concluded that the greatest public health menace to the population of the Earth is nuclear war, and that physicians, therefore, have a special responsibility —connected with their Hippocratic oath—to prevent nuclear war. That conference made a set of stirring and, at the same time, very rational pleas for nuclear disarmament. However, concern was expressed that, if the conclusions of the meeting were widely disseminated in the United States, while no one in the Soviet Union heard about them, it would redound to the strategic advantage of the Soviet Union, being tantamount to an advocacy of unilateral, American nuclear disarmament.

I wonder how many of us heard about the Airlie House conclusions? There was, in fact, very little public attention given to that conference in the United States. But in the Soviet Union, the leader of the Soviet delegation, Eugene Chazov[1], personal physician to Russia's last four leaders, described in great detail the conclusions of that conference, in a television broadcast transmitted all over the Soviet Union. The conclusions were published in both *Pravda* and *Izvestia*. At least in this particular case, there was significantly wider exposure of the dangers of nuclear war in the USSR than in the United States. In June of 1982, some of these same physicians met at an international cardiology conference in Moscow. Six of them, three Americans and three Russians, held a televised discussion on the dangers of nuclear war that included a straightforward and impassioned denial, by Bernard Lown of Harvard[2], of the utility of shelters in a full nuclear exchange. For many years, the Soviets have advocated such shelters, and have built a number of them. This discussion was shown in prime time, more than once, on the principal television channel in the Soviet Union. In the first showing, the only alternative television offering was the also-rans in the Tchaikovsky piano competition. The Soviets claim that 200 million people in the country saw the broadcast. In the United States, all three commercial networks refused the program. It was shown, eventually, on the much smaller Public Broadcast System, at 11 P.M. So much for the argument that the Soviets are afraid to exhibit arguments on the perils of nuclear war.

AN EXTRATERRESTRIAL VIEW

I sometimes imagine an extraterrestrial being, cavorting through the universe, minding his, her, or its own business, and coming upon the Earth, examining it with no prior knowledge of what had happened here, and discovering, after finding out what the local units of currency are, that something approaching a trillion dollars or rubles a year is spent on preparations for war—that the global, nuclear and conventional arms budget of all nations approaches a trillion dollars per annum. I imagine that extraterrestrial trying to calculate what good could be done with a trillion dollars, how much misery and hunger and ignorance could be undone with that kind of investment. I don't think it's too much to say that such an investment, sustained over a substantial period of time, could solve a very large number of the problems that most people of the planet Earth confront in their everyday lives. That

---

[1,2] Eugene Chazov and Bernard Lown, both among this book's contributors, today are co-presidents of the organization spawned by the 1981 Airlie House Conference—the 150,000-member (in 38 nations) International Physicians for the Prevention of Nuclear War, recipient of the 1985 Nobel Peace Prize.

being would, of course, wonder why we don't do something about it, why we consent to or, even worse, ignore the peril we have placed ourselves in.

Such an extraterrestrial being might also note that a few nations, one of them being the United States, actually have organizations devoted to peace as well as to war. The United States has something called the Arms Control and Disarmament Agency. But its budget is less than one-hundred-thousandth of the budget for the Department of Defense. This is a numerical measure of the relative importance we place on finding ways to make war, and finding ways to make peace. Is it possible that the intelligence, compassion and even self-interest of the American people have been thoroughly exhausted in the pursuit of solutions to the threat of nuclear war? Or, is it more likely that so little attention is given to it, so little encouragement is provided to bright young people to consider this issue, that we have not even begun to find innovative and imaginative solutions? It seems to me that a substantial increase in the budget of this agency, and a creative rededication to its function of actually seeking disarmament and arms control, and breaking out altogether from the lockstep logic of the arms race, would be an excellent token of the devotion of this government to peace, and not to war. Comparable remarks apply, of course, to other nations.

A GLOBAL INVITATION

I invite you to study these issues. Your future, and the future of all who come after you, depends upon it. It is possible that you might achieve an important new insight into this problem. If you exercise denial, if you refuse to think about these issues because they're too difficult or too agonizing, or because you feel nothing can be done about them, then you yourself are making a contribution towards the nuclear holocaust we all wish to avoid. Through the courageous examination of these deep and painful questions, and through the political process, I am convinced we can make an important contribution towards preserving and enhancing the life that has graced our small world.

CHAPTER I

The Problem

Over all these years, the competition in the development of nuclear weaponry has proceeded steadily, relentlessly, without the faintest regard for all the warning voices. We have gone on piling weapon upon weapon, missile upon missile, new levels of destructiveness upon old ones.

We have done all this helplessly, almost involuntarily, like the victims of some sort of hypnotism, like men in a dream, like lemmings heading for the sea, like the children of Hamelin marching blithely along behind their Pied Piper.

—GEORGE KENNAN, *former U.S. Ambassador to Russia; Princeton Institute for Advanced Study emeritus professor*

Hugh M. Downs

"It is, rather, as though two people in a vat of gasoline up to their necks are arguing over who has the most matches."

UNTIL RECENTLY, I felt that because decision-makers in our country had access to more and better information than I have, they would probably do the right thing in the long haul, and that the seeming drift to Armageddon was something like feint on both sides, under control and shortly to be reversed by deeper levels of policy.

I no longer see it this way.

There may be no long haul. Examining the old theories of deterrence, and the views of those who favor ever stronger nuclear arsenals, I now find only wrong axioms and a rigidity of course so alarming it no longer matters whether a military expert has more information. It is no longer a military matter. (Many of the experts have acknowledged that thermonuclear weapons have no military value.) It is, rather, as though two people in a vat of gasoline up to their necks are arguing over who has the most matches.

Why are not more acting to save our world? Among the reasons, I believe, are:

    (a) A psychological barrier to acceptance of facts too horrible to cope with...a kind of denial that allows an indi-

HUGH M. DOWNS, *U.S. TV and radio broadcaster; host, ABC's "20/20," TV Magazine of the Air; former host, PBS series "Over Easy" (1977-80), and of NBC's "Today" program (1962-71); chairperson, National Space Institute, Washington, and of U.S. Committee for UNICEF, New York.*

vidual to retain sanity, to defer action, and to sleep. Unfortunately, as a survival trait, this is not appropriate to the unique threat now facing us. There isn't time for the techniques suitable to the pace of evolution.

(b) Too many people may still regard a thermonuclear bomb as simply a much more powerful bomb than a ton of TNT. By habit, they may still believe they'll be safe outside the blast zone.

(c) Many have trouble fighting off a feeling of impotence. The mystery that no sane person or nation wants this to happen, but all seem impelled toward it by an unexplained force, breeds despair.

I believe we are approaching a threshold of horror and general awareness that will kindle, first, a feeling that 'there is nothing to lose' on a personal level, by speaking out, shouting out... no political disadvantage, no personal ostracism that could weigh against the alternative of general destruction.

On a national level (and this will call for political pressure, in the sense of keeping leaders sensitive to the will of the people), I believe a policy change is possible. Two large nations, facing this unique confrontation, will survive it if one of them breaks the drift by a sort of 'judo' technique of stepping aside—refusing to up the ante, and taking the lead in backing away from the brink.

It will be the greater of the two nations that does this. By 'greater,' we must mean having more nerve and wisdom, for 'greater,' in terms of excess destructive strength, has no meaning. And since the U.S. is a democratic republic, with significant input from a better-informed electorate, it must be the nation to initiate such policy. I believe the United States to be the greater nation.

There is no guarantee we'll survive—and I don't think we will without the kind of activism now arising everywhere—but we are not doomed in the way we would be if the sun were scheduled to become a nova in a few years. We have it in our power to reverse our course.

Bernard Lown

"The fact that nuclear war has not yet happened is largely irrelevant, for it only has to happen once.... This brutal fact can be simply stated: If the superpowers continue in their present course, none of us will see the year 2000, a mere 13 years away."

Today, our world confronts a crisis of unprecedented magnitude and danger. The possibility of nuclear war haunts our age. And the nuclear threat grows inexorably, fueled by the accumulation of weapons and their growing sophistication. Sooner or late, the *bomb* must take command, while we humans become puppets to our own technologic monstrosity.

An issue of such cosmic dimension is difficult to examine steadily and objectively. It is natural and even healthy to get on with the chores of our individual lives, rather than to focus on the mortal danger. Additionally, many think the responsibility lies somehow 'outside' of their own profession. For example, many have argued that this is an issue outside of the province of physicians.

But does medical ethics stop with debates over abortion or how long to sustain life of the terminally ill? Does preventive medicine stop with declaiming the hazards of tobacco? Can we limit medical concerns to lead paint on our walls, asbestos in our insulation, or toxic chemicals in our dumps? Is our social involvement to be preoccupied with seat belts and ignore the most critical fact of our

Bernard Lown, *U.S. physician; co-president of the 150,000-member International Physicians for the Prevention of Nuclear War (recipient of the 1985 Nobel Peace Prize); professor of cardiology and director, Cardiovascular Research Lab, Harvard University School of Public Health.*

time? This brutal fact can be simply stated: If the superpowers continue in their present course, none of us will see the year 2000, a mere 13 years away.

I do not believe physicians—or those in any other profession, for that matter—can acquiesce to the continued stockpiling of weapons of mass extermination as guarantors of national security. The fact that nuclear war has not yet happened is largely irrelevant, for it only has to happen once. We must speak out against the search for peace through overt flirtation with the death of millions. The horror is obscured by its magnitude, by the sophisticated technology ever readied to accomplish the slaughter, and by the aseptic Orwellian language crafted to describe the attack—"delivery vehicles" produce an "exchange" in which the death of untold millions is called "collateral damage".

Presently, the world is moving inexorably toward the use of nuclear weapons. The atomic age and space flights demonstrate the awesome power of science and technology. These developments have also brought humankind to a bifurcation—one road of unlimited opportunity for improving the quality of life, the other of unmitigated misery, devastation and death. The road we follow will determine whether modern society has a future.

We need an unprecedented people's movement. But a substantial impediment to mobilization of our citizenry for their own survival is the deeply-implanted misperception about the Russians. "You can't trust the Russians" is a major reason accounting for widespread helplessness. We are now paying an inordinate price for these muddle-headed words. This misperception has crippled our capacity for crisp, analytic thought, and has stereotyped our adversary as the embodiment of all evil. P.M.S. Blacket, over 30 years ago, predicted such collective paranoia: "Once a nation bases its security on the absolute weapon, such as the atom bomb, it becomes psychologically necessary to believe in an absolute enemy."

Clearly, our society is afflicted with moral lassitude and resignation. The idea of pointing nuclear missiles at entire nations is without precedent in moral depravity. We think of nuclear war as war, but with magnified consequences. But 'nuclear war' is a term of deception. It is not war, but an act of mindless, suicidal genocide.

Just as the Challenger explosion, the Chernobyl disaster, and repeated failures of U.S. Titan and Delta rockets demonstrate the fallibility of modern technology, the Korean airliner tragedy underscored an aspect of the nuclear threat that the International Physicians for the Prevention of Nuclear War has been emphasizing from its very inception—we have unleashed a nuclear golem that will increasingly dominate human affairs. Until the advent of the atom, history was the expression of *human* activities; increasingly, however, *things* will determine events. While on Sept. 1, 1983, the finger inappropriately pressed a trigger, the next time, it may be pressing a button. Hiroshima provided a glimpse of some aspects of nuclear war. The 007 flight provides a view of how it is likely to start.

Thomas Mann counseled that we must behave as though the world was created for human beings. Optimism, although a subjective emotion, becomes an objective factor essential in unleashing the energy for shaping historic events. Ethical considerations compel optimism as a Kantian moral imperative. Nuclear war *can* be prevented. I am optimistic that an aroused citizenry *can* pull us away from the precipice. And many years hence, when reason and sanity have returned, the role physicians are now playing will be considered their greatest historic and social contribution.

Erich Honecker

"We consider it as the needs of the hour that all political and social forces who sincerely want peace act together, putting aside all that divides them, in order to save the peoples of the world from the catastrophe of nuclear war."

N EVER IN ALL the milleniums of human history has the very existence of humankind been so much threatened as it is today, in the face of the danger of a nuclear inferno. The nuclear menace has very much increased since influential quarters in the U.S. attempt to achieve military superiority over the Soviet Union and the other socialist countries. With the MX, Trident and Pershing 2 missiles, they started to build an entire system of nuclear first-strike weapons for that purpose. The Strategic Defense Initiative ('Star Wars') continues their plan.

It is quite certain that they will not gain the military advantage they are seeking, for the socialist countries will take the necessary countermeasures for their own protection, and the defense of peace. Still, the nuclear arms race is bound to enter into a new round. The huge stocks of those weapons of mass destruction, alone, signify a heightened risk of nuclear conflict.

It comes, in addition, that those who've been instigating the arms race have also expressed extremely dangerous military doctrines. Top Reagan Administration spokesmen have talked of a "decapitation" blow against the Soviet Union, and of "limited" and "winnable" nuclear wars. What will happen if some irresponsible people

ERICH HONEKCER, *General Secretary of the Central Committee of the Socialist Unity Party of Germany; Chairperson, Council of State of the German Democratic Republic.*

should one day try to translate their theories into practice? In the present circumstances, where both sides have the capability of mutual, nuclear destruction, a nuclear war, once started, could not be contained anymore. It would be the beginning of the end of humankind—the nuclear holocaust.

To save humanity from drifting into a nuclear catastrophe, it is essential to do everything to divert the East-West relations from confrontation, back to the road of normal and mutually-beneficial cooperation in the service of peace. There is no reasonable alternative to peaceful coexistence between nations having different social systems.

I am definitely optimistic about the future of humankind. Optimism is one of the main features of our ideology. Despite a good many problems and setbacks, the people's desire for peace will, in the end, prove to be stronger than those who endanger the world's continued existence with their irresponsible policies.

Pessimistic or fatalistic moods that the 'bomb' will overwhelm us one day can, at best, be useful to those who have included nuclear war in their plans. Such moods can only have a demobilizing effect on the peace movement. As already said, we do clearly see the danger to humankind resulting from the arms race. Therefore, we will not grow weary of warning against that danger and of doing our share to avert it. But we also see the great power of the world peace movement, which we feel to be part of, and we know about the strength of our friends and allies, and about their determination to preserve peace for humankind. All this is reason for us to be optimistic about the future.

What our country's citizens yearn for is a life in a secured peace, enabling everyone to go about her or his day's work without having to worry about the danger of nuclear annihilation. A great many members of the older generation experienced—themselves—World War II, with all its horrors. They saw enough of death and dying, and have learned how essential it is to fight for survival. And youths, from childhood, acquire an awareness that peace does not come as a present. With that in mind, they actively participate in shaping their own future.

We have created a socialist society in the German Democratic Republic which guarantees all its citizens social security, prosperity and happiness, and has peace as its supreme national-policy objective. All this is what the people in our country really desire. That is what they are working for, and that is what they are passionately committed to.

Above all, it is important to stop the arms race, to freeze nuclear weapons at the existing levels, and to agree on effective steps towards disarmament. The recognition is gaining momentum that in our era, more weapons do not at all mean more security. It is essential to make peace, with ever fewer weapons.

The conclusion of a treaty on the non-use of force between the two major military coalitions, as proposed by the Warsaw Treaty States in Prague in early 1983, would be a very significant step in that direction. It should relate to both nuclear and conventional weapons, and include commitments to the maintenance of peaceful relations among States. Initially concluded between the Warsaw Treaty Organization and NATO, it could later on be open to all States, and thus become the nucleus of a stable and peaceful world order.

It is well known that the socialist States have submitted a whole series of proposals for the safeguarding of peace, which could, in part, be realized without lengthy negotiations. Hence, the question is why the United States does not emulate the Soviet Union's solemn pledge not to be the first to use nuclear weapons. The will of both sides to achieve constructive agreements, on the basis of equality and equal security, is the decisive factor. With full justification, pressure is mounting in the international disarmament discussions that the United States of America finally give up its obstructionist policies and make a serious effort to settle the problems. With their stereotype rejection of all proposals of the socialist countries, or their delaying formula to 'consider' them, NATO politicians do, in no way, live up to the responsibility they bear for the life and security of the people in their countries.

One may certainly differ on many things. This is, in fact, inevitable in face of the different political and social systems that confront each other today. However, the overriding, common objective should be to safeguard and to strengthen peace. Therefore, we consider it as the needs of the hour that all political and social forces who sincerely want peace act together, putting aside all that divides them, in order to save the peoples of the world from the catastrophe of nuclear war.

George Bush

"We cannot afford a hasty approach that sends hopes soaring, only to end in dashed expectations."

VERIFIABLE AND BALANCED reductions in nuclear arms are indeed an important means of diminishing the threat that such weapons could be used. Precisely for that reason, the Administration is currently engaged in serious negotiations with the Soviet Union across the spectrum of military capabilities: strategic nuclear forces, intermediate-range forces, and conventional forces. In each of these negotiations, the United States has proposed dramatic reductions intended to achieve an equitable and verifiable, as well as militarily significant, outcome that would reduce the risk of war and contribute to international security and stability.

While remaining committed to negotiate in good faith and to consider all reasonable proposals on their merits, the United States must also maintain sufficient military strength to deter aggression and to assure the security of ourselves and our allies. The Administration is determined to seek significant reductions in all major weapon categories. It is persuaded, however, that unless we see to our own security needs, negotiations will be fruitless.

We also know all too well from past experience that negotiations with the Soviet Union must be carefully conducted. We cannot afford a hasty approach that sends hopes soaring, only to end in dashed expectations.

GEORGE BUSH, *Vice President of the United States.*

Lord Zuckerman

"There is no need to threaten to use nuclear force in order to defend our liberties. These would be destroyed more quickly by nuclear war than they ever would by ideological arguments between the West and the Communist bloc."

THE IMAGINATION OF the ordinary person, by which I mean most of us, seems to be incapable of grasping the nature of the disaster which would result from a nuclear exchange.

U.S. Secretary of Defense Caspar Weinberger must have been dismayed by the leak to the *New York Times* [1982] of a Pentagon document which ostensibly set out the Reagan Administration's "guidelines" of a five-year plan designed to prepare the United States for a "protracted and winnable nuclear war" with the Soviet Union. If he wasn't, he certainly had every reason to be, even though as the responsible civilian head of his Department, he had, at first, to admit publicly that he had endorsed the document.

But then came the retractions—alas, probably too late to undo the harm caused by the leak. In a speech delivered a few days after the piece appeared in the press, Weinberger admitted there is no justification for the idea that a nuclear war can be won, and also that it was unlikely such a war, if it occurred, could be protracted.

He is right, even though he is now reported as saying the United

LORD ZUCKERMAN, *British anatomist; fellow, University College, London; fellow commoner, Christ's College, Cambridge; professor of anatomy emeritus, East Anglia and Birmingham Universities; adviser, more than 20 years, to British government—chief scientific adviser to Secretary of State for Defence, 1960-66, and chief scientific adviser to the Government, 1964-71;* Nuclear Illusion and Reality *(1982) and* Scientists and War *(1966) are among his published works.*

States must have such a plan to counter a corresponding Soviet plan. Wars that could be won—in a protracted, nuclear exchange—belong to the genus of video-computer games such as Space Invaders, which children and adults with time to spare now play out on television screens. The strategic advisers in the U.S. Defense Department who produced the document appear to know little of real warfare and destruction, and less about the way human beings react to the idea of being involved in nuclear war, or about the fragile strands which hold civilized society together. They are certainly ignorant of the strength of the protest movement against any idea of nuclear war, which is now sweeping Europe.

Whoever leaked the Pentagon paper on the eve of the opening of the Second U.N. Special Session on Disarmament probably sensed what the worldwide reaction would be to what was declared to be in the official American mind. It was a disloyal act, but it was presumably intended, on the pattern of Daniel Ellsberg's disclosures about the Vietnam War, as a blow for the forces of reason.

Some days after the leak, Gen. David Jones, then Chairman of the Joint Chiefs of Staff, stepped down from his high office as the United States' chief professional military adviser. He used the occasion to condemn the policy document, voicing serious doubts as to whether any nuclear exchange, once started, could be prevented from escalating to all-out war. As a military man, he knows full well that as soon as one side fires a nuclear warhead, the initiative will pass to the other.

His judgment is now joined to that of a growing number of European and Soviet military chiefs, who have declared that the chances are overwhelmingly against the containment of any nuclear exchange; who accept the view that the one 'battlefield' on which an exchange of such weapons could be expected to occur—the European mainland—would be devastated, with millions of civilian deaths, and with West Germany the first to go. And all this in the opening rounds of an exchange.

The Germans know this; so do the British, and so do the Russians. Equally, every analysis that has been made shows that an all-out exchange of intercontinental weapons would utterly devastate the United States, and at least the western part of the Soviet Union, with scores of millions of deaths, and no hope of recovery. It took years for Europe to recover from the destruction caused by chemical bombs and artillery fire in World War II, when an unscathed America was there to help the process of recovery.

There would be no unscathed America to step in after a nuclear exchange. In denouncing the Pentagon's policy document, General Jones was also making clear what would, or should be the professional, military advice to the civilian authority of any country which, in order to achieve some political objective, had it in mind to undertake military operations against an opponent also armed with nuclear weapons...Don't.

Ideas of protracted nuclear wars, and of rapid recovery after nuclear exchange, are more than a hoax on the American public. They are a threat to all of us, insofar as our future might well depend on the influence of men who profess such beliefs. Their message is also a serious threat to the cohesion of NATO. If the European members really believed that the declarations of T.K. Jones*, and others who think like him, imply serious U.S. policy, they might well find it safer to seek security without the help of America's nuclear umbrella.

There is no need to threaten to use nuclear force in order to defend our liberties. These would be destroyed more quickly by nuclear war than they ever would by ideological arguments between the West and the Communist bloc. Above all, as Winston Churchill put it in his book, *My Early Years*, we must remember that no one should ever believe that "any war will be smooth and easy, or that anyone who embarks on that strange voyage can measure the tides and hurricanes he will encounter. The statesman who yields to war fever must realize that once the signal is given, he is no longer the maker of policy, but the slave of unforeseeable and uncontrollable events."

---

*Editor's Note: Since the Reagan Administration came to power, world leaders in *all* fields have been stunned by declarations such as the following, from top U.S. policy-makers:

T.K. JONES, as Deputy Undersecretary of Defense: "That dirt is the thing that protects you from the blast and radiation. . . . if there are enough shovels to go around, everybody's going to make it."

RICHARD PIPES, as Presidential Advisor: "The [nuclear] contest between the superpowers is increasingly turning into a qualitative race whose outcome can yield meaningful superiority."

EUGENE ROSTOW, as arms-control chief: "We are living in a prewar and not a postwar world."

GEORGE BUSH, Vice President: "If you believe there's no such thing as a nuclear winner, the argument [that nuclear superiority is meaningless] makes sense. I don't believe that."

RONALD REAGAN, President: "Could we survive a nuclear war? It would be a survival of some of your people and some of your facilities, but you could start over again."

Uncertain whether or not a saner manner of thinking *has*, in fact, overtaken Reagan policy-makers, the majority of America's top physicists, in 1986, took the unprecedented step of signing a massive, nationwide petition saying 'no' to Star Wars, calling the President's Strategic Defense Initiative "deeply misguided and dangerous". More than 6500 scientists and engineers, including 53% of those teaching in the nation's top 20 universities, have signed a pledge *not* to work on 'Star Wars'.

Many among these have expressed fears not only that SDI's militarization of scientific and technological research will hinder academic freedom, but also that it leads to the politicization of American science. Says *VOS* contributor Richard L. Garwin, a professor at Columbia and Cornell universities, as well as an adjunct research fellow at Harvard: "SDI is a disaster not only for security and for democracy, but for science as well."

Herbert F. York

"We seem to be heading for a state of affairs in which the determination of whether or not doomsday has arrived will be made either by an automatic device designed for the purpose, or by a preprogrammed President."

THE NUCLEAR THREAT involves two absurd situations. The first of these has been with us for some time. It lies in the fact that ever since World War II, the military power of the United States has been steadily increasing, while our national security has been rapidly and inexorably decreasing. The same thing is happening to the Soviet Union.

The second of these absurdities, for reasons of secrecy, is not yet so widely recognized as the first. It lies in the fact that in the United States, the power to decide whether or not doomsday has arrived is in the process of passing from statesmen and politicians to lower-level officers and technicians and, eventually, to machines. Presumably, the same thing is happening in the Soviet Union.

The first absurdity is the simple, direct, and probably inevitable result of the interaction of modern science and technology with the chronic, military confrontation between the two superpowers. The nuclear-arms race, then, is simply an especially dangerous manifestation of a deeper struggle.

HERBERT F. YORK, *U.S. professor of physics and director, Program on Science, Technology and Public Affairs, University of California at San Diego; U.S. Ambassador, Comprehensive Test Ban Negotiations, 1979-81; former chief scientist, Advanced Research Projects Agency, Department of Defense; former director, Defense Research and Engineering, Department of Defense; former director, Lawrence Livermore Laboratory, University of California;* The Advisers *(1976),* Arms Control *(1973), and* Race to Oblivion *(1970) are among his published works.*

Only concerted action by the two superpowers can completely do away with this first absurdity. The long series of closely interrelated actions and reaction, by each of them, has led to a situation of such complexity that only a similar series of interdigitated arms-control and disarmament steps can undo it.

But even if the basic causes of the arms race have been, and remain, beyond the reach of American statesmen and politicians, its rate and scale have been largely subject to our control. Over the last 40 years, we have repeatedly taken unilateral actions that have unnecessarily accelerated the race. These actions have led to the accumulation of unnecessarily large numbers of oversized weapons. In short, these actions have led to the present situation of gross overkill.

I do not mean to imply by anything I have written that the Soviets are blameless for accelerating the arms race. I have emphasized American actions partly because I shared responsibility for some of them, partly because I know the details involved in most of the rest and, hence, understand them far better than I do Russian actions, but most importantly because of a fact that many people sense, but do not quite grasp: in the large majority of cases, the initiative has been in our hands.

Our unilateral decisions have set the rate and scale for most of the individual steps in the strategic-arms race. In many cases, we started development before they did, and we easily established a large and long-lasting lead, in terms of deployed numbers and types. Examples include the A-bomb itself, intercontinental bombers, submarine-launched ballistic missiles, and MIRV [multiple, independently-targetable, reentry vehicles].

In other instances, the first development steps were taken by the two sides at about the same time, but immediately afterward, our program ran well ahead of theirs, both in the development of further types and applications, and in the deployment of large numbers. Such cases include the mighty H-bomb and, very probably, military space applications.

In some cases, to be sure, they started development work ahead of us, and arrived first at the stage where they were able to commence deployment. But we usually reacted so strongly that our deployments and capabilities soon ran far ahead of theirs and we, in effect, even here determined the final size of the operation. Such cases include the intercontinental ballistic missile and, though it is not strictly a military matter, manned space flight.

The second absurdity — the steady transfer of life-and-death authority from the high levels to low levels, and from human beings to machines—stems from two root causes. One of these is the development and deployment of weapons systems, designed in such a way as to require complex decisions to be made in extremely short times. The other is the sheer size and wide dispersal of our nuclear-weapons arsenal.

As we have seen, deployment of MIRV by both sides, coupled with advances in accuracy and reliability, will put a very high premium on the use of the frightful, launch-on-warning tactic, and may place an even higher premium on a preemptive-strike strategy. Under such circumstances, any fixed, land-based-missile system must be able to launch its missiles so soon after receipt of warning that high-level human authorities cannot be included in a decision-making process, without seriously degrading the system, unless perhaps such authorities have been properly preprogrammed to produce the "right" decision in the short time that might be available to them.

And an identical situation applies to any ABM [anti-ballistic missile, or "Star Wars"] system. After years of waiting, but only minutes of warning, it must repond at the precisely correct second. In order to have any chance of being effective, it must have a 'hair trigger'. Thus, we seem to be heading for a state of affairs in which the determination of whether or not doomsday has arrived will be made either by an automatic device designed for the purpose, or by a preprogrammed President who, whether he knows it or not, will be carrying out orders written years before by some operations analyst.

Such a situation must be called the ultimate absurdity. It would involve making the ultimate decision in an absurd manner, and it would almost surely be more dangerous and insidious than the situation that would result from the invention and deployment of what others have called the ultimate weapon.

The sheer size of the huge, nuclear-weapons arsenal, and its very great dispersal, is leading us in the same direction. The proper command and control of these weapons requires a correspondingly large and complex system, reaching down from the President, whose authorization to use nuclear weapons is required by law, to the many soldiers and technicians at lower levels who actually have physical custody of the weapons and the buttons that fire them.

All kinds of complicated technical and organizational schemes have been invented and introduced to inhibit any unauthorized use of a nuclear weapon. These include the so-called "permissive-action link" (PAL), the "two-key" type of control system, and the "fail-safe" technique employed by our SAC bombers. So far, these have worked, but no one can be certain they will continue to do so indefinitely.

Some of these controls, schemes, and devices are cumbersome and awkward, and they reduce the state of readiness of the various elements of the stockpile. A number of the schemes have been unpopular with the military services from the beginning, and the introduction of some of them has been resisted. Some people would like to eliminate the distinction between ordinary and nuclear weapons that now exists in most people's minds. If they succeed, even in part, can we expect these extraordinary control measures to continue in force?

Can we rely on the Soviets to invent and institute the same kind of controls? What will happen as advances in our weapons technology require them to put more and more emphasis on the readiness and the quick responsiveness of their weapons? How good are their computers at recognizing false alarms?

It cannot be emphasized too strongly that unfavorable answers to these questions about *their* capability mean diminished national security for *us*. Yet there is no way for us to assure favorable answers to them. The only way we can reestablish something like our former level of national security and safety is by eliminating the need to ask them. Strategic weapons must be designed so that no premium is put on a preemptive attack, and so that there is no need for the kind of 'hair trigger' epitomized in the launch-on-warning concept. Their numbers must not be so great, and their dispersal not so wide, that such long and complex chains of command are necessary. Weapons systems that do not fit these characteristics must be eliminated. The distinction between ordinary weapons and nuclear weapons must be reinforced, and not weakened.

What underlies these overreactions and technological excesses? The answer is very largely patriotic zeal, exaggerated prudence, and a sort of religious faith in technology. Malice, greed, and lust for power are not the main sources of our trouble. In a way, that's too bad; if evil men were the progenitors of these dangerous errors, we could expose them and root them out, and all would be well. But dealing with errors committed by sincere men acting in good faith is extremely difficult, if not impossible. And the guilty men and organizations are to be found at all levels of government, and in all levels of society.

These human failings are exaggerated by a widely held myth: that technical experts—generals, scientists, strategic analysts—have some special knowledge making it possible for them, and only them, to arrive at sound, political judgments about the arms race. This belief is held not only by much of the general public, but also by many of the experts themselves. And it is made all the more plausible by lavish use of secrecy, whenever the debates begin to get tough.

The net result of all this, over the years since World War II, has been the creation of a defense establishment and an arms industry that are very much bigger than they need to be. The people who inhabit this oversized, military-industrial complex, in turn, form the constituency supporting those elements of the Congress that automatically endorse any weapons development program. Thus, a vicious spiral has been created that gives the arms race a "mad momentum" of its own, and drives it forward blindly and faster than necessary, without regard for, and in spite of, the absurd situations that have been steadily arising from it.

We were all surprised by the sudden emergence of the Soviet Union as a first-rate, technological power; the reaction Sputnik engendered was nearly universal. But being surprised once ought to be enough; continued overreaction to a series of lesser surprises cannot be condoned. On the contrary, the public safety demands that they be stopped.

Elisabeth Kubler-Ross

'I truly believe that about five generations from now, we will have learned our lesson—maybe the hard way, maybe through some major, catastrophic events—and we will finally learn that we are all brothers and sisters, all people of all nations, of all colors and all creeds."

THE NUCLEAR THREAT is a disaster, and a reflection of the chaos and negativity in the present world. It is something that nobody wishes, but that all the large nations are preparing to use, a contradiction in itself.

It is a result of our ever-increasing greed, of our ever-increasing destructiveness...to have more and more and more of everything. In order to have more, we have to be more destructive with our resources, with our wildlife, with our animal life, with our mineral resources, and with our forests. If we want to be the domineering nation of the world, we have to interfere with disputes abroad and, therefore, get involved in wars like Vietnam and others. One negativity leads to another. Since there is a universal law that negativity only feeds on negativity, unless we stop our own negativity and stop comparing, there will be an incredible increase in death on our planet Earth.

I do not believe the average citizen has any inkling how to save our world. He's confused and torn apart, and with all the negativity

ELISABETH KUBLER-ROSS, *Swiss physician; founder, Shanti Nilaya Growth & Health Centers (worldwide);* Ladies Home Journal *"Woman of the Decade," 1979;* Working it Through *(1981),* Death: The Final Stages of Growth *(1975) and* On Death and Dying *(1969) are among her published works.*

over the news media in his neighborhood and, last but not least, in his own family, how can he save the world when he feels he can't even save a small group of people who are supposed to live lovingly together?

I truly believe that about five generations from now, we will have learned our lesson—maybe the hard way, maybe through some major, catastrophic events—and we will finally learn that we are all brothers and sisters, all people of all nations, of all colors and all creeds. When we again remember our origin—that we are, in the most literal sense, all children of God—we will learn unconditional love and raise our children with that kind of love, combined with firm, consistent discipline. Then, our world will truly be a paradise.

First, we have to learn to become honest again with ourselves ("Become ye as children.") and acknowledge our fears, because it's the fear in all of us that makes us defensive, aggressive and unloving. Fear is the only *real* enemy of man, and if each individual who reads these lines would get in touch with his or her own fears, he/she would contribute to world peace. It would become the phenomenon described in *The Hundredth Monkey**. And it's up to us—each individual—to make peace a reality by first and foremost making peace with ourselves.

*By Ken Keyes, Jr.; Vision Books, 790 Commercial Ave., OR 97420, USA.

William F. Buckley, Jr.

"The best work in the service of world peace is to ensure that the potential provokers —chiefly, the Soviet Union—are handled with firmness, and a clear and public determination to resist their machinations."

I VIEW THE NUCLEAR threat as an aspect, albeit a grave aspect, of the political threat of totalitarianism, which has, here and there, taken the lives of about one-hundred-million people, and blighted the lives of a billion more.

It should be evident to any honest observer that the free nations of the West will never initiate a world war, or a nuclear exchange, unprovoked. The best work in the service of world peace is to ensure that the potential provokers—chiefly, the Soviet Union—are handled with firmness, and a clear and public determination to resist their machinations.

WILLIAM F. BUCKLEY, JR., *U.S. editor and author; editor-in-chief,* National Review; *syndicated columnist; host of television series, "Firing Line";* High Jinx *(1986),* Henri Tod, *(1984),* Overdrive *(1983) and* Atlantic High *(1982) are among his published works.*

Aleksandr Braunstein

M Y VIEWS ABOUT the nuclear threat are the same as those held by the great majority of people in my country, by all mentally-sane and morally-sound citizens of all land on Earth—including the U.S. and the allied NATO countries—as opposed by a small minority of war-mongers (mainly in North America; also in the South African Republic) who either gain immense profits from arms production, or madly desire to dominate the whole globe.

In incessant, worldwide manifestations, millions of concerned citizens claim and publicize, ever more insistently, what can and must be done, namely:

1. Put a halt to the arms race.
2. Freeze the production of nuclear and chemical arms, and then destroy the existing, devastating weapons of all levels—from strategic, to medium-range and tactical.
3. Educate all those who are unaware of the deadly danger (or pretend to be unconcerned) and urge them to condemn and oppose every aspect of menacing activities of the imperialist "shakers and breakers of peace".

The Soviet Union lends support to all initiatives contributing to a lessening of the danger.

ALEKSANDR BRAUNSTEIN, *Soviet biochemist; laboratory director, Institute of Molecular Biology; member, U.S.S.R. Academy of Sciences; foreign associate, U.S. National Academy of Sciences; Lenin Prize, 1980; Hammer and Sickle Gold Medal; Hero of Socialist Labor.*

John W. Gofman

"A virtual obsession with nuclear weapons diverts attention from the real event: a force more brutal and tyrannical than Nazi Germany is conquering the world by nonnuclear means."

A VIRTUAL OBSESSION WITH nuclear weapons diverts attention from the real event: a force more brutal and tyrannical than Nazi Germany is conquering the world by nonnuclear means. And decent people are morally degraded into paralysis by a carefully cultivated terror of "the nuclear threat". Whether naively or cynically, disarmament leaders deliberately use terror on a far bigger scale than the PLO, Kaddafi, etc.

Teach the truth stated 40 years ago by Winston Churchill: "Disarmament is never the route to peace." When peace is achieved, disarmament will follow. The human problem, as any survivor of the Khmer Rouge, Auschwitz, or the Gulag will attest, is bully-removal...not hardware-removal. Big-time bullies use small-time bullies to expand the realm of tyranny. Either we must commit ourselves to the Brother's Keeper rule, or watch bullies nibble up the whole world until we are told to serve up Hawaii, Maine, and Florida as the next payment on our own survival.

I'm confident that nuclear holocaust is very unlikely. But the odds do favor installation of a permanent "universal gulag," even though that is *not* the necessary alternative to nuclear holocaust. The permanent extinction of human rights on this planet is the necessary

JOHN W. GOFMAN, *U.S. physicist; professor of medical physics emeritus, University of California at Berkeley; co-discoverer, Uranium-232 and -233; Manhattan Project plutonium chemist; founder, Biomedical Research Division, University of California Lawrence Livermore Laboratory;* Radiation and Human Health *(1981) is among his published works.*

consequence of something *else:* pacifism, masquerading as the moral high ground.

Good people have been activated in exactly the wrong direction by falsehoods, especially about mindless, accidental holocaust. Faster, more accurate nuclear-delivery systems do *not* necessitate hair-trigger, launch-on-warning systems on either side; they only necessitate making a retaliatory force mobile or hidden—for potential use without haste—days or weeks later. Accurate missiles cannot threaten retaliatory weapons which they cannot locate. The Soviets mobilized and hid their ICBMs years ago. When the U.S. takes this safety step, too—over opposition from 'peace' movements—the awful, hair-trigger prospect will vanish.

In the nuclear-disarmament movements, I see no moral high ground, or any agitiation to save the millions of Cambodian, Afghan, Ugandan, Chinese, and Soviet 'citizens' who were slaughtered since 1945. I see simply Americans and West Europeans displaying their natural *survival* wish, plus manipulation of this wish by those who present the false choice: nuclear holocaust (suicide) or pacifism (surrender).

Philip W. Anderson

*"If everyone were busy
'cultivating his own garden'
as Voltaire suggested, we
would have no problem of
nuclear war, at all."*

A VERY GREAT many people are much more psychologically disturbed by the threat of nuclear war than they admit even to themselves. The result is a lot of what the psychiatrists call "inappropriate responses". Two of these that are very common are, first, the feeling that if one can only identify an enemy, one can transfer the threat to that enemy, and everything would be all right if that enemy were only defeated.

I feel this is behind much of the irrational, anticommunist hysteria, and behind much of the polarization of the people of the two superpowers. Many Americans feel that somehow, if we could just defeat the Russians everywhere in the world, we would be all right (and vice versa, for the Russians). Unfortunately, it is clear that the threat would still be there. The second inappropriate response seems to be dogmatic acceptance of one belief system or another; for instance, Marxism-Leninism, or fundamentalist religion of one kind or another.

If everyone were appropriately busy "cultivating his own garden" as Voltaire suggested, we would have no problem of nuclear war, at

PHILIP W. ANDERSON, *U.S. physicist; 1977 Nobel Prize in Physics; consulting director, AT&T Bell Laboratories; professor of physics, Princeton University; National Medal of Science, 1982;* Basic Notions of Condensed Matter Physics *(1984)*, Concepts in Solids *(1963) and research papers on nuclear physics and quantum chemistry are among his published works.*

all. The Shiite Moslems of Iran, the right-wing death squads of El Salvador, and the KGB all undoubtedly believe they are acting to 'save the world' as they see it, by enforcing their fanaticisms on the rest of us. I am afraid our American point of view can be equally dogmatic; for instance, in equating socialism with sin, and atheism with evil.

Today, however, we can't afford the luxury of another world war, and must learn to find mechanisms for change and accommodation which do not involve great-power conflicts.

Viktor G. Afanasyev

A POLITICIAN IN A position in Washington once said that there are things more important than peace. This is a cynical statement. I share the view of millions of my fellow countrymen, and hundreds of millions of other people throughout the world, that nothing can be more important than peace. The issue at stake is whether your children and my children, and our grandchildren, will live, and whether our fellow countrymen and all people living on our wonderful planet will stay alive.

I am not Albert Einstein, I have not won the Nobel Prize, and I have not made any great discoveries. I am a philosopher, a member of the USSR Academy of Sciences, and editor-in-chief of the newspaper *Pravda*. This, however, does not prevent my having two grown children and three grandchildren—two boys and a little girl; she is just five years old. Her name is Polya, which sounds very much like the Russian word *pole* (that means 'field' in English) and brings to mind the vast expanses of Russian fields.

Between 1946—the first year after the war that claimed 20 million Soviet lives—and November, 1981, the Soviet Union advanced 131 peace proposals. In recent years, the late General Secretaries of the Central Committee of the Soviet Community Party, L.I. Breshnev and Y.V. Andropov, advanced a new series of proposals, whose implementation could have lowered the nuclear-war danger by many orders of magnitude. General Secretary Mikhail Gorbachev has continued to do the same, going so far as to initiate a unilateral, one-year nuclear-test moratorium, in hopes of negotiating a nuclear test-ban agreement with the U.S. The Reagan Administration, however, not only ignored his proposal, but decided to abandon U.S. adherence to the 1979 SALT II treaty, as well.

Look at the facts. The Soviet Union assumed a solemn pledge never to be the first to use nuclear weapons. And in the face of innumerable threats to our country, and thousands upon thousands of nuclear warheads trained on Soviet territory—even sited at different points near Soviet frontiers—that pledge and commitment to peace are truly unprecedented. If the other nuclear powers assumed a similar pledge, nuclear war would be ruled out.

VIKTOR G. AFANASYEV, *Soviet philosopher; editor-in-chief of* Pravda; *a leading member of the Communist Party of the Soviet Union's Central Committee; member, USSR Academy of Sciences.*

In December, 1982, when the Soviet people celebrated the 60th anniversary of the formation of the USSR, the Supreme Soviet and the Central Committee adopted an appeal to parliaments, governments, political parties, and peoples of the world. The plenipotentiary representatives of our people solemnly declared that the Soviet Union will make every effort, and do everything within its power, to prevent war. In their appeal, they reaffirmed the Soviet Union's pledge never to be the first to use nuclear weapons; the proposal for freezing the Soviet and US nuclear-weapons arsenals, on a reciprocal basis; the proposal for reaching an agreement on the complete and universal banning of nuclear-weapons tests, and other proposals for preserving and strengthening peace. That appeal aroused great interest among the international public.

Likewise, the other countries of the Socialist community are engaged, together with the Soviet Union, in an active struggle for peace. At a conference several years ago, the Political Consultative Committee of the Warsaw Treaty countries proposed that a treaty be concluded between the Warsaw Treaty countries and the NATO nations, whereby the two sides would undertake not to use force against each other, to maintain relations of peace, and further, that the treaty be open to all other nations. Neither the United States, nor NATO, responded positively, but instead speeded the installation of new weapons for war, Europe being the prime target.

Negotiations are a complicated, long, and responsible process. Is there any reason why the present nuclear weaponry should not be frozen, to facilitate talks? Is there any reason why the testing and deployment of new weapons should not be stopped, as the Soviet Union has proposed? This sober-minded approach has been supported by many U.S. Senators and Congressmembers. And support for this approach is not confined to them alone; demonstrations by millions of American peace supporters confirm this most vividly. The signs are, however, that the White House is not inclined to take into account the opinion of the American people.

I would like to hope that American politicians have enough political vision to abandon "zero option" thinking, which provides for unilateral disarmament of the Soviet Union, and is therefore unacceptable for us. History may never forgive the White House for continually missing these chances to reach agreement.

The human race wants to live on. And it must, to leave a place—to live in—for its children and the coming generations. The peoples are joining the struggle for peace. And I believe their voice will be the decisive factor, in the final analysis. But it all depends on their unity, their commitment to their purpose, and concerted action. There will never be a war, if we all—political leaders and ordinary working people, alike—everywhere pull together as a team.

Phyllis Diller

"If all nations which have nukes pop them off and destroy all Earthbound humankind, it's a good thing they're including women in outer spacecraft, because when that rocket gets back, they will have to start over and give credence to that Adam and Eve story."

I VIEW THE NUCLEAR threat as real, mainly because of possible madness in a suicidal leader, or a computer accident. Suppose one person with a hot button is dying of terminal cancer and decides to take us all with him! It could happen.

If all nations which have nukes pop them off and destroy all Earthbound humankind, it's a good thing they're including women in outer spacecraft, because when that rocket gets back, they will have to start over and give credence to that Adam and Eve story.

As long as Russia, with its totalitarian philosophy, makes no bones about wanting to enslave the entire world, I feel it is madness to disarm. If we were helpless, I truly believe they would be here tomorrow. In Russia, the guys who run the country live in luxury. Everybody else is monitored, spied on and poor. It is a wretched life, with no way out.

We destest that idea. In the United States, most people live a free-to-do-what-you-will-providing-you-don't-hurt-anybody-else system. Most of our population live happy lives. They are free to come and go as they please. They can leave the country if they like. When you live in Russia, you don't go anywhere.

Humankind has always wrestled with current problems. The possibility of nuclear warfare is one of our current problems. A quote from Gertrude Stein fits today as it fits all times, from the very beginning: "The answer is there is no answer."

PHYLLIS DILLER, *U.S. comic, actress.*

Christopher Cross

"I'm a father, and so I want so much to be optimistic about our future; but sometimes, it seems hopeless."

"You put your gun down; then I'll put mine down." That's part of the problem. Sometimes I think the powers, and sometimes even the people, feel that way . . . just no human trust. And the stupid part is that *we* can begin to reduce arms, and certainly stop production. I mean, how dead can you kill someone? Total destruction is fine, thank you.

America can't control the whole world, although some of our leaders think so. But we can easily start the ball rolling at home, to show good faith, without one ounce of threat to our 'national security'. "We the people remember "WE" are the masters of this part of our destiny.

As the powers of the world, large and small, struggle for power—which, sadly enough, seems to be the human condition we have grown to—the least we all can do, to give ourselves a chance for a future, is to remove nuclear weapons as a means to the end . . . and I do mean The End.

I'm a father, and so I want so much to be optimistic about our future; but sometimes, it seems hopeless. Still, there are people like you, showing people like me and lots of others, how to show we care. So though our real chances may, in fact, be small, I'll take the odds, and hope we all work together . . . before it's too late.

CHRISTOPHER CROSS, *U.S. singer, songwriter;* Every Turn of the World, Christopher Cross *and* Another Page *are among his albums.*

Zhores Medvedev

"When people in nations everywhere realize that the deterioration of their living standards is directly related to this arms race ... then it will be possible to start the positive trends."

T HE THREAT OF nuclear war is apparently increasing these last few years, mostly because of the appearance of the new genereations of nuclear weapons, along with sharply (and often artificially) increased tension between the Soviet Union and United States. But if we consider the number of 'real' nuclear alerts, or crises, during which the possibility of real use of nuclear stikes was under consideration, one can see most such alerts occurred before 1963 (the Cuban crisis being among the most serious).

The last was in 1973, during the Arab-Israeli War. There've been no nuclear alerts since then, which means that the practical use of nuclear weapons was considered feasible until 1973, and there was the will to use them, if necessary. So during the last decade or so, the enormous growth of nuclear arsenals has not been related to any *real* crisis. Rather, the growth of nuclear arsenals, the deployment of new nuclear systems in many new countries, and the creation of still more new systems, has, in itself, become a permanent source of international crisis.

ZHORES MEDVEDEV, *Soviet (now stateless) geneticist at National Institute for Medical Research, London, since deprived of Soviet citizenship in 1973;* Andropov *(1983),* The Nuclear Disaster in the Urals *(1979),* Khrushchev: The Years in Power *(with Roy Medvedev, 1971) and* Protein Biosynthesis and Problems of Heredity, Development and Ageing *(1963) are among his published works.*

Before 1973, nuclear arms were military weapons. Now, nuclear weapons have been transformed into political weapons, and have become an integral part of economic systems (more so in the West than in the USSR, because in the West, the 'nuclear economy' is mostly in private hands and connected with profit-making, employment problems, political lobbies, etc.; all these factors are much less important in the Soviet Union). So it's become necessary to *create* conflict situations, artificially, in order to justify the enormous arms race. Therefore, if before 1973 the conflicts were periodical, they've now become a permanent condition of superpower relations. And the nuclear threat has become an institutional part of our lives.

Movements against nuclear weapons and nuclear war are certainly growing. However, political factors are not yet strong enough to reduce the level of superpower confrontation, so antinuclear campaigns, alone, can hardly force governments to reverse the arms-race momentum. What *is* necessary is to reduce the level of hostility between different political systems.

In the Soviet Union, commercial interests are certainly less influential in maintaining this high level of confrontation. However, the political interests of the ruling elite make it necessary for them to restrict civil-rights freedoms, the free exchange of information, and the freedom to travel abroad, all of which contribute to the government's ability to create a 'confrontation psychology' and 'siege mentality'. It's the same in China, as well.

Nevertheless, the most educated people now recognize that cooperation between world powers, not confrontation, offers a better chance for prosperity and survival. But the prosperity of nations, and the prosperity and privileges of ruling elites, are not yet complementary everywhere. (Prosperity, as I understand it, includes not only material benefits, but political, cultural and intellectual freedoms, as well.)

Like any living species, human beings have strong instincts for survival. And one reason the arms race is so successful is because arms makers misuse this survival instinct for their own ends. Nevertheless, I am optimistic, although I think it will get worse before it gets better.

I think that not only political, but mostly economic factors make it necessary to try to reduce this arms race, and to cooperate for more economic use of our world's limited resources. For when people in nations everywhere realize that the deterioration of their living standards is *directly* related to this arms race, and when political leaders discover that internal instability could better be controlled by *cooperation*, rather than confrontation, then it will be possible to start the positive trends.

The majority of populations, even in industrialized countries, are politically illiterate, and can easily be manipulated into one extreme or another. In the West, most mass-media information sources are based on commercial interests, and thus work to preserve this political illiteracy. In the Soviet Union and China, mass-media sources are not commercially oriented, but are under severe censorship, and thus reflect the interest of only one political doctrine. So they support not so much political illiteracy, but political dogmatism.

The main task of activists in peace movements in the West is to work to reduce this level of political illiteracy. In the communist countries, it is to reduce political dogmatism and intolerance. This will gradually reduce the level of psychological confrontation, and diminish the ability of ruling groups to manipulate public opinions. Military actions are almost impossible without psychological hostility. And all major wars have been first prepared in the minds of nations, before being started on battlefields. Thus, peace movements should not concentrate all their energy in demonstrations, but should make much stronger efforts in explanations/education at the national and international levels.

Jan Tinbergen

"I am not optimistic, but pessimism is counter-productive, so I continue to think about how we could, perhaps, escape a holocaust."

I AM NOT OPTIMISITC, but pessimism is counterproductive, so I continue to think about how we could, perhaps, escape a holocaust.

The policies followed so far have been polarizing, and have caught us in a disastrous spiral of ever-increasing armament on both sides. We must change this policy at once, and *not* continue it because we want to negotiate "from a position of strength".

The new policy must be one of cooperation on matters of common interest: the maintenance of a clean environment, research on energy and agricultural productivity, a major common interest in security, etc.

The tendency to polarize opinions and policies on the social order should also be replaced by a scientific discussion of the best social order, characterized by the willingness to learn from each other—already recommended by Karl Marx—and to adopt from other countries their positive elements, while avoiding the negative ones.

For example, the Soviet order is not completely socialist, since there is a private sector. And the American order is not completely capitalist, since there is a system of social insurance. The real ques-

JAN TINBERGEN, *Dutch economist; 1969 Nobel Prize in Economics; professor of development planning emeritus, Rotterdam and Leiden Universities;* Income Distribution *(1975)*, Development Planning *(1968)*, Shaping the World Economy *(1962)*, *and* On the Theory of Economic Policy *(1952) are among his published works.*

tion is: which mix of socialist and capitalist elements is best? The answer need not be the same for all countries. We can learn, for instance, from both Japan and Hungary.

While the search for an optimal order continues, armaments should be reduced, more or less equally. Alva Myrdal [1982 Nobel Peace laureate] is quite right that "equilibrium" is not very important, as long as the overkill capacity exists. So reductions to one-half the present level of armament can be undertaken, even unilaterally.

Sir Neville Mott

"I think that as the stockpiles increase, the chance of a catastrophe decreases—the catastrophe, if it came, becomes worse, but even the hawks who want to 'prevail' know there would be pretty little left of the U.S. or U.S.S.R. after a nuclear exchange."

OF COURSE THE possibility of nuclear annihilation exists, and an all-out war would be an unbelievable catastrophe. The 'probability' of such an event is impossible to assess, in any scientific sense. All the propaganda about it does little but induce despair, and a kind of defeatism...not the cool thought about what ought to be done to minimise the risk. I think, in fact, that as the stockpiles increase, the chance of a catastrophe decreases—the catastrophe, if it came, becomes worse, but even the hawks who want to "prevail" know there would be pretty little left of the US or USSR after a nuclear exchange.

I think, too, there is too much fear of the 'nth country problem'. Suppose two hostile countries in the Middle East each had a few bombs and used them. This would certainly be horrible, but it seems incredibly unlikely it would lead to a worldwide catastrophe. It is much more likely that the superpowers would act together, in their own interests, to put out the fire. It is even possible that the shock of such an event might put the world on the path to real control, or even abolition of these weapons.

SIR NEVILLE MOTT, *British physicist; 1977 Nobel Prize in Physics; professor of physics emeritus, Cambridge University; former director, Cavendish Laboratory, Cambridge;* The Theory of Atomic Collisions *(with H. Massey) and Elementary Quantum Mechanics (1972) are among his published works.*

We in Europe face the massive power of the Soviet Union. We know they use it in Afghanistan or Poland, and we do not want to feel helpless, as we would if we disarmed unilaterally. Those who advocate that we should, feel you can trust the Soviet Union. I am afraid I do not.

I believe that a nuclear-free Europe would fall under Soviet influence without any war. On the other hand, it seems to me quite incredible that our side—the NATO alliance, defenders of the free world—should be the one to threaten the *first* use of nuclear weapons, if the Russians attacked. To cross the nuclear threshold could be the supreme crime against humanity. So I believe NATO should build up its non-nuclear forces, developing electronic anti-tank weapons, to the point where we can negotiate with the Russians a no-first-use agreement. A no-first-use agreement could be the first step to a general acceptance of 'no-use,' and a gradual withering away of these horrible things.

Of course, there is a great deal of literature on this matter, including the famous article in *Foreign Affairs* (June, 1982) by Bundy, McNamara, and others, plus lots of arguments against it, too. If you ask what can be done, other than just demonstrate against nukes, I would say, first read the above article, and much else. Liddell Hart wrote: "If you desire peace, *understand* war." So I would say to anyone concerned, try, before you join a movement, to read some of the major books and articles that discuss war in the nuclear age. You can leave out those that discuss the nuclear horrors; that we can take for granted. What is important is how the build-up of weapons happened, and what the doctrines of the two sides are.

I think the two worst dangers before humankind are, first, the stockpile of nuclear weapons, and second, the threat of over-population, together with the exhaustion of energy resources. In the long run, the second may be the more serious. Nevertheless, I believe that in the future, as in the past, there will be times and places where happy and civilised lives can be lived.

Robert S. McNamara

"Do we favor a world free of nuclear weapons? If so, should we not recognize that such a world would not provide a 'nuclear deterrent' to Soviet conventional aggression? If we could live without such a deterrent then, why can't we do so now?"

HAVING SPENT SEVEN years as Secretary of Defense dealing with the problems unleashed by the initial nuclear chain reaction 40 years ago, I do not believe we can avoid serious and unacceptable risk of nuclear war until we recognize—and until we base all our military plans, defense budgets, weapon deployments, and arms negotiations on the recognition—that *nuclear weapons serve no military purpose whatsoever. They are totally useless—except only to deter one's opponent from using them.*

This is my view today. It was my view in the early 1960s.

At that time, in long private conversations with successive Presidents—Kennedy and Johnson—I recommended, without qualification, that they never initiate, under any circumstances, the use of nuclear weapons. I believe they accepted my recommendation.

I am not suggesting that all U.S. Presidents would behave as I believe Presidents Kennedy and Johnson would have, although I hope they would. But I do wish to suggest that if we are to reach a concensus within the Alliance on the military role of nuclear weapons—an issue that is fundamental to the peace and security of both the West and the East—we must face squarely and answer the following questions:

ROBERT S. MCNAMARA, *former U.S. Secretary of Defense and World Bank president.*

Can we conceive of ways to utilize nuclear weapons, in response to Soviet aggression with conventional forces, which would be beneficial to NATO? Would any U.S. President be likely to authorize such use of nuclear weapons? If we cannot conceive of a beneficial use of nuclear weapons, and if we believe it unlikely that a U.S. President would authorize their use in such a situation, should we continue to accept the risks associated with basing NATO'S strategy, the weapons *would* be used in the early hours of an East-West conflict?

Would the types of conventional forces recommended by General Bernard Rogers [NATO's Supreme Allied Commander, and Commander-in-Chief, U.S. European Command], MIT Professor William Kaufmann [an experienced Pentagon consultant] and the European Security Study, serve as an adequate deterrent to non-nuclear aggression by the U.S.S.R.? If so, are we not acting irresponsibly by continuing to accept the increased risks of nuclear war associated with present NATO strategy, in place of the modest expenditures necessary to acquire and sustain such forces?

Do we favor a world free of nuclear weapons? If so, should we not recognize that such a world would not provide a 'nuclear deterrent' to Soviet conventional aggression? If we could live without such a deterrent then, why can't we do so now—thereby moving a step toward a non-nuclear world?

Willy Brandt

"One immense danger is obviously in the fact the real decisions in the realm of armaments are still increasingly made by the 'military-industrial complex' (Eisenhower)—on both sides."

ONE IMMENSE DANGER is obviously in the fact the real decisions in the realm of armaments are still increasingly made by the 'military-industrial complex' (Eisenhower)—on both sides; one should perhaps add the secret service agencies of the big states. In addition, the threat which grows out of computerized answers to a real or suspected attack is growing: the fate of us all, here in Europe a little earlier than elsewhere, can depend on whether a data machine works correctly. One wonders whether the Soviet machines are more reliable than the American ones? Thirdly, I see with great concern how more and more, the East-West conflict pushes itself into the North-South dimension. The sum total of the risks, on the avoidance or overcoming of which depends the survival of humankind, has powerfully increased.

I have already hinted that it is not easy for me to maintain the moderate optimism which has accompanied me through life, in spite of Hitler and all. Still, it seems reasonable to me to submit the working hypothesis that solutions are possible. No, certainly, as long as there is life, there's hope.

WILLY BRANDT, *former Chancellor of West Germany; 1971 Nobel Peace Prize; chairperson, W. German Social Democratic Party, since 1964; president, Socialist International; chairperson, Independent Commission on International Development Issues;* Arms and Hunger *(1986),* Common Crisis *(1983) and* North-South: A Programme of Survival *(1980) are among his published works.*

Many have begun to take action, and I salute that. Most, however, are dominated by a feeling of impotence. Or they are prisoners of an outdated or even perverted thinking in regard to defense and balance-of-power. We can overcome such thinking only when we arrive at the insight that we are dealing with something very concrete: the survival of one's own nation and particularly, one's own family. With all that is debatable and will remain so, especially between the world powers, there is only one hope: to recognize, define, and acknowledge common interests.

Many more people—and especially, many more scientists and technicians—should express with vigor what they know, and what others should know: that nuclear arms first have to be limited, and then destroyed; that other armaments, too, have to be reduced; that the extreme amount of today's armament expenses adds essentially to poison the international economic relations, and that we, if we want to survive, have to make up our mind to reduce international armament loads in favor of international developmental enterprise. World hunger could be eliminated, and a concept of common interests would be—as implied in the choice of the word—of benefit not only for others, but for ourselves; i.e., to those who will come after us, if they come.

Mary Jo Deschanel

"Perhaps we must admit evil, as well as good, to effectively cope and deal with this problem."

THE NUCLEAR THREAT is so scary that it is difficult to think about it, dwell on it, or to act on it in any sustained or concrete manner.

I believe that people feel impotent to stop, or change, or 'save' our world. I cannot understand the love of war and violence that man has always seemed to have. Perhaps we must admit evil, as well as good, to effectively cope and deal with this problem.

As a mother, I feel one important way to change the world is to act in a small, but day-by-day effort, to educate children to love themselves and each other, to turn away from the easy, age-old method of aggression and revenge.

I see much good around me. I feel love and giving every day, from all sorts of people I know and don't know. I cannot help but believe in the basic goodness of most human beings, and so am optimistic about our future. I feel hope, but there is a lot of work to be done, as nuclear war is so close, so easy, and so accessible to people who do not seem to understand at all what it is, or what it means.

I guess just this is what is to be done. We all have to talk to each other about IT; to educate our young (and old) about it, and to convince ourselves that we *can* change, that we *can* change things, that we *have* an effect, that we *can* be powerful and save ourselves, and our planet.

MARY JO DESCHANEL, *U.S. actress;* The Right Stuff *is among her films.*

Colin Wilson

"It seems to me quite possible that the nuclear bomb could be one of the best things that has ever happened to the human race."

How do I view the nuclear threat? I'm inclined to think that it could be one of the best things that has ever happened to the human race. I have written an enormous *Criminal History of Mankind* (1984 publication). When I began to study the subject, it emerged very clearly that cruelty and violence seemed to have emerged fairly recently in the history of the human race. I sometimes suspect that Julian Jaynes may well be right in saying that the date is around 1250 B.C. Men were going to war up to 2000 years before this, but there do not seem to be any definite records of cruelty or mindless violence. In fact, many of these early conquerors seem to have been singularly unruthless. You might note, for example, Winwood Reade's comment in *The Martyrdom of Man* that everything we know about the ancient Egyptians seems to indicate that they treated their defeated enemies with great courtesy.

What seems to have happened is that man developed what might be called 'left-brained concentration'. He *had* to, in order to survive in a world that suddenly became appallingly complicated. He had to develop the equivalent of a watchmaker's eyeglass, to be able to examine things *close up*. Animals find this very difficult, for the same reason that a drunken man finds it difficult to find the keyhole—his relaxed and blurry consciousness makes precise concentration difficult. Man *had* to develop the ability to concentrate precisely, for long periods, if he was going to survive at all. The result was the sudden, tremendous spurt forward taken by the human race around 3000 years ago, which in a mere 500 years had produced Plato and Aristotle. But now that he was no longer 'drunk,' he tended to be far

COLIN WILSON, *British writer;* The Personality Surgeon *(1986)*, The Psychic Detectives *(1985)*, Life Force *(1985)*, Criminal History of Mankind *(1984)*, Starseekers *(1980)*, New Pathways in Psychology *(1972)*, The Occult *(1971)*, *and* The Philosopher's Stone *(1969) are among his published works.*

more narrow, far more obsessive. And we all know how bad-tempered obsessive people can be. This, I think, is the basic explanation of man's propensity to violence.

The result is that the so-called 'great conquerors'—from Alexander the Great onwards—have treated war as a kind of sport, rather like hunting. People like Frederick the Great and Napoleon looked around for causes for quarrels, that would enable them to engage in this sport. (Frederick the Great chose a very thin pretext to start a war with the Empress of Austria.) But the trouble was that by that time, history had changed its rules, and it was no longer possible for people to go to war in the spirit of Alexander the Great. Europe had somehow become too small. The result is that in all the really great wars—from the Hundred Years War onwards—there were no real winners. *Everybody* lost. Yet, as we can see, the fact that the china shop was getting smaller and smaller still did not prevent enthusiastic bulls from wanting to rush into it. If the human race had any sense, Napoleon would have been the last 'great conqueror'. Instead, we've had Bismarck, the Kaiser, Mussolini, Hitler, Stalin, and so on.

This explains why I am optimistic. With the hydrogen bomb, there is at last a very good reason—the most powerful of all reasons—why future 'Alexanders' should learn to restrain themselves. It is no longer possible to treat war as a sport. And even the stupidest person can see this. So it seems to me quite possible that the nuclear bomb could be one of the best things that has ever happened to the human race.

In any case, the bomb is here, and there is no going back. This is really what worries me about all these anti-nuclear campaigners. In fact, what they really want is to go back to the old pre-nuclear age. And this simply is not possible. It is rather as if somebody in a mountain-climbing team suddenly lost his nerve when they were halfway up some particularly difficult rock face, and began screaming that he wanted to go down again, because it was dangerous. In fact, he would merely endanger the whole team. This is certainly no time to lose our nerve about nuclear power.

I, personally, don't think thousands of nuclear protesters make the slightest difference to the safety of our world, one way or the other.

It is perfectly apparent to me that Russia contains as many 'men of goodwill' as England or America, and that the chief problem is for someone to attempt a completely new initiative. The problem at the moment seems to be that Russia is in the hands of a great many, very old men* who are still determined to uphold Communist dogma as taught by Marx, Lenin and Stalin. This is not a situation that will go on forever, and I suspect that there might be something of a change for the better in another decade, in the same way that there was in China, after the death of Mao.

---

*Editor's Note: Apparently, Wilson here refers to the same Politburo membership which reportedly decided Gorbachev should *not* immediately 'go public' on the Chernobyl disaster.

I also feel strongly that perhaps some kind of alliance between Western and Russian intellectuals might help to bring about a better understanding between the two power blocs. It cannot, I am quite certain, be impossible. Shelley said that poets are the "unacknowledged legislators of the world," and certainly, writers and philosophers have had an enormous influence at various times, often through a single book. It seems to me that it is time the 'intellectuals' began to take their responsibility seriously, and try to do something about it.

Harry S. Ashmore

"Detente once enjoyed majority support in the United States; it can again."

Aт тне end of World War II in Europe, where I had served as an infantry officer in Patton's Third Army, I was convinced that what are now called conventional weapons had already altered all previous tactical and strategic considerations. So long as an army's striking power was limited by the range of its artillery, it was possible to largely confine combat to military forces, and there was practical support for the so-called rules of civilized warfare. Long-range aircraft had changed all that. The Germans had introduced the concept of total war, in which the objective was not to destroy the enemy's fighting force, but its supporting infrastructure—that is, the urban concentrations upon which it depended for war material. We had replied in kind, and so had undermined the philosophical concept of the just war; Hitler's Third Reich surely represented evil incarnate, but so did our wholesale slaughter of unarmed civilians.

After V.E. Day, I was ordered to the Pentagon for service with the War Department General Staff, and assigned to the group working on plans for invasion of the Japanese home islands. Faced with the estimates of our own and Japanese casualties—civilian as well as

HARRY S. ASHMORE, *U.S. journalist; senior fellow, Center for the Study of Democratic Institutions, Santa Barbara; Pulitzer Prize, editorial writing, 1958;* Fear in the Air *(1973),* Mission to Hanoi *(with W. Baggs, 1968),* The Other Side of Jordan *(1960) and* An Epitaph for Dixie *(1957) are among his published works.*

military—that were certain to result from kamikaze-style resistance, I greeted the atomic bombing of Hiroshima with relief. I still cannot fault the judgment of those who believed it the most humane and economical means available for forcing an end to the conflict.

After the war, I shared the hope that the quantum leap in destructive capacity, represented by missile-borne nuclear weapons, might make global-warfare obsolete. That hope diminished as it became evident that the great powers would not yield the degree of national sovereignty necessary to give the United Nations the authority required to enforce arms control, and provide nonmilitary means of settling international dispute. In the absence of any effective, international rule of law, the deterrent effect of nuclear armaments was bound to erode, and it has now done so to the point of extreme hazard.

Those who live in nations with nuclear capacity, or access to it, have been taught that their society, as they know it, cannot survive without such a deterrent. In this sense, their society *is* the world, and the threat of universal nuclear destruction is no more compelling than the threat of national defeat. Hence, unilateral disarmament is a political impossibility, and the effort to frighten the populace into supporting it has proved to be counterproductive.

Until a few years ago, the military strategists on both sides assumed there was no way to win a nuclear war—that retaliatory striking power was sufficient to guarantee mutual destruction. So long as this view held, deterrence was an effective basis for international negotiation; it made possible detente between the USSR and the USA, and with this came a tentative beginning toward arms control, looking to ultimate reduction. When the strategists began to profess belief that technical advances could provide means of nullifying retaliatory force, detente—which depends upon a degree of mutual trust—was undermined, and the arms race resumed.

The task now is to restore the conditions that produced detente, thereby making possible a resumption of the admittedly difficult negotiations that will be required to bring about arms reduction. This will require a change in the basic attitudes of the leadership of the USA and the USSR. We can't know what will be required to bring about such a change in the Kremlin, but we can be certain that it will *not* take place without a change on our side. And that will require replacement of intransigent leadership; for example, we could not expect President Reagan to abandon, or significantly modify, his conviction that we can only deal with the Soviet Union from a position of overwhelming military superiority.

The emotional change provided by the nuclear-freeze movement will continue to affect coming elections. The moral argument provided by the Catholic bishops, who contend that nuclear weaponry is incompatible with the Church's historic doctrine of 'just war,' will further mobilize religious opposition to military-based foreign policy. But the issue also must be drawn on the rational ground that the risk inherent in the futile effort to gain effective, nuclear superiority over our adversaries, is far greater than that admittedly entailed in seeking a diplomatic solution to our ideological and economic differences.

In addition to a cry from the heart, we need one from the head. Detente once enjoyed majority support in the Untied States; it can again, if we elect leaders who genuinely believe it is not only possible, but essential, and make the case in terms that reassure the electorate. The nomination and election of such candidates is the most critical business for all of us.

Flora Lewis

"The most important first step, I think, is for as many people as possible to educate themselves in the facts of modern weaponry and strategy, so that they do not feel obliged to abdicate their right of expression and influence to 'experts,' nor to reject knowledge of the world, as it is, as 'madness'."

THERE HAVE BEEN wars since the beginning of human history. Nuclear weapons change the meaning of war, because they can wipe out humankind, and perhaps most kinds of life on Earth. Therefore, they represent a totally different kind of threat than we have ever known. But there are other threats, perhaps equally menacing, in other weapons being developed or considered— biological, chemical, etc. Even conventional weapons have been developed to a level where destructive capacity is unprecedented, and could profoundly change civilization, as we know it.

Certainly, it is urgent to reverse the arms race, in many domains, not only nuclear. But I do not think it is possible, now that the nuclear genie has escaped, to will or wish it away. Therefore, we must learn to live with it, which means a dramatically new kind of prudence, and some important changes in basic assumptions. This is very difficult, but perhaps the effort to know our world, and to understand the menace of our actions, is what we can do to try to save it.

I am optimistic because the urge to survive, to be decent, to be

FLORA LEWIS, *U.S. foreign affairs columnist,* The New York Times; One of Our H-Bombs is Missing *(1967) and* Case History of Hope *(1958) are among her published works.*

kind, is just as profoundly rooted in the human spirit as the urge to destroy and to harm. We are not helpless. We *can* influence our destiny.

I do not think there is any simple formula, any simple measure that can resolve the dilemma. Arms control and reduction are needed. I oppose the Freeze idea, because I do not think it will lead to reduction of arsenals, nor the development of better ways to settle conflict. I support the "build-down" proposal. MIRVs [multiple, independently-targetable, reentry vehicles] were a terrible mistake, which can be corrected in this way. Now it is urgent not to repeat that mistake by opening an arms race in space.

President Reagan speaks of yearning for a world where "war means victory or defeat," where warfare is "civilized," as he says it used to be. This is the most dangerous illusion of all. There is no way for the superpowers to move their hostility onto some other level—space or ultimate defense—where it can be settled by force, without endangering all of humankind.

The demand for security cannot be ignored. It is rational, even in the irrational world of nuclear weapons. And it is overwhelmingly emotional, even in the cold world of nuclear logic. The need, therefore, is to seek, in every way we can, how to enhance mutual security, instead of increasing insecurity. Many partial measures are possible and needed; none should be rejected on the grounds of being incomplete. The most important first step, I think, is for as many people as possible to educate themselves in the facts of modern weaponry and strategy, so that they do not feel obliged to abdicate their right of expression and influence to 'experts,' nor to reject knowledge of the world, as it is, as 'madness'.

David P. Barash

"Americans, particularly, have a unique responsibility, as the only nation to have used nuclear weapons against other people, and as the leaders and pacesetters in the nuclear-arms race."

I VIEW THE NUCLEAR threat as, quite simply, the most important issue facing the world—not just today, but the most important that human beings have ever faced. I see it as something that demands my total and committed attention as nothing else ever has before, and as nothing else ever will. It also provides an enormous opportunity for each of us, an opportunity to become involved in something that *really matters*, something that can give our personal lives 'relevance' as nothing else can.

I am not optimistic, yet I am totally committed to seeking to assure our future. I find that my approach to nuclear war is increasingly an existential position: despite the gathering gloom and the low probabilities of ultimate success, I see no alternative for human beings than to struggle. Indeed, it is precisely because of that threat that the struggle becomes imperative, and in the process, we can realize the deepest resources of our own humanity.

Americans, particularly, have a unique responsibility, as the only nation to have used nuclear weapons against other people, and as the leaders and pacesetters in the nuclear-arms race. Fortunately, we also have a unique opportunity, as inhabitants of a great democracy that is ultimately responsive to the will of its people. So, we must get busy and use our precious democracy to demand an end to the arms race, and drastic reductions in nuclear weaponry.

DAVID P. BARASH, *U.S. professor of psychology and zoology, University of Washington;* The Hare and the Tortoise *(1986),* The Caveman and the Bomb: Overcoming the Neanderthal Mentality *(1984, with J. Lipton),* Stop Nuclear War! A Handbook *(1982, with J. Lipton), and* The Whisperings Within *are among his published works.*

Mario Cuomo

"I regard the danger of a nuclear showdown as probably the gravest it has been in our history."

BECAUSE WE ARE among the living, we should always be optimistic. I feel that way strongly. I have fathered five children, pursued a career, and taken part in public life. Why? Because I hold a positive attitude toward life. I believe things can be changed in our world.

There is no question that the peril of nuclear war, nonetheless, haunts us all today. I regard the danger of a nuclear showdown as probably the gravest it has been in our history. Thus, we should never be lulled into a false sense of peace, simply because we have survived 40-plus years since the end of the Second World War, without a conflagration.

War can come about through an accident, a misinterpretation of facts, a show of macho politics, and a deliberate first strike. In other words, small incidents as well as large ones, in our tense era, can trigger military responses by either the United States or the Soviet Union, or by some other nation with the capacity for waging thermonuclear war.

What should we do? We must educate all citizens, here and abroad, about the dangers of nuclear armaments. We must organize voters to press for an end to the arms race. We must work to break the present deadlock between the U.S. and U.S.S.R. over arms negotiations. We must push for the inclusion of every member of the family of nations, in a common agreement to control nuclear arms. As civilized peoples, finally, we must try every reasonable approach that will avert us ever having to answer the question of whether to push the button or not.

MARIO CUOMO, *U.S. Governor of New York.*

Eugene I. Chazov

"As a physician, I know that medicine will not be able to aid the victims of nuclear strikes, those millions of burnt and maimed. Nuclear war, if unleashed, shall be the final epidemic."

THE NUCLEAR THREAT is real. Indeed, the matter concerns not only the stockpiling of nuclear weapons and their continuing improvement. In my view, more danger lies in the consistently disseminated ideas of the admissibility of their use in a conflict, of the possibility of waging a "limited" nuclear war, and of winning such a war. These are dangerous illusions, which may result in irreparable tragedy for humankind. As a physician, I know that medicine will not be able to aid the victims of nuclear strikes, those millions of burnt and maimed. Civilization, in our sense of the word, will virtually cease to exist. Nuclear war, if unleashed, shall be the final epidemic.

There are those among us who, in their daily chores, forget about the nuclear threat. This is a typical psychological reaction to a permanent irritation source. But the number of unconcerned is going down. Humans cannot be rid of the insticnt of self-preservation. Moreover, hope is peculiar to humankind. And hope is nurtured (in a broad social sense) by the growth of forces coming out against nuclear war. Undoubtedly, I am optimistic about our future. Reason should prevail. It is not too late, as yet, to stop the dangerous trend.

EUGENE I. CHAZOV, *Soviet cardiologist; Soviet Deputy Health Minister; director general, USSR Cardiology Research Centre; co-president of the 150,000-member International Physicians for the Prevention of Nuclear War (recipient of the 1985 Nobel Peace Prize); Presidium member, USSR Academy of Sciences; personal physician of the last four Soviet leaders.*

First of all, it is necessary to open the eyes of peoples and governments to the terrible prospect of nuclear war. It is necessary, further, to incessantly unmask various illusions concerning nuclear weapons: illusions of nuclear superiority, and of the possibility of restricting a nuclear war to a local conflict. Lastly, it is necessary to persuade the governments of nuclear powers to renounce the first use of nuclear weapons, to freeze nuclear arms, and beyond that, to finally destroy them.

To these ends was addressed the call of the Third Congress of the International Physicians for the Prevention of Nuclear War, held in June, 1983, in Amsterdam. I would like to draw your attention to the fact that the Soviet Union supports these very measures. In particular, it undertook, already in 1982, not to be the first to employ nuclear weapons.

As for the situation in Europe—which has become the 'nuclear powder keg' of this planet—the main task is to exclude the appearance of *more* new American missiles that make the situation a hundred times more dangerous. Then, this new cycle of the nuclear arms race would be avoided. As far as my country is concerned, it will—of this I am sure—go as far as is necessary...to the point of freeing the Continent from nuclear weapons, whether medium-range or tactical.

John McCarthy

"A nuclear war in the Third World is more likely than a Soviet-American war. There are more and more countries with nuclear capability, and more crazy leaders."

A FULL-SCALE NUCLEAR war between the Soviet Union and the United States would damage civilization severely, but probably not destroy it. It might be comparable in its impact, on the countries involved, to the Khmer Rouge destruction of Cambodia. Let me assure you that this opinion is based on considerable thought and computation, and is not casual, wishful thinking—even though I may be wrong.

It seems to me, however, that such a war is not more likely than it has been. I do not see any process inexorably advancing towards a war between the U.S. and the Soviet Union. The arms race itself (more a walk than a race, at least on the U.S. side, where a mere six percent of the GNP—as compared to 10 percent in 1960—goes to the Military) does not make war more or less likely. That depends on political factors.

I do not believe that there is any chance that the U.S. will initiate a war. And the present Russian leaders are very unlikely to begin it unless, perhaps, their system starts to collapse. However, every time the top man dies in such an oligarchy, there is a chance of civil war. And a civil war in Russia or China might become nuclear, if a side possessing nuclear weapons will otherwise be defeated. All these are dangers, but not very likely dangers. As you see, I see the danger of world war as coming primarily from the specific characteristics of communist society.

A nuclear war in the Third World is more likely than a Soviet-American war. There are more and more countries with nuclear capability, and more crazy leaders. Probably, we wouldn't be

JOHN McCARTHY, *U.S. computer scientist; professor of computer science, Stanford University; inventor of the computer language Lisp; pioneer in artificial intelligence.*

involved. But I cannot predict whether the devastation of such a war would make further nuclear war more or less likely.

We are not acting to save our world because we cannot agree on what action will save it. There is no unilateral American action that would necessarily save the world from nuclear war—not even surrender to the Russians. The last ten years have shown that communists are even more inclined to fight among themselves than are democracies. Surrender might result in our becoming an expendable resource in an intra-communist battle.

Our present dithering between detente-oriented and defense-oriented policies is more likely to avoid war than either extreme. A steadier policy would reduce our nervousness, but we are unlikely to adopt it.

James E. Muller

"Must we drift passively toward that moment when chance brings together the critical mass of plutonium and drugs, alcohol, psychosis or computer error that will destroy us and all we value?"

WHEN THE HORROR of nuclear war forces its way to consciousness, many cling to the belief that it is so horrible that no rational person will ever push the button. This discounts our stated policy that we *would* push the button in self-defense, but it does provide comfort ... until the possibility of *accidental* nuclear war is considered.

The U.S. military, to whom we Americans have delegated the task of managing nuclear weapons, well understands the danger of unintentional nuclear war. A special program called the Personnel Reliability Program (PRP) exists for individuals with access to nuclear weapons. More than 100,000 are included in the program; to enter it, an individual must show evidence of emotional stability and good social adjustment, and not have had a problem with alcohol or drug abuse. Physicians assist in the screening process and period-ically monitor those selected.

The results of this surveillance are *shocking!* In 1975, 5128 person-nel were removed from access to nuclear weapons because of viola-tions of the PRP; in 1976, 4966, and in 1977, 4973—an annual rate exceeding four percent. Reasons for removal in 1977 included alco-hol and drug abuse; the primary drug abused was marijuana, but

JAMES E. MULLER, *U.S. cardiologist; co-founder and former secretary of the 150,000-member International Physicians for the Prevention of Nuclear War (recipient of the 1985 Nobel Peace Prize); assistant professor of medicine, Harvard Medical School.*

more than 250 were removed for abuse of drugs such as heroin and LSD. In the same year, 1289 were removed for a "significant physical, mental or character trait or aberrant behavior, substantiated by competent medical authority," which might "prejudice reliable performance of the duties of a particular critical or controlled position."

In addition to these medical disqualifications, 828 were disqualified for negligence, 350 for court-martial or civil convictions of a serious nature, and 885 for evidence "of a contemptuous attitude toward the law." Description of this misconduct should not be interpreted as a criticism of the military, for it is we who have asked them to accomplish the impossible in handling nuclear weapons safely.

Computers, which occasionally tell us we have died, or never existed, or must pay a bill a second time, are also intimately involved in the nuclear arsenals. The record of mistakes is extensive. During one 18-month period, the North American Air Defense Command had 151 false alarms. Four resulted in orders that increased the state of alert of B-52 bomber crews and intercontinental-ballistic-missile units. A major false alert, lasting a full six minutes, occurred when a technician mistakenly mounted on an American military computer a training tape of a Soviet attack. Mechanical malfunction and human errors have also led to a number of accidents with nuclear weapons.

The risk of accident increases as we increase the size of our arsenal and the number of personnel involved. Our move to 'counterforce' warfare, in which each side becomes concerned that it must fire its missiles before they are destroyed, decreases to less than 30 minutes the time available to evaluate the computer signals of a possible attack, and decide to launch. The spread of nuclear weapons to less-developed countries with limited technical sophistication also increases the risk.

What are the implications of this understandable, but somehow startling, evidence of technical and human fallibility? Can a group of individuals whose judgement is impaired decide to launch a nuclear weapon without authorization, or fail to respond properly to a computer error? Although the Pentagon has stated that no single person can launch a nuclear weapon, under certain conditions, the crew of a submarine can fire nuclear weapons on its own. Our survival also depends on the proper conduct of Soviet personnel and computers. Alcoholism is a major health problem in the Soviet Union, and is at least as likely to exist among their military as it is among ours.

An unauthorized launch would undoubtedly require a combination of failures, but the opportunities are numerous and increasing. Must we drift passively toward that moment when chance brings together the critical mass of plutonium and drugs, alcohol, psychosis or computer error that will destroy us and all we value?

We are moving inexorably and unwittingly toward a finale similar to that so powerfully described in *Hamlet*. At the play's conclusion, Fortinbras enters and finds the recently-slain Hamlet, Laertes and the King and Queen of Denmark, and Hamlet's friend, Horatio, explains how such a disaster occurred:

> *And let me speak to th' yet unknowing world*
> *How these things came about. So shall you hear*
> *Of carnal, bloody and unnatural acts,*
> *Of accidental judgments, casual slaughters,*
> *Of deaths put on by cunning and forced cause,*
> *And, in this upshot, purposes mistook*
> *Fall'n on th' inventors' heads.*

We are now the "inventors". We have set the stage for "accidental judgments", "forced cause" and "purposes mistook" to lead us, not to a series of palace murders, but to an event of unimaginable horror in which *millions* of innocent people will die agonizing deaths. Physicians who survive will be unable to provide even minimal pain relief for most of the dying.

There is really only one cause for optimism: the phenomenal growth of the mass movement for total nuclear disarmament. Hope and a sense of common purpose have replaced despair and isolation for hundreds of thousands. If others with similar concerns act on their belief, the movement can become an unstoppable force.

Now is time for renewal of the belief that humanity can survive. Such progress is needed: the hour is late. We can live with the threat of accidental nuclear war for 10 or 20 or 30 years, as we have—but not forever.

CHAPTER II

The Response

A SOCIETY that systematically shuts its
eyes to an urgent peril to its survival
and fails to take any steps to save itself
cannot be called psychologically well.
—JONATHAN SCHELL, *U.S.*
author, The Fate of the Earth

John Money

*"The nuclear threat is the
equivalent of being lured to
Jonestown to be subjugated,
by the Reverend Jim Jones
and his lieutenants, into
being an obedient, self-
immolating participant in his
cyanide-and-koolade
apotheosis."*

THE NUCLEAR THREAT is the equivalent of being lured to Jonestown to be subjugated, by the Reverend Jim Jones and his lieutenants, into being an obedient, self-immolating participant in his
cyanide-and-koolade apotheosis. The leader closes all ways to
escape. This applies to both 'us' and 'them'.

It is a fundamental principle of human nature that those who are
the victims of sufficient brainwashing and abuse become addicted to
brainwashing and abuse. Like all addicts, they return for more. They
are robots of obedience, even though obedience requires self-
destruction. In the present age of nuclear threat, it is touch and go as
to whether so many of 'us' and 'them' are already programmed for
self-destruct, that there are too few others to hold back the
self-destroyers.

For abuse-addicts, the risk of more abuse is intoxicating. They get
high from it. (Scientifically, it is quite likely that their brains actually
get flooded with endorphin, the brain's own morphine-like sub-
stance.) The more dramatic the risk, the higher the intoxication.

JOHN MONEY, *U.S. psychologist; professor of medical psychology and associate professor of pediatrics, Johns Hopkins University; founder, psycho-
hormonal research unit, Johns Hopkins Hospital; president, American Foundation of Gender and Genital Medicine and Science; Hofheimer Prize, American
Psychiatric Association, 1956;* Lovemaps *(1986),* The Destroying Angel *(1985)
and* Love and Lovesickness: The Science of Sex, Gender Difference and
Pairbonding *(1980) are among his published works.*

Hence, detailed images and predictions of total nuclear annihilation make warnings against it all the more challenging and dreadfully exhilarating. Addicts of abuse ride a high-wire of tempting fate. So, also, do those who preach nuclear superiority as deterrence. They are players at the global casino of Russian roulette. They are intoxicated by 'if?' and 'when?'. Like all addicts, they are impervious to rationality and logic.

Another fundamental principle of human nature is the principle of sudden conversion (which can be secular, as well as religious). Thus, there is the possibility that the victims of abuse can, *en masse*, rebel against acquiescence to nuclear annihilation. It will require great orators to bring about this rebellion, just as it requires great revivalists to lead mass religious conversions.

IN CULTURAL ANTHROPOLOGY, it is an established principle that new technology, whether discovered, invented, or borrowed from one's cultural neighbors, is a sure-fire way of bringing change into a nation or community, and into the customs and behavior of its people.

Gradual change, like a drifting current, often leads to an unforeseen destination. Guided change toward a definite destination is legislated. There are three steps in legislated, guided change. First, there is public debate and a decision to make the change. Then follows a period of technological preparation and public education. Finally, change goes into effect, by law, at the proverbial stroke of midnight. Next morning, the disobedient are subject to prosecution or arrest! As a life-and-death matter, it had to be that way in Sweden when the change was made from left- to right-hand drive on the highways.

The lessons of change to right-hand drive in Sweden, as well as of the guided change to the metric system in America, apply also to change to the exclusively life-positive use of the technology of physics. This new technology, invented once, has diffused globally. Like all new technologies, it has imposed change on the customs and behavior of the peoples to whom it has diffused, and whose governments now manufacture nuclear power. This imposed change began as life-negative in its military application as the atomic bomb in 1945, and subsequently became life-positive in industrial and biomedical applications. The balance between the two, negative and positive, has subsequently been a drift toward an unforeseen destination, rather than a navigated journey toward a foreseen destination.

Change by drift, since it requires no navigator, is seductively effortless. Guided change needs to be legislated. It requires a navigator, and is laboriously burdensome.

The navigators of guided, legislative change toward life-positive nuclear policy will need to be immensely charismatic leaders whose appeal will be globally effective. If this appeal convinces first the power-brokers and decision-makers of nuclear policy, everywhere, to adopt a life-positive nuclear policy, then the masses, including the police and the military, can be charismatically led to follow suit. Alternatively, the masses in their millions may be converted ahead of their regional and national leaders, who then will be coerced, by the sheer weight of numbers, to follow suit.

The risk, at this point, is that the leaders may become tyrants who, rather than lose their power, will turn upon the masses from whom their power derives, and destroy them and themselves as well, perhaps even with the nuclear weapons originally intended for their enemies. This risk of suicidal genocide, on the model of Jonestown, is a risk that may have to be run as the alternative to the risk of homicidal genocide—in other words, the risk of nuclear war between enemies. The evidence of history is that attempted destruction of an enemy has been more frequent than attempted destruction of one's own people.

Once the international unity of intention to be nuclear life-positive has been universally agreed upon, the pragmatics of what follows, no matter how time-consuming, will be as straightforward as the pragmatics of changing to the metric system is proving to be.

In summary, the first and greatest challenge is to reach universal agreement that global nuclear policy will be life-positive, and not life-negative. Then will follow a period of implementing the technology of the change, from a mixed positive-negative to an exclusively-positive nuclear policy. This implementation will need to include a universally-applicable, self-policing system so that when the bell rings at midnight, no life-negative nuclear minority can sabotage the life-positive majority.

Ralph K. White

"To prevent nuclear war, the primary goal should be to drastically reduce the exaggerated, unhealthy, 'paranoid' form of fear on both sides."

As a POLITICAL psychologist, I view the nuclear threat as by far the most serious aspect of the problem of war's causes, in general. We've got to understand better why war, itself, has occurred so often—even in our supposedly enlightened, 20th century—in order to understand how to prevent nuclear war.

The chief thing we can learn from both history and psychology is that most of the wars, and in fact most of the acts of aggression in our century, have grown out of some kind of fear. They have been defensively, more that offensively, motivated. Hitler is the great exception. Nearly everyone thinks of Hitler's aggressions first, as a prototype of how wars start. That puts the emphasis in exactly the wrong place.

Defensively-motivated aggression occurred on both sides at the outset of World War I; in Japan's behavior, at the outset of World War II, and in the aggressions of both sides in the East-West conflict, such as Afghanistan on the Soviet side, and Vietnam on ours. (I elaborate on all of this in a book, *Fearful Warriors: A Psychological Profile of the East-West Conflict.*)

It follows that to prevent nuclear war, the primary goal should be to drastically reduce the exaggerated, unhealthy, 'paranoid' form of fear on both sides. Retaining the necessary minimum of healthy, realistic fear on each side (e.g., by an adequate, second-strike capability), is necessary, but much less vitally important. And in order to proceed intelligently in reducing the fear of the West in the minds of the Soviet people and their leaders, we need to start with an under-

RALPH K. WHITE, *U.S. professor of psychology emeritus, George Washington University;* Fearful Warriors: A Psychological Profile of the East-West Conflict *(1984) is among his published works.*

standing of the reality of their fear, especially their fear of being 'encircled' by a hostile, aggressive coalition that includes Western Europe, as well as China, the United States, and perhaps Japan.

Many concrete things can be done, among which I give top priority to these six:

A. U.S. Adm. (Ret.) Noel Gayler's* formula for drastic, equal, verifiable destruction of nuclear weapons, based on each side making its own free choice as to which of its weapons it will publicly destroy. He has done the most outstanding, creative, but realistic thinking on *how* really drastic reductions might be brought about. The destabilizing weapons should, of course, be destroyed first, and Gayler's proposal makes that likely. This and any other deep cuts should be done in stages, taking into account the GRIT principle (Graduated and Reciprocated Initiatives in Tension-reduction) of U.S. psychologist Charles Osgood.

B. A drastically-lowered ratio of warheads to missiles (the Midgetman principle). No MIRVs (multiple, independently-targetable, reentry vehicles).

C. A joint, no-first-use statement.

D. A freeze agreement, modified to allow substitution of less-destabilizing for more-destabilizing weapons.

E. A comprehensive test ban.

F. Elimination of Pershing II's, ground-launched cruise missiles, and SS-20s.

---

*Ret. Adm. Noel Gayler was U.S. National Security Agency director, 1969-72; commander-in-chief of the U.S. Pacific Forces, 1972-76, and deputy director of the U.S. Joint Chiefs' Strategic Target Planning Staff.

Michael York

"It is only by thinking—and thinking hard—about the unthinkable, that the full measure of the threat to our endangered lives and planet will become apparent. We need to be scared and alarmed, for most of us are in a trance."

THE UNLIMITED ENERGY provided by nuclear power is a testament to the creative genius of humankind. However, there is now a very real danger that this dynamic discovery will serve as nothing but a monument to death and destruction—that is, of course, if monuments can survive nuclear holocausts.

Leaving aside, for a moment, moral and ethical considerations, I think that the danger—and, perversely, maybe our salvation—lies in the prevailing process whereby nations' economies are being maimed and crippled by an international arms race in which there can be many losers, and no one winner. No country can afford this burgeoning madness, and there is a growing awareness that the time has come to draw the line. But where? And by whom? And with what?

Fundamentally, of course, it is not a question of economic survival, but of physical survival. So massive is the arsenal of weaponry that is poised for blast-off that any accidental unleashing of this power is as unimaginable as it is unthinkable. There would be no forgiving, forgetting or redress for our Promethean crime. It is only by thinking—and thinking hard—about the unthinkable, that the full measure of the threat to our endangered lives and planet will

MICHAEL YORK, *British actor;* Space, Cabaret, The Three Musketeers, Justine, Fedora, Logan's Run, Murder on The Orient Express, The Master of Ballantrae, The Weather in the Streets, For Those I Loved, Final Assignment, Great Expectations, *and* Romeo and Juliet *are among his films.*

become apparent. We need to be scared and alarmed, for most of us are in a trance. If a good hard slap is required to restore reality, then so be it.

Early 20th-century human beings were conditioned to think of themselves as, essentially, creatures of limitations. Unlike their Renaissance counterparts, who gloried in themselves as creatures of unlimited possibilities, they accepted their place in the pigeonhole, and wore with resignation the label that hung round their neck, and which marked their specific function in the scheme of things. The vast masses of Us were cowed into accepting the unquestioned, totalitarian authority of Them. There was a rarely questioned assumption that the people in control knew what was best for them.

Today, these assumptions are being challenged, as the balance of power teeters on a knife's edge, so that equipoise is delicate and ultimately destructive. The rules of war have suddenly changed. To borrow an earlier, military term, we run the risk of being hoist with our own petard. We can no longer allow the politicians to deal with our politics, and the soldiers to wage our wars. Nor should we abrogate the authority we have over our lives to human-made, electronic software. The machine can ape and even outdistance our intelligence, but it is essentially, and irremediably, soulless.

Those who will now act from heartfelt instinct will run the inevitable risk of being termed—by Them—as irresponsibly irrational. To counter that, I am reminded of what George Bernard Shaw said: "The reasonable man adapts himself to the world; the unreasonable one persists in trying to adapt the world to himself. Therefore, all progress depends on the unreasonable man."

Scientific progress was always assumed to be on a traditional, forward-moving path—from the bogs of primeval knowledge towards the lofty summits of Olympian superpower. There is now an uncomfortable realisation that that knowledge has diverted us to a path that leads over a precipice. There is a feeling that the designated leaders are in front, but not in control. The time has come to invent new rules for international behaviour, and to replace fear with trust.

I am optimistic, because I must be. Modern psychiatry has testified eloquently to the damaging, nullifying effects of negative thought. It seems that for over 40 years, we have let pessimism and suspicion hold sway. Now—before it is too late—we should, in the interests of democratic fair play, allow optimism and faith a free run, and their spokespersons a free voice. We have everything to gain, and nothing to lose.

Vietnam showed that unpopular wars can be terminated by the involvement of the concerned masses. In the same way, the campaign for a mutual, verifiable, nuclear freeze could be converted into a genuinely popular, worldwide movement, one that crosses frontiers and other barriers erected by prejudice, ignorance and bigotry.

Nothing can bloom in a climate of fear; at best, growth is stunted, subterranean, and ultimately fruitless. We have the statistics that present a terrifying testament to the folly of our ways. Nuclear missiles in Europe now take only five to eight minutes to reach their targets, reducing the margin of error, reconsideration and renegotiation to a perilous thinness. Humankind is still in an evolutionary process, albeit an accelerated one. It is still a process, however, fraught with trial and error. But the nature of the potential Great Error that adumbrates the beauty of our lives is so cataclysmically irreversible, that it cannot be allowed to happen. So we can disarm, or die.

We must turn away from the battlefield and—either by an act of faith or political strategy—cast away the first stone...before our civilisation becomes, itself, a mere statistic in some cosmic memory bank.

Paul Smyth

*"If we cannot love our neighbours, if our
intentions are not good, or if they are not
understood as being good, then we have
little hope."*

H UMANKIND HAS DEVELOPED, through technology, at an incredible rate. We have wiped out killer diseases; we can save thousands of lives by predicting and preparing for natural disasters, and we can communicate across oceans in a matter of seconds, all for the betterment of humankind. And yet we can let two-thirds of our people starve; we can hold back the progress of developing countries by refusing them aid, and worst of all, we can, in a matter of minutes, destroy everything and everyone, because we have allowed our countries for so long to study and wage war.

The nuclear threat is the most horrendous of all our developments. 'Civilized' human beings are prepared to destroy eveything. But if we lose everything, what can there possibly be to gain? I am not prepared to fight my brother, nor will I shoot him, nor will I ever have anyone else shoot or threaten to shoot him on my behalf. How much more ridiculous, then, it is for the government of my country to threaten to wipe out an organisation, a country, or a nation, in my name, or on my behalf! I will not let them do it, and I will ask my sister that she does not let them do it in her name either.

More are not acting to save our world because our politicians and so-called leaders carefully manipulate the weapons of mistrust and fear, to make one human hate another, and nation hate nation. We are encouraged to hate, when our only hope for survival is to love. Man's capacity for self-destruction is so total, so horrific, so disgusting that we find it difficult to comprehend.

My belief is that human beings are basically good. Circumstances make them evil, and in the modern world, it is becoming increasing-

---

PAUL SMYTH, *Irish administrator, Youth for Peace division, Community of the Peace People, Belfast, Northern Ireland.*

ly difficult for people to distinguish the difference between good and evil. If we can renew our faith in ourselves and our neighbours, and in our community, we can survive and prosper. If we cannot love our neighbours, if our intentions are not good, or if they are not understood as being good, then we have little hope.

My answer may sound simplistic; it is purposely so. If I am not optimistic about our future, who will be? It is up to us—the peacemakers—to forge the way forward. If we have no faith in what we are doing, or if we lose our love for humankind, we are doomed.

Daniel Berrigan

"The Bomb is the preeminent moral issue of our time. Everyone has one foot over the nuclear precipice."

WE HAVE SUCCEEDED in 'normalizing' murder as a socially-respectable method of dealing with human conflict. In such a way, both the truth of the primordial myth (Cain-Abel, the first sin) is verified, and its consequence revealed. Which is to say, every human, like it or not, is my brother or sister; and second, war is essentially fratricide, which the Bomb has elevated to omnicide.

The Bomb is the preeminent moral issue of our time. *Everyone has one foot over the nuclear precipice.* So for at least ten years, I have tried to live, act and write, believe and hope, as though I had one clear call...to say, in whatever way was open to voice and hands: Thou shall not kill. At last, and most ironically, the full force of this primordial command is coming home. We shall either resolve not to kill, or we shall all die.

Every act of God, rightly understood, corresponds to an act of humans. This relieves us of both magic and despair. So if I say, a future of humans depends on an act of God, I am not rubbing a genie bottle. We are required, in Auden's phrase, "to choose to be chosen"...for survival, that is. Or in Martin King's insight, the choices are narrowed: nonviolence, or extinction. Therefore, what can be done, in the short run, is what each and all are doing. Dorothy Day used to advise: "Fill the jails with our people." Exactly.

DANIEL BERRIGAN, *U.S. priest, author, lecturer; Catonsville 9 and Plowshares 8 activist (received three-to-twelve-year sentence for destruction of two Mark 12-A reentry vehicles—which carry W-78 nuclear warheads—at King of Prussia, Pennsylvania); co-founder, Catholic Peace Fellowship;* The Nightmare of God *(1982),* Commandments for the Long Haul *(1981),* We Die Before We Live *(1980) and* The Disciples of the Mountain *(1979) are among his published works.*

Hannes Alfven

*"Planet Earth cannot accommodate both life
and nuclear technology. One of us—life or
nuclear-weapons technology—has to be
buried forever. We have to choose."*

M OST SCIENTISTS ARE specialists. To them, the most important
thing is their latest discovery or technical innovation. Whether this is
to the benefit or the detriment of humankind is often of secondary
interest. They are happy to pass that responsibility to the businessmen, the military men and the politicians who pay their research
grants and their salaries. Usually, destructive results are rewarded
much more generously than other results, so scientists are often
under pressure to accelerate the 'race to oblivion'.

Scientists are often—but not always—very 'intelligent' people.
However, in our context, there seem to be two different types of
intelligence. One kind is what we may call 'nuclear intelligence'. The
people who possess this count their achievements by how many
people their devices can kill, how large a figure they can enter in the
'megadeath' column. (One 'megadeath' means one million people
killed.) Their aim is to make this figure as large as possible for the
'enemy' and as small as possible for their own masters.

What 'megadeath' means in human terms is something they do not
understand, or refuse to think about. In particular, they never mention that the nuclear 'megadeath' is not comparable to a 'conventional' killing of the same number of people, because radioactive
death is not a 'heroic' death, in the old sense. It is very often a slow,
torturing to death, as we know very well from Hiroshima.

The other kind of intelligence we may call a 'humane intelligence'.
Those who possess it cannot avoid seeing the meaning of megadeath

HANNES ALFVEN, *Swedish physicist; 1970 Nobel Prize in Physics; professor of
electrical engineering, University of California at San Diego; professor of
plasma physics emeritus, Royal Institute of Technology, Stockholm;* Cosmic
Plasma *(1981),* Evolution of the Solar System *(1976, NASA SP-345),* Atom, Man
and the Universe *(1969) and* Worlds-Antiworlds *(1966) are among his published
works.*

in human terms. Their intelligence is combined with empathy in such a way that it compels them to identify *themselves* with those who would be killed. They imagine that they, themselves, constitute one-millionth of what the people with nuclear intelligence call a megadeath.

What I am referring to is best explained by a reference to the International Physicians for the Prevention of Nuclear War (IPPNW) or the Physicians for Social Responsibility (PSR) who, inspired by Bernard Lown, Evgeny Chazov, Helen Caldicott and many others, have started a movement for saving humankind from 'The Final Epidemic'. This movement is now the spearhead of a rapidly increasing popular movement. The Union of Concerned Scientists is another example of a group of scientists with humane intelligence.

How do you separate those who have nuclear intelligence from those who have humane intelligence? It's very easy. You need only listen to what they say for a few minutes. You can judge them from what they advocate; *more* nuclear arms . . . or *less*.

At present, a general madness is sweeping the world. Humanity is obviously preparing for 'omnicide,' the killing of us all . . . the result of an irresponsible propaganda for more nuclear arms, which is possible only because so many people are uneducated enough not to react against it.

The arms race is escalating, the nuclear situation gets increasingly unstable, and the threat of omnicide more horrifying. Further, we cannot completely exclude the possibility that a partial defense against missiles (by laser beams, etc.) can be constructed in the future, and this is the basis for what is called SDI, which stands for 'Strategic Defense Initiative,' usually nicknamed 'Star Wars'.

This project has been severely criticized by practically all who've studied it *without* being corrupted by the billions of dollars which are spent on buying scientists to work on the project—it aims at developing a new, utterly destructive technology.

How can this be referred to as defense? It is claimed that in principle, an utterly destructive technology can be used even to destroy destructive missiles before they reach their targets. This is possible if only one or a few missiles are launched, but is unrealistic if thousands of them are launched simultaneously.

The concept of a 'strategic defense' is used only to camouflage the real character of the project, which is to develop a super-destructive technology. What should we call the project if we want to use a correct and honest terminology? We could very well call it SDI, but this abbreviation should rather stand for *Super Destructive Initiative*.

It is not 'realistic' policy to limit our actions for saving ourselves from omnicide to those which are acceptable to the political, military, commercial and scientific establishments of today. We have all seen clearly enough that their actions lead to an escalating risk of omnicide. A policy which has such consequences cannot be called 'realistic'. If we believe that humankind has a brain to be used for saving the human race from extinction, we cannot allow the present establishments to eliminate the use of the human brain in promoting their short-sighted interests.

The only possible definition of a realistic policy is one which aims at rescuing us from the nuclear threat. Hence, the only realistic policy is to stop all nuclear activity as soon as possible.

Why do we not do so? The Physicians for Social Responsibility have shown there is no cure for the consequences of a nuclear war. Those physicians who are psychiatrists have diagnosed the present state as a severe psychic disease of humankind. Humanity is threatened by a general madness of destruction, a most serious illness.

It is contagious. If one leading politician has been infected, his colleagues in other countries run a risk of also being infected. It is a fatal disease, but unfortunately, not fatal only to those who've been infected. It also threatens those who are not. The disease should be called the Super Destructive Illness, or shortened to SDI.

And for everyone who wants to survive, who wants to save our children and grandchildren, who wants to preserve our culture and everything humankind has achieved, the highest priority *must* be to cure humankind of SDI—the Super Destructive Illness. Planet Earth cannot accomodate both life and nuclear technology. One of us—life, or nuclear-weapons technology—has to be buried forever*. We have to choose.

---

*Exceptions are very small-scale nuclear-activity use for medical purposes and as tracers, the purely scientific investigation of the structure of nuclei, etc.

Germaine Greer

"The future is not ours, because we have abandoned responsibility for it."

THE NUCLEAR THREAT is more devastating in its effects—even before the threat becomes actuality—than anyone appears to realise. Nobody is really certain that there is a future, and that takes a whole dimension away from human behaviour. We have become irresponsible and desperate in our pleasures, and in our frustrations. Those of us who are aware of the gross absurdity of a technology which is irresistibly attracted towards its own destruction, have stopped bearing children. The people who still bring them forth, in pain and optimism, are the ones who will inherit the poison and the anguish that we will unleash upon a world we can no longer care about.

Our civilisation has lost its energy, thrown it away in two world wars which were the culmination of a period of mad expansionism, in which Caucasians allowed themselves to believe they were the lords of the Earth. We are tired, and the few children we have are more tired than we are. When they have to pay the bill for our declining years—which get longer and longer—they are going to get even tireder, even faster. All we can offer in exchange is commercial fun, which is no substitute for joy.

The nuclear weapons exist; the only deterrent to them is more of the same, and more deadly. The rest of us are trying to interpose

GERMAINE GREER, *Australian feminist and author;* Sex and Destiny *(1984),* The Obstacle Race *(1979) and* The Female Eunuch *(1970) are among her published works.*

hearts and minds against fissile materials, yet we can find no tangible way of expressing our energy which could counterbalance what is in the silos. If dying would defuse a fraction of the warheads, I would die; but it won't. And I will die, willy-nilly.

If every man, woman and child could be mobilised to block roads and fill the landscape, even if they did no more than rock and moan, in mourning for the cruelty and madness of it, we might still lose, but we would lose honourably. Instead, we leave the job to tiny groups of dedicated agitators, who are driven to crazy extremes by their isolation.

The future is not ours, because we have abandoned responsibility for it. We have also refused to people it. My prayer is that the people we despise—the poor and powerless—will take the future away from us. My fear is that we will destroy it, rather than let them have it.

Barbara Garson

"Based on reality, the chances of averting nuclear war are as likely as the chances of taking power away from the statesmen and industrialists who currently divide up the world."

DURING THE CUBAN missile blockade, I assured my worried parents (remember how families were calling long-distance to say goodbye) that it was all under control. Kennedy and Khrushchev had been on the phone all along working it out, so that they'd each emerge looking good in their hometown papers. And no one would blow up the world.

I was wrong.

When I hear grown-up generals talk so earnestly about their pre-emptive strikes and mobile missile-launching systems, I feel sorry or embarrassed for them. Obviously, they haven't been let in on the secret. There's nothing in those silos. They're just empty holes in the ground. Surely, the real insiders must know that nuclear missiles are for show, not for use.

I guess I'm wrong this time, too.

There must be something wrong with me. I can imagine soldiers scheming for promotions, industrialists hustling sales, and politicians unifying their countries around pre-election crises. But somehow, I can't believe that we're being ruled by people who take these nuclear games seriously. They may be cynical, but surely there's someone on top who's sane.

Maybe other people aren't acting (though, of course, many are) because they share my incredulity, or ostrich-like lack of imagination. It's not that I don't act; I go on plenty of peace demonstrations. But that's primarily to be with my friends. I still don't believe that the world I live in is likely to be blown away.

BARBARA GARSON, *U.S. author, playwright;* Macbird *and* The Meaning and Demeaning of Routine Work *are among her published works.*

Most people imagine themselves alive after a nuclear war. They can see themselves heroically helping others, stoically bearing pain, or nobly starting again to lay brick upon brick, despite the grief (and relief) of losing so many dear ones. (Perhaps the really sad sacks envision themselves taking decisive control in the catastrophe.) The problem isn't a death wish, but a lack of imagination. I don't think anyone really imagines himself dead.

Based on my own lack of imagination, I'm optimistic. But based on reality, the chances of averting nuclear war are as likely as the chances of taking power away from the statesmen and industrialists who currently divide up the world.

What can be done? Take power away from these sober-sounding madmen. How? I don't know. So far, as a peace activist, I spend most of my time petitioning maniacs to please be more careful.

Stacy Keach

"If there is nothing left for us but to dream of what might have been on Planet Earth, then trying to make the dream into a reality is at least a noble task, even if it does not succeed. If we are doomed to die... let us die trying."

As THE WORLD seems poised on the brink of total annihilation, due to ever-growing and perhaps irreconcilable conflicts between the USA and the USSR, it is not easy to muster the human spirit toward affirmative action. For "What can we do to prevent such a horrible war?" is a question answered only by seemingly futile, insignificant gestures and demonstrations.

And yet, somehow, we must not forget or overlook a personal responsibility. If we are to die in a nuclear holocaust, if, in fact, nothing can be done to prevent it, then the inevitability of this death, and the knowledge that that is what we are all facing, reaches down and touches our humanity. And in so doing, a paradoxical condition emerges which seems to activate a deeper sense of self-respect, of self-preservation, in short... of survival. For, if there is nothing left for us but to dream of what might have been on Planet Earth, then trying to make the dream into a reality is at least a noble task, even if it does not succeed. If we are doomed to die... let us die trying.

I would encourage independent contact with similar types of organizations in the USSR (if, in fact, they exist; if not, then encourage their formation). I would try to form an international coalition of people. I would address a unified, collective energy both to the leaders of the world (by means of film, video, active demonstrations), and to the peoples of all nations... that we must join together to abolish nuclear weapons and nuclear testing.

STACY KEACH, *U.S. actor, director, producer, writer.*

Robert A. Hinde

"The behaviour of individual nations can be seen as a sort of collective madness, leading towards nuclear suicide. Sanity may prevail, but the forces that are at the moment propelling the world towards destruction must be stopped, and stopped soon."

THE THREAT OF nuclear war has for long been like a sword of Damocles, threatening the continued existence of civilization and, perhaps, of the human race. The current atmosphere of distrust between East and West, at all levels, makes the threat even more acute. And the continued accumulation of nuclear weapons makes the situation ever more desperate.

I think more people are not acting to save our world (a) because the enormity of the issues defies comprehension; (b) because individuals feel themselves to be ineffective against the political-military-industrial forces that fuel the arms race, and (c) because distrust of the other side is explicit or implicit in the statements of so many leading politicians and so much governmental propaganda.

The behaviour of individual nations can be seen as a sort of collective madness, leading towards nuclear suicide. Sanity *may* prevail, but the forces that are at the moment propelling the world towards destruction must be stopped, and stopped soon.

ROBERT A. HINDE, *British ethological psychologist; research professor and honorary director, Medical Research Unit on the Development and Integration of Behaviour, Cambridge University; foreign associate, U.S. National Academy of Sciences; Leonard Cammer Medal in Psychiatry (Columbia), 1980;* Defended to Death *(jointly),* Ethology *(1983),* Toward Understanding Relationships *(1979) and* Biological Bases of Human Social Behaviour *(1974) are among his published works.*

The most important issue is to build trust—both in the short term, so that the immediate confrontation can be ameliorated, and in the longer term, so that the world can find new ways of ordering its affairs. One means to that end lies in unilateral steps in the reduction of armaments, and a reduction in the dissemination of arms.

Those who *do* perceive the dangers of the arms race must stand up and be counted, and help others to see the issues clearly. Pressure from individuals and groups *can* influence government decisions. But much else is needed besides—the abrasiveness of politicians must cease, and we must take positive steps to encourage new values embracing the quality of life, and to build tolerance and understanding for other ways of life.

Kay Boyle

"As long as the most popular sport in our country is football... no overwhelming majority of our fellow citizens is prepared to engage in actions of peace."

I VIEW THE nuclear threat as William Butler Yeats viewed the succession of discoveries and occurrences we call progress. Many decades ago, he saw it as the sentencing of humankind to extinction. And he asked how the arts could overcome the dying of men's hearts, and "lay their hands humbly on men's heartstrings, again without becoming the garment of religion, as in the old time?"

We are all desperate, *all* of us—those who look on material possessions as success; those of us who don military uniforms to mask our uncertainties, or those of us who abruptly recognize ourselves in soap operas on the TV screen. If we can come to the belief that to dominate, to win, is not recommended, then we can accept the 'moral law', a law that is accepted by all rational human beings. It is a pragmatic, a secular law, that requires no idolatry to validate it. But at present, we are not guided by rational human beings.

Far too many of the habits we have formed, and the values with which we have learned to live, never cease putting us at ease with violence. As long as the most popular sport in our country is football, with ice-hockey a close second in violence (a war game featured, as well, in the Olympics), no overwhelming majority of our fellow

KAY BOYLE, *U.S. author; O. Henry Award (twice), year's best short story; Guggenheim Fellowship (twice); professor emeritus, San Francisco State University;* The Underground Woman, Generation Without Farewell, His Human Majesty, Nothing Ever Breaks Except the Heart, *and* Gentlemen, I Address You Privately *are among her published works.*

citizens is prepared to engage in actions of peace. From childhood on, we are encouraged to take part in these war games, to prove ourselves, to compete.

British political scientist Ronald V. Sampson has pointed out that the individual develops, to a greater or lesser degree, in one or the other of two directions: he orders his relationships—both with other individuals, and nations not his own—on the basis of power, or on the basis of love. To the extent that we progress in our ability to love, we disqualify ourselves for success in the competition for power. And only in the triumph of compassion, Sampson tells us (*The Psychology of Power*, 1965), can equality among men prevail. It is obvious that equality among men is antithetical to the war games we have been taught to applaud and shout aloud over. When the arts— all the arts—speak to men more effectively than any other vocabulary, individual action will be recognized as eloquence.

What can be done? In responding to this question, I would like to speak of a law, of which Benjamin Ferencz (a man whose choice has been unequivocal compassion) says: "In an interdependent world, the sovereignty of the State must yield to the sovereignty of the law." Ferencz is speaking of the enforcement of international law. A former U.S. prosecutor at the Nuremburg war-crime trials, and now a New York attorney, Ferencz has documented, in six remarkable volumes*, the actions to be taken that would lead to world peace. The most recent of the six was published in 1983, and includes a detailed inventory of the alternatives to violence that were available at the time of the Falkland Islands War, and the alternatives available now in the present conflict in the Middle East. Ferencz believes that the ending of the nuclear threat, and the establishing of lasting, world peace, can be achieved by the actual prosecution of those heads of state guilty of acts that offend the moral law and the conscience of humankind.

It is because of the dedicated works of Benjamin Ferencz, British political scientist Ronald Sampson, and others who share their convictions, that I cling, almost hopelessly, to a modicum of hope.

---

*Defining International Aggression: The Search for World Peace, two volumes; An International Criminal Court: A Step Toward World Peace, two volumes, and Enforcing International Law: A Way to World Peace, two volumes (Oceana Publications, Inc., Dobbs Ferry, NY 10522, USA).

Ronald V. Sampson

*"Great forces of evil are loose
in the world."*

THE SEPARATE INDIVIDUALS who make up the million-bodied
Leviathans have no quarrel with one another. How can they fear or
quarrel with people whom they have never seen, whose language
they do not know, with whose literature and culture they have only
the barest familiarity? For these very reasons, however, they are an
easy prey to the vicious propaganda ceaselessly conducted by the
ruling groups of the world's major alliances against their rivals, in the
interests of perpetuating their own power.

People do not fear the Russians (Americans), but unconsciously,
soaking up the propaganda of the media, they *do* fear what they
imagine their relatives, colleagues, friends and work-mates would
think of them if they adopted a stance inconsistent with the expectations of distrust and fear, with which the officially-controlled political atmosphere is imbued.

I am asked if I am optimistic. It depends on the efforts of every
one of us. Great forces of evil are loose in the world. Ultimately, love
always prevails over hate, but often, not until humankind has undergone terrible and wholly-unavoidable suffering. But love is more
tenacious, more long suffering, more enduring than the will to
power.

RONALD V. SAMPSON, *British political scientist; professor of politics emeritus,
University of Bristol;* The Discovery of Peace *(1973) and* The Psychology of
Power *(1965) are among his published works.*

William E. Colby

"...nuclear war is too important to be left either to generals, or to statesmen..."

NUCLEAR WEAPONRY IS awesome, complex, and surrounded by secrecy. As a result, most world citizens delegated this subject to the experts. Today, the world citizens demand an accounting from the experts, but are confused by a cacophony of conflicting voices as to the dangers involved in the weaponry, and their fears of their adversaries.

However, world citizens are increasingly applying Clemenceau's dictum—that nuclear war is too important to be left either to generals, or to statesmen—and feel that the threatened, human family must assert its responsibility and its voice, to demand that these weapons be brought under control. Unfortunately, the special authority of governments successfully impedes communication among the simple people of the world, and some world leaders profit by exploiting fears of hostility from other nations. While this is more true of the Communist and totalitarian powers, the problem also exists in the West.

I am optimistic, because we see the rise in the influence of the ordinary citizens of the world, insisting that their governments lessen the danger that this weaponry has created. While this is certainly true in the democratic countries, the march of technology, partic-

WILLIAM E. COLBY, *U.S. lawyer; former CIA director; founder, International Business-Government Counsellors, Inc.;* Honorable Men: My Life in the CIA *(1978) is among his published works.*

ularly in the information and communications sectors, has forced even totalitarian countries to begin to open channels of communication for and with their peoples.

I look for no dramatic opening of the closed Communist societies of the East, as occurred with the Meiji Restoration in Japan in 1860; but I do see an erosion of their capability of maintaining the kind of regimented discipline over their peoples that another age permitted. The real question is whether this process can move sufficiently rapidly to meet the escalating danger of nuclear weaponry.

Chad Everett

"If the people of the nations of planet Earth do not rise up in one loud voice now, 'next time' *may not come."*

I DO NOT VIEW the nuclear threat as a threat, but as a reality. Threats are four-letter words spoken in anger, ususally without the force to back them up. But there can be no question in any logical, human mind that there is more than enough force to turn threat to reality.

I don't believe that my contemporary in Russia wants to lose his family to nuclear holocaust. Yet politics has become an almost laughable chess game . . . a few players in a Planetary Tournament. So it's time—if we are to be saved (with the help of our Lord)—for we pawns to instruct the players.

I further believe that if we would take the consensus of all children in our world* between the ages of five and 12—those who are really the most open and troubled re: this ultimate issue—and publish these responses in and on every media . . . MAYBE the *powers* and the *people* will react.

As a Christian, I am always praying for peace, and for the humaneness of the people to be reflected through our leaders. We in the U.S.A. have given in to the habit of complacency on issues of magnitude: "Our leaders know more, so they will handle it. After all, that's why we elected them, and if I don't agree, I won't vote for the bastard next time." . . . democracy at its best! Yet if the people of the nations of planet Earth do not rise up in one loud voice now, "next time" may not come.

I can't speak of other political persuasions—dictatorship, monarchy, socialism, communism. I don't know if it's more difficult for some of my brethren to make themselves heard. But we all *must* try.

---

*Editor's Note: A 1986 survey of teenagers in 59 nations (excluding the Soviet Union) revealed that more than a third—39 percent—now believe nuclear war is inevitable during their lives.

CHAD EVERETT, *U.S. actor;* The Rousters, The French Atlantic Affair, Medical Center, *and* The Dakotas *are among his TV series.*

Blase Bonpane

"We must give no allegiance to any policy involved in plotting, planning or conspiring to commit a nuclear war."

I AM OPTIMISTIC ABOUT our future. The alternative would be the very cynical non-action which already characterizes our culture.

Some people have become convinced they are powerless, and have sought the services of professionals who practive cottage-industry in retailing 'adjustment' to the victims of wholesale depression. Essentially, however, more are not acting to save our world because of their spiritual and intellectual formation; i.e., the existing cultural mode promotes spectators of life, not makers of history.

For example, good people 'keep their mouth shut,' are not 'agitators,' stay out of 'politics,' talk about 'positive things' (Disneyland and other nice things), and do not discuss 'negative things' (intervention in Central America, or nuclear war). We can assume that Russians, despite living under a different social system, are similarly programmed to avoid discussing *their* 'negative things' (intervention in Afghanistan, or *their* contribution to the madness of the nuclear-arms race).

We North Americans, however, are formed in a culture of silence (e.g., "Stay out of controversial issues!" or "Don't you think President Reagan knows more about this than you do?"). Such cultural

BLASE BONPANE, *U.S. director, Office of the Americas; senior research fellow, Council on Hemispheric Affairs; former Central American specialist, University of California and California State University; former Maryknoll priest, Central America.*

paralysis can only be cured by direct opposition to the popular assumptions; i.e., only by viewing ourselves as *makers* of history can we understand our responsibility.

First, we must acknowledge the problem. Then we must lay aside the counterproductive and malicious attitudes which identify our 'national interests' as paramount; the human family is paramount. Hence, we must accept the fact that the nation-state, as a terminus of sovereignty, is outdated. There can only be international law and order.

Certainly, less than one percent of the people of the U.S., for instance, are in the state of mental illness required to promote nuclear-war fighting. Therefore, the vast majority must demand sanity—the removal of all politicians who promote nuclear war and nuclear weapons, and in the interim, absolute non-cooperation with any individual or administration looking upon nuclear war as a solution to world differences.

And as a nuclear war could begin as a result of an interventionary war which a major power is unable to win—e.g., the US in Central America, or the USSR in Afghanistan—one way to stop nuclear war is to stop the interventionary wars which could trigger The End.

Further, *we must give no allegiance to any policy involved in plotting, planning or conspiring to commit a nuclear war.* Taxation without representation is tyranny. The crisis demands massive civil disobedience: non-payment of taxes, general strikes, boycotts of government directives, and more importantly, boycotts of products from companies profiting from the arms race ... companies such as GTE, AT&T, General Electric, Westinghouse, General Tire & Rubber, Honeywell, Singer, Monsanto, Bendix, du Pont, Union Carbide, Litton, Tenneco, Avco, Proctor & Gamble, etc.

Lance E. Mason

*"How can we take seriously the threat of
holocaust and catastrophe when we have
Magic Mountain, Monday Night Football,
and a taste for consumptive living orchestrated by Madison Avenue and fostered by
relative wealth and leisure?"*

A LACK OF VISION and a jaded idleness has crept into our lives. We
do not see the future and do not work for a better life, because the
drive to do so has been eviscerated by the double-edged sword of
abundance. How can we take seriously the threat of holocaust and
catastophe when we have Magic Mountain, Monday Night Football,
and a taste for consumptive living orchestrated by Madison Avenue
and fostered by relative wealth and leisure?

And if, by some chance, we creep up to the edge and look out into
the world in which most of humanity lives, and if we open our eyes
and our minds to the awesomely dangerous existence we may be
living, and if we ask the first question—"Whose responsibility *is* it to
change this?"—are we not too readily drawn back into the soft and
well-heeled comfort of ski boots, hair dryers, hot tubs and a lifestyle
that caters to the acquisitive and concern-less mind? Contentment
breeds apathy. Consumption breeds greed. Ignorance breeds veg-
etative indifference. There is not so much a death wish, as a wish to
be left alone to enjoy, enjoy, enjoy.

Americans need to face their global responsibilities. The feeling
and the voice of the American people ought to dictate the U.S.
government's choices, laws, and decision-making regarding nuclear
weapons (and atomic power). And since the U.S. controls perhaps
the largest component of this force, in the world, the American
people have a tremendous and honorable responsibility to choose
actively and wisely how that component will be used. If they ignore

LANCE E. MASON, *U.S. dentist, author; taught dentistry at the University of
California at Los Angeles;* Halcyon Home *(forthcoming) is among his works.*

that choice, they abdicate their power, their dignity, and their honor.

Therefore, I view the nuclear threat as the proving ground for human morality, for *American* morality. If history, progress, technology and all the other 'inevitables' of our experience have ever tested our morality of choice in human issues, they do so now. If we could depend on those people in positions of precise and crucial decision-making to *make* decisions in concert with the highest principles of this morality, then no threat from nuclear power would exist.

But, history and our experience show us we cannot depend on that. What we can depend on is self-serving ideology, moral prostration to the mutually-fueled dictates of greed and power, and choices more concerned with extension of political and corporate influence than with the extension and quality of life. That is how I view the threat, and it is a very real threat, one that can strangle all the vision and hope and spirit of the time and humankind, if it is allowed to burgeon and dominate our lives.

These thoughts and words speak of fear. But, do not confuse fear with cowardice. Only a fool does not experience fear in the face of a real threat. But a coward allows that fear to dominate his will, his spirit, and his resolve to act well. Whoever said that a coward dies a thousand deaths, a hero dies but one, stated one of the great truths of the human condition. For surely, if the human race lives by cowardice now, it will die a thousand horrible deaths in the future.

Jules H. Masserman

"The mere anticipation of such a holocaust has caused overt, covert, but always disruptive anxiety in every sentient man, woman and child on Earth."

I AM NOT OPTIMISTIC about our future, but am doing everything I can to change the odds. Presently, more are not acting to save our world because delusions of macho invulnerability, and immortality under the protection of whishfully subservient deities, constitute our most precious—and most dangerous—obsession.

The mere anticipation of such a holocaust has caused overt, covert, but always disruptive anxiety in every sentient man, woman *and child* on earth, and has contributed demonstrably to economic deprivations, physical and psychologic dysfunctions, drug escapisms, group violence and crime.

All we can do is an intensive educational campaign to engender political movements that will depose, dethrone and immobilize militantly ignorant, dereistic, paranoid or vicious warlords everywhere in the world. The campaign should not emphasize the threat of the vivid prospects of (inconceivable) personal deaths, but of helplessly witnessing the agonies of loved ones.

JULES H. MASSERMAN, *U.S. psychoanalyst; professor of neurology and psychiatry, Northwestern University; honorary life president, World Association for Social Psychiatry; past president, American Psychiatric Association, American Academy of Psychoanalysis, American Society of Biological Psychiatry, American Society of Group Therapy, and American Association for Social Psychiatry; Taylor Manor Psychiatrist of Year, 1972; Lasker Award, 1946; A Psychiatric Odyssey is among his published works.*

Adam Yarmolinsky

"It is not a characteristic of human societies that they deal very well with remote or unprecedented dangers, however terrible it is agreed they would be."

M OST PEOPLE IN the world are caught up in a cycle of poverty and population growth that denies them the minimum essentials of adequate food, clothing and shelter. Most people live under varying degrees of political repression, which denies them effective citizenship. And too many people—even in Western, industrial democracies—are, in increasing numbers, denied the opportunity to contribute their work to society, which is the first essential of human dignity.

We can attack all these problems, and we may, to some degree, succeed. But a major nuclear exchange would make our efforts all for naught, and return the few survivors—if any—to a hunter-gatherer way of life. Whatever the probability of this occurrence—and I believe it is not insubstantial—it overshadows all the other dangers and difficulties we face.

It is not a characteristic of human societies that they deal very well with remote or unprecedented dangers, however terrible it is agreed they would be. We are much better at dealing with more immediate or repetitive risks, even very minor ones. This characteristic of human behavior is, in the present situation, exacerbated by the fact

ADAM YARMOLINSKY, *U.S. educator, lawyer; served in the Pentagon, White House and Arms Control and Disarmament Agency under Presidents Kennedy, Johnson and Carter;* Paradoxes of Power: The Military Establishment in the Eighties *(1983) is among his published works.*

that a solution to the nuclear-weapons dilemma is not immediately apparent in a world of nation-states, particularly with the large gap, in principles and practices, between the two superpowers. No utopian solutions are possible, in my view, and more limited steps— arms agreements, confidence-building measures, etc. —may not be able to keep pace with technological advances.

There are three immediate and imperative tasks for each of us:

1. To educate everyone we can reach—from our circle of friends and acquaintances on outward—to the fact that a nuclear exchange between the two superpowers would almost certainly mean the end of the human race, and that any employment of nuclear weapons would create an unacceptable risk of escalation to a major exchange. The logically inevitable consequence of these propositions is that nuclear weapons are only useful to discourage the other side from using them.

2. To press our Congress and our President to take practical steps to reduce the probability of a nuclear exchange. In priority order, I would list: (a) agreements with the Soviets to reduce surprises and misunderstandings, in crisis conditions, and to improve crisis communications between the two sides (in the jargon of the arms controllers, these are called "confidence-building measures"); (b) to pursue a steadier policy in foreign affairs, avoiding commitments we cannot hope to meet, and simplistic overstatements of the degree of Soviet involvement in complex situations; (c) to encourage increasing contacts between U.S. and Soviet officials, in the Executive Branch and, particularly, in the Legislative Branch (I exclude transparently artificial 'people-to-people' contacts), and (d) to keep alive the most promising arms-control proposals—a genuine build-down, a comprehensive test ban, a production cutoff for weapons-grade fissionable materials, and some form of verifiable freeze—until negotiations can be resumed.

3. To work for the election of a Congress and a President who understand the problem of avoiding nuclear Armageddon.

Howard M. Temin

"One can only hope that as a new generation takes hold, they will be more ready to accept the change in political behavior that must occur as a result of the introduction of nuclear weapons."

I REGARD THE recent increases in nuclear arms as profoundly destabilizing and decreasing our own world security.

Why are more not acting? I think that short-term political and economic considerations are paramount. In addition, the pace of technological progress has been so much faster than the evolution of our political thinking and institutions.

Unfortunately, I have no original ideas as to what can be done. One can only hope that as a new generation takes hold, they will be more ready to accept the change in political behavior that must occur as a result of the introduction of nuclear weapons. We can only hope that the weapons are not used until such time.

HOWARD M. TEMIN, U.S .virologist; 1975 Nobel Prize in Physiology/Medicine; professor of oncology, University of Wisconsin; Lasker Award, 1974.

Vivienne Verdon-Roe

"The Chinese word for 'crisis' is the same word used for 'opportunity'. If our country is to move forward to its best promise, we must move forward to our best promise."

As SHIRLEY CHISHOLM pointed out in *Women—For America, For the World:* "The most important resource any society has is its children."

In the United States, 10,000 children die every year as a direct result of poverty. Yet since 1981, every child-nutrition program has been cut back or eliminated. At the same time, our bloated military budget continues to balloon, as we stockpile ever faster, more accurate, more deadly nuclear weapons for fighting a nuclear war.

How, in a country of such high ideals, can we American people allow such gross overkill-capacity to continue accumulating, at the expense of our people? It's because we feel overwhelmed by the seeming enormity of such problems, and thus helpless. Also, we're intimidated from speaking up about our concern because we fear we'll be told to "leave it to the 'experts'," or that it's "un-American" to criticize 'official' policy.

What's essential is that we understand that human problems require human solutions. Children die of hunger and disease because we've not made it our priority to see that their suffering is prevented,

VIVIENNE VERDON-ROE, *U.S. film producer, director; co-director, Educational Film & Video Project, Berkeley, CA, a nonprofit distribution company making nuclear-awareness and peace programs available globally;* Women—For America, For the World *(1985),* The Edge of History *(with I. Thiermann, 1984),* What About the Russians? *(ibid., 1983) and* In the Nuclear Shadow: What Can the Children Tell Us? *(ibid., 1983, Academy Award nominee) are among her films.*

and their needs met. While draining our national resources into weapons, we've forgotten how powerful the individual is. Social change may be slow, but U.S. history shows that when a significant number of citizens decide to humanize our priorities, *nothing* can stop us (e.g., we abolished slavery, won the vote for women, began the civil rights movement, and ended the Vietnam War).

Personally, up until four years ago, I was a political blob...an ostrich with my head buried firmly in the sand. I felt there was nothing I could do about the world's problems, so I looked away. Then I saw a documentary film—*The Final Epidemic*—which showed what would happen to a city and its inhabitants if just one nuclear bomb was dropped. The film changed my life: it forced me to face *reality*, to look at the nuclear problem straight on.

And because I knew—very directly, from personal experience—the power of film to break through the numbness, to inspire, and to motivate action—I learned to make films. Likewise, each of us is called upon, at this critical moment in history, to find her or his own unique way of contributing.

The Chinese word for 'crisis' is the same word used for 'opportunity'. If our country is to move forward to *its* best promise, we must move forward to *our* best promise. And as we do, it helps to reflect, from time to time, on anthropologist Margaret Mead's words of wisdom: "Never doubt that a small group of thoughtful, committed citizens can change the world. Indeed, it's the only thing that ever has."

CHAPTER III

The Prognosis

Humanity, as never before, is split into two apparently irreconcilable halves. Psychological rule says that when an inner situation is not made conscious, it happens outside, as fate.

That is to say, when the individual remains undivided and has not become conscious of his inner contradictions, the world must perforce act out the conflict and be torn into opposite halves.

—CARL JUNG, *Swiss psychologist and psychiatrist*

Indira Gandhi

"Those who know the disastrous consequences of a nuclear war must make themselves heard. Silence at this juncture is treason against humankind."

Oᴜʀs ɪs ʙᴜᴛ a small planet, in a small galaxy, in an immense universe. Nuclear war threatens extinction of our species, and life as it has evolved on Earth. This may not be much of a loss to the universe. But as human beings, we are proud of the human spirit, and the achievements of the human mind. The human race is far from perfect, but it does have the capacity to reach out beyond its grasp. Surely, the annhilation of life cannot be its ultimate achievement, nor can we willingly accept such a calamity.

I cannot afford not to be optimistic. I cannot believe that the achievements of humankind were meant to end ignominiously, through its own folly.

Peace movements are growing, cutting across political and other affiliations. The Non-Aligned Movement, which represents more than a hundred nations, has dedicated itself to resisting the threat of a nuclear conflagration. Unfortunately, those who are against nuclear armaments are not strong enough to prevent their use, without the cooperation of the big powers.

The future is a question mark. Although rival blocs remain, countries within them try, in their own way, to affirm their identities. Tension grows, but at the same time, there is a parallel peace movement. Either nuclear war will annihilate the human race and destroy

---

Iɴᴅɪʀᴀ Gᴀɴᴅʜɪ, *assassinated Prime Minister of India and chairperson, Organization of Non-Aligned Nations (101 members).*

the Earth, thus disposing of any future, or men and women all over must raise their voices for peace and for an urgent attempt to combine the insights of different civilizations with contemporary knowledge. We can survive in peace and good will only by viewing the human race as one, and by looking at global problems in their totality. Human beings must rise to a higher level of evolution. But how can this be done?

First of all, the superpowers must agree to arms limitations, after which there can be further discussion on gradual, and eventually total, elimination of nuclear stockpiles. Nuclear powers must be made to realise that the world's resources are too precious to be squandered on destructive purposes when millions of people are still poverty-stricken.

Also, those who know the disastrous consequences of a nuclear war must make themselves heard. Silence at this juncture is treason against humankind. Those who are ignorant or misled must be awakened to reality in all its grimness.

In the ultimate analysis, individuals, wherever they happen to live, have to decide whether or not they want their world to survive. If they care for the human race, they must fight for it. In this struggle, the path of nonviolence, to which India is devoted, can be most effective. In essence, it is an unrelenting effort to convert the hearts of the powerful.

Gerhard Herzberg

"What's needed is somebody sufficiently persuasive, who understands the situation and has access to the two world leaders. The trouble is that neither one is very anxious to listen."

THE NUCLEAR THREAT is certainly the most serious one that has ever faced humanity. There is no question that if anyone should initiate a nuclear holocaust, it will be the end of human life as we know it on this planet.

I'm very pessimistic about the future of humankind. Even if the nuclear threat could be eliminated, we still have the threat of over-population—*another* threat many people still don't take seriously. I'm sure there are millions of people who'd like to 'save our world,' but what can they do?

I'm not qualified to make good suggestions about what can be done, other than negotiations between the two superpowers. But how can we trust the Soviets when they send—to concentration camps—their own people who report violations of human rights even the Soviet Union agreed, at Helsinki, to honor. If it weren't for this treatment of dissidents, one might argue "better Red than dead". Yet how can anyone be persuaded to appreciate their system of government, when one reads of the innumerable violations of human rights in the Soviet Union?

It is very difficult to influence the opinion of the leaders of the two superpowers. What's needed is somebody sufficiently persuasive, who understands the situation, and has access to the two world leaders. The trouble is that neither one is very anxious to listen.

GERHARD HERZBERG, *Canadian physicist; 1971 Nobel Prize in Chemistry; research scientist, National Research Council, Ottawa;* Molecular Spectra and Molecular Structure *(4 vols., 4th with K. Huber, 1945-79) and* The Spectra and Structures of Free Radicals *(1971) are among his published works.*

Peter Nichols

*"I don't have much hope we shall learn how
to live with this technical tragedy, until we
have some more terrible example than
Hiroshima and Nagasaki."*

ATOMIC OR NUCLEAR weaponry is a fact that paralyses our capacity to think. I, myself, try to grasp it by comparison with other lethal toys of the past, but neither long-bow, cannon nor machine-gun were more than advanced catapults. We need to think *more,* not less clearly, now that we have the means for self-destruction. Didn't Einstein say The Bomb would change everything except the way men think?

The most hopeful I can be is to say that some kind of limited nuclear event will happen, some cities be destroyed, and many people killed and maimed. When the interests, territory, and capital investment of the big powers are threatened, they will find some way to avert total war. Some places, in other words, are at greater risk than others.

All the wars since 1945—the start of the atomic age—have been in backward countries. I live in Airstrip One, as Orwell saw it. This island is bristling with missiles...the only aircraft carrier in the world with thatched cottages on the decks. U.S. forces have such control here that our own Defence Minister has to ask American officers if he wants information about how many, or where they are.

A calm assessment of our position here in Britain gives only one reason the Russians would attack us—to cancel all the missiles. So a first step towards the reduction of weaponry would be for the U.S. to take home the ones they've put here.

Between the sincere and disastrous United States and the Tsarist, paranoid U.S.S.R., the rest of us feel helpless. We are all, in fact, satellites. We have precious little power of decision. We seek to

PETER NICHOLS, *British playwright;* Georgy Girl *is among his films;* A Better Mousetrap *and* Poppy *are among his musicals.*

assert spurious authority in little wars we know we can win—against Argentina, in our case; Egypt, in Israel's.

I suppose that neither of the two great powers really likes the responsibility, but they don't dislike it, either. As a subject of an ex-imperial country, I watch the American people fretting and exulting in the exercise of global power. They don't enjoy it, but they wouldn't be without it.

I don't have much hope we shall learn how to live with this technical tragedy, until we have some more terrible example than Hiroshima and Nagasaki.

Bernard T. Feld

*"In the 41 years since I've been aware of the
threat—and working, in my way, to avert
it—I have never been so frightened about
the probability of a nuclear war."*

IN THE 41 years since I've been aware of the threat—and working,
in my way, to avert it—I have never been so frightened about the
probability of a nuclear war.

Most people think that if nuclear has been averted for 40 years, we
are not likely to get into one now (if they think about the problem at
all, as compared to their concerns about their economic problems).
Others think our 'leaders' will take care of us and that, anyway, this
is much too complicated and technical for the 'man on the street'.

The following can be done: (a) wake up the people; (b) let the
politicians know that they are being watched and judged on their
actions relating to this issue; (c) bring it into every political campaign
at every level, and (d) retire Ronnie.

BERNARD T. FELD, *U.S. professor of physics, Massachusetts Institute of Technology; former editor-in-chief,* Bulletin of the Atomic Scientists; *former secretary general, Pugwash Conferences on Science and World Affairs; Manhattan
Project physicist; worked with Enrico Fermi in developing the first nuclear
chain-reaction.*

Noam Chomsky

"Considering how close we have come to nuclear war in the past, and how frequently, it seems to me a near-miracle that we have survived so far."

I T SHOULD BE obvious to any sane person that a nuclear war would be a devastating catastrophe. Presently, there are at least four major factors that may contribute to this outcome: (1) the scale and character of the nuclear arsenals of the superpowers; (2) conflicts and tensions in the world that may lead to superpower confrontation; (3) proliferation; (4) the forces that drive the arms race.

As for (1), the present moment is one of extraordinary danger, since the new systems being developed and put into operation appear to have a first-strike capacity, or to be so threatening as to drive the adversary to preemptive or launch-on-warning strategies that virtually guarantee nuclear war, if only by error, misinterpretation, or concern over rising international tensions.

As for (2)—the most neglected, but in my view, most important factor—while it is difficult to imagine that either superpower will attack the other, or that war will break out in Europe, nevertheless, tensions and conflicts in the Third World, to which the superpowers regularly contribute, have in the past repeatedly brought the superpowers close to confrontation, and are very likely to do so again. Any such confrontation is likely to lead to the use of nuclear weapons, and there is little reason to believe that such use will be limited.

NOAM CHOMSKY, *U.S. professor of linguistics, Massachusetts Institute of Technology;* Turning the Tide *(1986)* and Fateful Triangle: The U.S., Israel and the Palestinians *(1983) are among his published works.*

As for (3), like the superpowers, others, too, will resort to any weaponry they control, if they regard their survival or fundamental interests as threatened. Given the prevalence and character of international conflicts, proliferation of nuclear weapons makes it very likely that they will be used.

Turning finally to (4), a review of the history of the post-World War II arms race shows very clearly, I think, that security threats have played a very minor role in driving it onward. Rather, it has been driven by internal domestic factors (in the U.S., the regular resort to 'military Keynesianism' as a device for stimulating the economy and subsidizing high-technology industry), and by the commitment to subversion, intervention, and sometimes outright aggression to secure what is regarded as 'the national interest,' meaning, in practice, the special interest of dominant social groups.

Considering how close we have come to nuclear war in the past, and how frequently, it seems to me a near-miracle that we have survived so far. I see little reason to be optimistic about the future, unless there are massive changes in general consciousness, and a commitment—on a scale so far unimaginable—to carry out substantial institutional changes.

There are no magical formulas. Whether we are considering a potential nuclear war, or the actual catastrophes to which much of the world is subjected today, those who are concerned with something beyond their own short-term welfare will, in the first place, make the effort to understand the nature of the society and world in which they live, a task that requires a major effort, given the effectiveness of contemporary systems of indoctrination and thought-control. They will then devote themselves to bringing this understanding to others, and will join in efforts to organize effective action which, in the capitalist democracies at least, can range from electoral politics to various forms of resistance.

There are many options and opportunities. What is lacking, primarily, is imagination and will. The doctrinal system, in fact, is designed to induce passivity, to make it appear that what happens in the world is beyond our control, either because it is the result of the machinations of whoever happens to be the current Great Satan, or because we are powerless in the face of grand and impersonal forces. We can only hope that such perceptions can be overcome, though it is difficult to see why much optimism is warranted.

Ragnar A. Granit

"Nordic sagas ended with the prophecy of Ragnarrök—*a world catastrophe, the final destruction. It is implied in the nuclear armaments race."*

THE BESTIALITY OF our century is, if anything, exceeding that of Genghis Khan. How could optimism be motivated?

In our Western states, we have replaced individual responsibility by a vote, delegating political action to those voted into power. In the Communist states, the few people who dare act individually against the accepted policy of the state, sooner or later will be treated as enemies of the state, with well-known consequences.

The balance of power has now prevented a nuclear catastrophe for some 30 years. The relevant question is: Will balance of power work indefinitely? Clearly, only as long as the balance is kept.

With all respect for peace movements, demonstrations, and peace 'marches' as expressions of concern and good will, I think the world must undergo a revolutionary change before its politicians become unanimous on a course that, to everybody else, seems the only sensible one: i.e., wholly to abandon the notion that international conflicts should be solved by the threat of reckless armaments.

Nordic sagas ended with the prophecy of *Ragnarrök*—a world catastrophe, the final destruction. It is implied in the nuclear armaments race.

RAGNAR A. GRANIT, *Swedish neurophysiologist; 1967 Nobel Prize in Physiology; professor of neurophysiology emeritus, Karolinska Institute, Stockholm;* The Purposive Brain *is among his published works.*

Desmond Morris

*"The bad news is that it only requires one
mentally-disturbed, button-equipped
individual to destroy us all."*

T HE GOOD NEWS is that nuclear weapons, unlike conventional weapons, will destroy the villains who start the fighting, along with
everyone else. Without such weapons, we might have had pro-
longed and savage war over the past 30 years, because the war-
mongers would stay safe inside their headquarters. But even deep
bunkers won't save them from the consequences of a nuclear holocaust. If all nuclear weapons were incapacitated tomorrow, I think
we would soon have a massive, 'safe' war that would cause untold
misery and bloodshed, but which would probably, in the end, allow
our society to survive, in the usual battered, post-war form.

The bad news is that it only requires one mentally-disturbed,
button-equipped individual to destroy us all. The nuclear stalemate
only works to protect us from war if all the military leaders are
enjoying life and wish to continue doing so. If one of them with
sufficient power decides to commit suicide, he could take us all with
him. This is a serious flaw in the system.

Obviously one day our species will become extinct. It is such a
high-risk species that this is bound to happen sooner or later. But I
think it might be later, rather than sooner, if only because people *are*
becoming more and more concerned about the rotten way we have
treated this planet, and the even more rotten way we might do so. In
any case, I suspect that there are small pockets of humans who
would survive almost any disaster, and they would gradually
rebuild. I am not talking about bunker-inhabitants, but rather some
of the more remote desert tribes who might escape global fallout
altogether. And it might take them another 10,000 years to rebuild
some sort of civilization.

DESMOND MORRIS, *British zoologist;* Bodywatching: A Field Guide to the
Human Species *(1985),* Inrock *(1983),* The Soccer Tribe *(1981),* Manwatching:
A Field Guide to Human Behaviour *(1977),* The Human Zoo *(1969) and* The
Naked Ape *are among his published works.*

Peter Matthiessen

I SEE THE PROBLEM as pervasive fatalism, apathy, and common laziness—What can a few little people do?, etc. The truth is, if *everyone* would do *something*, even one letter to a Congressmember, the wall of official ignorance would crumble.

I cannot be optimistic about the future so long as we put second-rate people of stunted vision and no imagination in high office. Our one chance is grass-roots organization of the painstaking kind that Cesar Chavez made successful against all odds in California.

PETER MATTHIESSEN, *U.S. author;* Nine-Headed Dragon River *(1986),* Indian Country *(1984),* In the Spirit of Crazy Horse *(1983),* Sand Rivers *(1981),* The Snow Leopard *(1979, National Book Award),* Far Tortuga *(1975) and* At Play in the Fields of the Lord *(1965) are among his published works.*

Karl Menninger

I VIEW THE NUCLEAR threat with utmost concern and alarm; it's suicidal.

More are not acting to save our world, I think, because of ignorance or disbelief. The dissemination of the facts is surprisingly incomplete, but even those of us who know about it are sluggish and uncertain.

I do not see how anyone can be optimistic, especially reading Schell's book [*Fate of the Earth*] and some of the others, like *The Final Epidemic*, and George Kennen's *The Nuclear Delusion*.

KARL MENNINGER, *U.S. psychiatrist; founder, The Menninger Foundation.*

Niko Tinbergen

"What I think I know of the history of our species makes me afraid that in the struggle between rational, long-term insight and non-rational, short-term motivation, it will be the latter that will win."

As a biologist who is convinced of the precariousness of survival of all forms of life, I have no doubt that an all-out nuclear war would cause the extinction of the human species, and of most, if not all, higher forms of life on Earth. Possible short-term survivors would soon perish in an uninhabitable environment. But even if I were wrong in this, plain common sense and decency would tell me that war must be prevented, as long as there is even the slightest *chance* of such total destruction. The Earth is not an 'experimental plot' that can be compared with a 'control plot,' and to gamble with life is irresponsible, stupid and criminal.

I am convinced that collectively, we do have the *rational knowledge* and *insight* that could prevent war, but that we will most likely not apply this insight, because our collective *will* is not strong enough for this. What I think I know of the history of our species makes me afraid that in the struggle between rational, long-term insight and nonrational, short-term motivation, it will be the latter that will win. Because I see so few signs of a radical change of our political behaviour, I have become pessimistic about our future.

I see innumerable indications that shortsighted personal and national interests are overriding rational, cooperative planning. War threatens, as long as there is anarchy *between* nation states which fear each other, and as long as *within* each nation state, those in power give priority to short-term, individual and, at best, national interests.

Niko Tinbergen, *British zoologist; 1973 Nobel Prize in Physiology; professor of animal behavior emeritus, Oxford University.*

Joseph Chilton Pearce

"We know, intuitively, that we are already
over the cliff. We ask only that our opiates
not be taken away."

OUR NUCLEAR BUILDUP isn't something unique, but it is the clearest
and most inescapable end-result, or final expression, of our whole
current mode of life and way of thinking.

We elect the people we elect; we reap as we sow. And we support
the system as we do—knowing full well where it must lead—
because to do otherwise would be inconvenient. For every overt
and feeble move we make against the Bomb, we make a dozen
covert moves that support it.

From where does our incredibly sophisticated arsenal of destruction come? From the Pentagon? They couldn't make a paper air-
plane. Our instruments of destruction come from our 'finest intel-
lects'—the academic-scientific community who, with one side of
their mouth, bemoan the stupid politicians, and with the other, beg
for DOD grants, money, fame and Nobels, by which they give the
'warlords' their swords. Withdraw the supporting think-systems of
Harvard, MIT, U. Cal., Stanford, Caltech, and so on, and the power
of the warlords would disappear.

We rage against 'forces' over which we have no control. But control would require effort, and our efforts go to self-comfort, personal
benefit, and living the good life.

At the same time, a half-conscious, cultural guilt grows over our
detruction of our planet, and self-damage brought about in achieving our 'high standard of living'. But, again, to stop the machine
would bring inconvenience or discomfort. We know, intuitively, that
we are already over the cliff. We ask only that our opiates not be
taken away.

Our reality operates by cause-effect. And effects rain on the just

JOSEPH CHILTON PEARCE, *U.S. author, lecturer, former humanities teacher;*
The Bond of Power, Magical Child, *and* Crack in the Cosmic Egg *are among*
his published works.

and unjust, equally. No culture in history has ever escaped the consequences of its acts. Why do we think we can be exceptions?

Cultures are causal processes—"morphogenetic fields," to use Rupert Sheldrake's term. A morphic field, once set in motion, only replicates, and never dissipates. It can only be superseded... absorbed into a larger, more powerful and complex causal field. As products of this self-replicating process, each solution we arrive at contains, at its core, the problem we would resolve. To quote Bergman's Law: "Each and every one of today's problems is the direct and inevitable result of one of yesterday's solutions."

No one is in charge of this morphic field of our culture. Not the Pentagon, nor its highest brass; not our Government, with its latest clown-in-charge. Nor is anyone in charge of the enemy camp—the mirror image of our own madness. 'It' is in charge, and 'it' is the morphic field of our own creation, which, once put into motion and supported by billions of people over many generations, must simply grind its way to oblivion.

There is no exit for us within any of our existing, self-engineered schematics. We can't bail ourselves out of this one, and we all know this, intuitively. To break the deadlock, and set up a new cultural field, would mean to abandon the behavioristic-mechanistic, scientific religion extant since Newton, Descartes and the rest. I see small chance of this.

The way out lies through a 'turning within,' to an inner Self. But this giving over of a self-encapsulated ego to some empty category involving faith, stands small chance in a culture glued to the television, where the fair-haired spokesman of 'Science Says' denies not only mind, but even consciousness (not to mention such cultural embarrassments as soul or God). As Susanne Langer once said: "The average man in the streets has no choice but to take his notions of who he is from those he assumes know." Our current assumption has been a deadly one.

The way out lies in a 'not-doing' of which Castaneda, the Zen and Yoga people, Jesus, and others such as Muktananda spoke: a surrender to the life-function which *still does*—in spite of our arrogance and stupidity—underlie the ground of things. From this point of surrender, and only from there, solutions need not contain, at their core, the problems to be solved. I see small prospect of such a giving-over; rather, we would rail at our scapegoat politicians, and waste our remnants of power to 'bring the rascals down'.

William L. Shirer

"I believe that unless we are terribly lucky, the Soviet Union and the United States will destroy the planet before we get into the 21st century."

I BELIEVE THAT UNLESS we are terribly lucky, the Soviet Union and the United States will destroy the planet before we get into the 21st century. We are rapidly drifting toward that confrontation. I have little reason to think that some damn fool in the White House or in the Kremlin will *not* push the button that will end our world.

Here at home, more are not acting to save our world because we are a nation of sheep. Also, unlike most other countries, ours has never been bombed, so that Americans have been lulled into a false sense of security..."It can't happen here."

However, recently I detect some signs that we Americans are waking up to the threat of nuclear war, and to the consequences of such a conflict. A hundred-million adults reportedly watched *The Day After*, a film on what a nuclear strike could do to an America city. Additionally, polls show the majority of Americans want a nuclear freeze, plus more and quicker progress toward nuclear disarmament.

So although I am pessimistic about the future, we must now arouse the people of this country to the danger and threat of nuclear

WILLIAM L. SHIRER, *U.S. author, journalist; president, Authors Guild;* Gandhi— A Memoir *(1979),* 20th Century Journey *(1976),* The Collapse of the Third Republic *(1969),* The Sinking of the Bismarck *(1962) and* The Rise and Fall of the Third Reich *(1960, National Book Award) are among his published works.*

war, and to the necessity of an immediate nuclear freeze, followed by a drastic reduction of nuclear arms and their elimination before the year 2000. Stir up the press on the subject, including—and especially—the TV news. Elect Congressmembers who are not, as Helen Caldicott accurately labeled most, "corporate prostitutes". And elect a President who conceives the danger and the threat, and is willing to do something immediate and drastic about it.

Lisa Peattie

"The power to move the system must come, I think, from a sort of great popular uprising, a refusal, a mass defense of human life."

LEARNING ABOUT THE Crusades, a student may think: Imagine, killing for that! Just so, on another planet, people might look at the nuclear threat we've created on Earth and say: How on earth did they come to think and do those things? But there is no other inhabited planet. We are the only people who can look at what we are doing, so we must do so now, and take action to stop the arms race.

What's happening is probably more appropriately understood by comparing it to other times and places, where human beings have joined material interest and passionate ideas into murderous or suicidal institutions: Hitler Germany's extermination of six-million Jews, the Jonestown massacre, etc. None of these represent the same scale as proposed in the various nuclear war-fighting scenarios, but the comparison may help us understand how such things are, indeed, possible.

The peace movement is now, I believe, larger than the movement against the Vietnam War ever was. But that is not enough. The Vietnam War could be opposed as a particular project, whereas preparation for nuclear war is more deeply institutionalized in the

LISA PEATTIE, *U.S. anthropologist; professor of urban anthropology, Massachusetts Institute of Technology;* Women's Claims: An Essay in Political Economy *(with M. Rein, 1983),* Making Work *(with W. Ronco, 1983),* Thinking About Development *(1981) and* The View from the Barrio *(1968) are among her published works.*

warfare states, which interlock in the arms race. The institutions of these states constitute the societies in which we live.

People are paralyzed into inaction by the sense of impotence which comes from being surrounded by and, to tell the truth, implicated in, the problem they have to solve. There seems nowhere to begin. Yet people must learn how, in this situation, to stand forth in opposition.

Presently, I am not optimistic about our future. But as Camus once said: Anyhow, we have no choice. We must do what has to be done, so we can live together. We cannot say, today, what in the end has to be done to live with the ability to exterminate ourselves, for the institutional means to a safe future are still to be created. But to have the possibility of building that future world, the political leaders of the great states must now be brought to freeze production of nuclear arms, and to negotiate seriously on arms control.

That, however, I believe will only happen if people *make* it happen. Scientists can help by exposing the consequences of nuclear war. Political leaders can help by offering channels to act on. But the power to move the system must come, I think, from a sort of great popular uprising, a refusal, a mass defense of human life.

Robert S. Mulliken

"I am slightly optimistic that something may unexpectedly be done to save the situation."

A NUCLEAR WAR would, I think, probably result in the end of the sometimes glorious, more often miserable, history of the human race, and possibly most or all life on Earth. *For the long run,* I am almost as worried about the 'population bomb' as about the more immediate threat of the cataclysmic use of the nuclear bomb.

I am slightly optimistic that something may unexpectedly be done to save the situation. But many people do not yet really understand the danger, or if they do, do not see what they can do.

If the people in the Kremlin could somehow be persuaded to replace their present devotion to the success of Soviet, imperialistic communism, by a devotion to the good of the whole human race, that would be enough to begin a solution to the problem. But I do not know who can persuade them, unless it be they themselves, and that seems highly improbable.

ROBERT S. MULLIKEN, *U.S. chemist and physicist; 1966 Nobel Prize in Chemistry; professor of chemistry, University of Chicago; worked on Plutonium Project at Chicago, 1942-45.*

Joan Baez

"I think we Americans will begin to seriously wake up over the next four or five years. I think we are beginning to be touched."

How do I view the nuclear threat? Overwhelming... but in order to build a real movement against it—and *for* a less violent, more decent world—we must attempt to organize *not* out of terror and hysteria, but out of a clear desire to live more decently for ourselves, our children, and the human race. Gandhi called it organizing love. In the face of the nuclear threat, there is a great need for calm determination, and a willingness to take risks.

Why are more not acting to save our world? Probably because either they have so blocked out the reality of the current danger that they don't think the world needs saving (that point of view is becoming less and less prevalent), or because they feel utterly impotent in the face of the enormity of potential destruction. As soon as one is touched directly, as were North Americans in the '60s when family members went to Vietnam, or as hundreds of thousands of Europeans are touched now by living on the superpowers' nuclear playground, it becomes easier to act. I think we Americans will begin to seriously wake up over the next four or five years. I think we are beginning to be touched.

Nevertheless, I am not optimistic. Somehow, in the face of our

---

JOAN BAEZ, *U.S. singer, songwriter, activist; founder and president, Humanitas International Human Rights Committee; founder, Institute for the Study of Nonviolence (now known as the Resource Center for Nonviolence); her works include nine gold albums.*

current ghastly, international deterioration of moral and spiritual values, the buildup of nationalistic frenzy and armaments (nuclear and otherwise), the 40 or so wars that are currently raging, and the dirty work of the two greatest terrorists in human history—the U.S.A. and the U.S.S.R.—optimism seems a little silly. BUT, I am resilient, hopeful, determined, active, and ready to take risks.

What can be done is to first, see Attenborough's *Gandhi* again, to give you inspiration; then get hold of an album of Martin Luther King's speeches, to give you more inspiration; then call up your local peace movement, and get involved. Take heart from the European peace movements, but keep nonviolence as your guide—because if we magically got all the nuclear weapons in the world to evaporate, but did not make basic changes within ourselves and our behavior with our adversaries, we could and would rebuild it all in the wink of an eye, and be back to square one ... or the Stone Age. And when you've finished reading this, reflect for at least a moment or two on the comedy amidst this tragedy, because a sense of humor is one essential ingredient, in times like these!

Arno A. Penzias

MY VIEW OF our future might best be described as guardedly optimistic, based on what I perceive to be a mutual recognition by both sides of the seriousness of the situation.

As to why more are not acting, it is difficult to know what to do. Adding further fuel to the present level of anxiety is likely to be dangerously counterproductive.

ARNO A. PENZIAS, *U.S. astrophysicist; 1978 Nobel Prize in Physics; vice-president for research, AT&T Bell Laboratories; visiting professor, Princeton University; discovered cosmic microwave background radiation, 1965.*

Olaf Palme

"It is very unlikely that disarmament will ever take place if it must wait for the initiatives of governments and experts. It will only come about as the expression of the political will of people, in many parts of the world."

I FIND THE present international situation, with regard to the nuclear threat, more dangerous than for many years, but also more hopeful. Relations between the United States and the Soviet Union have deteriorated sharply during the Eighties. The arms race is accelerating both in quantity and quality. The development of new nuclear weapons seems to suggest that the nuclear powers may actually consider fighting a nuclear war. The threat of a global war seems closer than for many years.

However, the world has also seen a tremendous popular and political awakening to the threats of war. Millions of people are taking part in the work for peace and disarmament. This gives us a certain reason for optimism. This involvement on the part of the man and woman in the street may eventually be decisive, when it comes to convincing the politicians in charge that the world needs less, not more, nuclear and other weapons.

In 1982, the Independent Commission on Disarmament and Security Issues, which I had the honour to chair, published its Report. The report contains the elements of a programme for arms limitation and disarmament, with short- and medium-term measures, as well as proposals for strengthening the United Nations and for action that could be taken at the regional level. The aim of the Commission was to promote a downward spiral in armaments.

OLAF PALME, *assassinated Prime Minister of Sweden.*

Among its proposals are the establishment of a zone in Central Europe free of battlefield nuclear weapons, as well as a chemical-weapon-free zone. We have also proposed a comprehensive test-ban treaty, a chemical weapons disarmament treaty, agreements to limit military activities in space, and other measures.

It is becoming increasingly obvious that a nuclear war can, in fact, never be won. In a nuclear war, the two sides would be united in suffering and destruction. They can only survive together. They must achieve security not against the adversary, but together with him. Thus, the doctrine of mutual deterrence known as Mutually Assured Destruction, or M.A.D., must be replaced by one of common security. To convince the world leaders of this is a most important task today.

I think that the involvement of millions of people in the struggle towards disarmament gives us reason for a cautious optimism. It is a considerable political force, and already has influenced events. It is very unlikely that disarmament will ever take place if it must wait for the initiatives of governments and experts. It will only come about as the expression of the political will of people, in many parts of the world.

Marilyn Ferguson

*"The main way to save the
world is for each of us to
change ourselves.
Unfortunately, for many
people, this is the most
difficult task of all."*

I ACTIVELY SUPPORT THE people trying to come up with creative
answers. Optimism and pessimism are not the issue. I realistically
believe that a great many people are engaged in a major change of
thinking that could affect all of humankind. We could also blow
ourselves up. I'm inclined to think we won't. If I had to be labeled,
I'd go for 'cautiously optimistic'.

Most of my friends are acting to 'save the world,' and so are most
of their friends. The main way to save the world is for each of us to
change ourselves. Unfortunately, for many people, this is the most
difficult task of all.

MARILYN FERGUSON, *U.S. publisher*, Brain/Mind Bulletin; The Visionary
Factor *(forthcoming) and* The Aquarian Conspiracy *are among her published
works.*

Albert Ellis

"As soon as it is possible for a small group of fanatics to manufacture nuclear weapons in their own bathtub, I am reasonably sure several of them will get together and deliberately use these weapons against the rest of us, in the name of God, Jesus, Mohammed, or what you will."

THE NUCLEAR THREAT is quite serious. I doubt whether one of the major powers will launch any nuclear attack in the next ten years or so, but as soon as it is possible for a small group of fanatics to manufacture nuclear weapons in their own bathtub, I am reasonably sure several of them will get together and deliberately use these weapons against the rest of us, in the name of God, Jesus, Mohammed, or what you will.

More people are not acting to save the world because they do not believe there is a great threat, or else do not believe they can do anything about it, or else are too goddamned lazy. Most people have abysmally low frustration-tolerance and think about doing something constructive to save themselves and the world, but do not actually carry out their thought.

People want to live, but they want to live easily and comfortably, without doing very much to make their lives more enjoyable or safe. Their main wish is for immediate gratification and ease. This wish may lead to death, but that is not the intention of the wisher.

Nevertheless, I am optimistic that humans will eventually think and plan themselves out of their present dilemmas, including their nuclear dilemmas, But I am pessimistic about their doing so soon,

ALBERT ELLIS, U.S. *clinical psychologist; executive director, Institute for Rational-Emotive Therapy;* Rational-Emotive Approaches to Problems of Childhood *(1984),* A Guide to Personal Happiness *(1982),* How to Live With and Without Anger *(1977),* A New Guide to Rational Living *(1975),* Executive Leadership: A Rational Approach *(1972) and* Reason and Emotion in Psychotherapy *(1962) are among his published works.*

and without a good deal of needless turmoil and strife before so doing.

Many, many things can be done, and I am not an authority on what most of these are, since I am mainly a psychotherapist. The most important thing I would recommend is trying to raise all humans so they think rationally, scientifically, and undogmatically. This will minimize, though not necessarily reduce to zero, the chances of a small group of devout fanatics deliberately doing us in with nuclear warfare. It will also minimize the chances of regular wars.

Most humans' hostility and homicide stems from crooked, dogmatic, absolutist thinking. The more we do to train all humans to eradicate this kind of thinking, the more peaceful and sane we will tend to make the world.

Art Seidenbaum

"The threat is as bald as an off-on switch. On, the world continues. Off, someone— anyone on any side—throws the switch and the world is condemned to eternal darkness."

To MEET THE morning requires optimism. Each day, for each person, is an affirmation of life. A centenarian once put it in the simplest terms: the secret of living to be 100 is the ability to wake up every day for 100 years. Pessimism serves no purpose, unless you are determined to take razor to wrist.

The threat is as bald as an off-on switch. On, the world continues. Off, someone—anyone on any side—throws the switch and the world is condemned to eternal darkness. If there is life after nuclear assault—lichen life or fungus life or even vestigial, human life—that life will not be recognizable in terms or values we now celebrate.

What can be done? Talk. Talk, educated talk, among citizens everywhere. Talk between competing governments and ideologies. Talk on campuses and in congresses. Talk in print and on electronic carriers, for mutual agreement is the only survival guarantee. And mutual recognition of mutual suicide is the only way to that agreement.

The answer is simple. But the mechanisms for arriving at that answer continue to be terrifyingly elusive. Mechanisms made in the streets are likely to fail. But the cries for new mechanisms are important. The education process is underway; so is the recognition process. The world is not so far away from necessary agreement. What

---

ART SEIDENBAUM, *U.S. Opinion Page editor,* The Los Angeles Times.

we need are governments willing to translate talk into that agreement.

Many people are acting to preserve our planet, including scientists, philosophers, physicians and attorneys, even journalists and some business interests. The problem, in past, is the paucity of politicians acting beyond chauvinism or provincialism. If a world governance is not required, then a sense of a world constituency must be fostered, established, and addressed by every representative leader.

Milton Schwebel

"Economic profits and the fear of losing jobs are powerful motivators for maintaining the arms race."

IN MY VIEW, even as we seem to be veering toward the edge of a precipice, it is realistic to be hopeful, just because the people of the world are now, as in the past, resorting to one means or another for letting their voices be heard. The current crisis is only several years old, yet many influential groups in the U.S.—like the Catholic bishops, and professional entities, especially the physicians—have taken a stand against proliferation, and in favor of arms reductions. And the American people as a whole, both in recent national polls, as well as in state and city elections in 1982, declared themselves for a nuclear freeze and for disarmament. The question is whether the mobilization of the people of the world will be sufficiently powerful to ward off the mounting perils later in this decade, and into the next one.

The demands of daily survival get a higher priority. For many, the struggle for a livelihood leaves little energy, or interest, in a threat that is seen as being in the unforeseeable future. And that is all the more true for the millions whose income depends upon the enormous armaments industry, and who have been given no reason to expect a viable alternative. Economic profits and the fear of losing jobs are powerful motivators for maintaining the arms race.

MILTON SCHWEBEL, *U.S. psychologist; professor of psychology, Rutgers University; president, National Organization for Migrant Children;* Cognitive Development and Its Facilitation *(1983)*, Student Teacher's Manual *(with A., B., and C. Schwebel, 1979)*, Piaget in the Classroom *(with J. Ralph, 1973)*, Who Can Be Educated *(1968) and* Behavioral Science & Human Survival *(1965) are among his published works.*

M.G. Krein

"As to whether reason will prevail over madness, I believe it will, because there presently are still conditions making it possible for normalization of the world situation."

I CONSIDER THE THREAT of nuclear war as a threat to the existence of humankind. This threat is real because: (a) It already exists, in the enormous compilation and perfection of nuclear weapons; (b) There exists an influential circle promoting the possibility and permissiveness of so-called 'limited' nuclear war, and (c) The broad masses still lack any idea of the extent of such a catastrophe, which *will* befall humankind if a nuclear war begins (limited or unlimited).

Therefore, it appears extremely essential that the movement towards peace, in the entire world, be broadened. Such movement already has the support of the Soviet Union, through a commitment not to be the first to use nuclear weapons, and its suggestion to the U.S. that both nations freeze present nuclear arsenals.

As to whether reason will prevail over madness, I believe it will, because there presently are still conditions making it possible for normalization of the world situation. However, it is necessary for the U.S. to also take upon itself a commitment not to be the first to use nuclear weapons (which it has *not* yet done).

Beyond that, all 'nuclear' states should agree upon freezing nuclear armaments, and then work out plans for the step-by-step annihilation of these weapons, in as short a time as possible.

Each of us can help reason prevail by bringing, to the consciousness and understanding of *every* adult, the facts regarding how terrible the consequences of nuclear war will be. In particular, more social and religious leaders, more statesmen and -women, and more leaders in the sciences, arts and literature should unite—get involved —in this movement to explain, by all possible informational means, the tragic consequences of a nuclear catastrophe.

M.G. KREIN, Soviet engineer; professor, Odessa Institute of Civil Engineering; foreign associate, U.S. National Academy of Sciences; foreign member, American Academy of Arts and Sciences.

Hans G. Furth

"We can as little 'discover' a correct solution to the nuclear threat as Beethoven 'discovered' the Ninth Symphony. *What is missing is not factual knowledge, but positive emotions and relations."*

Is THERE A FUTURE for our world? For the first time in history, this question can be meaningfully asked, and no sure, factual answer can be given. I do not think it makes sense to call a person an optimist who believes the nuclear arms will never be used, and the person with the opposite belief, a pessimist. In the eyes of those who today contribute to the nuclear build-up, I may well seem a pessimist: without a change in our emotional and knowledge perspective, I see no possibility to constrain the use of nuclear forces, indefinitely. On the other hand, I am persuaded that the psychological resources of humanity are not limited to our present power-perspective, and that all the talk about some form of innate death instinct is biological nonsense, and but a thin camouflage for denying personal responsibility in the shaping of our world.

I am optimistic that a critical mass of people will respond to the nuclear challenge in a psychologically-constructive manner, by preparing the emotional context of interpersonal openness. And this context—and only this context—provides the optimistic assurance that the present nuclear danger will become the object of communicative action, in which reason and a reasonable use of nuclear knowledge will prevail.

HANS G. FURTH, *U.S. psychologist; professor of psychology, Catholic University of America;* The World of Grown-Ups *(1980) and* Piaget and Knowledge *(1969, 1981) are among his published works.*

The nuclear threat is without parallel in the history of humanity, and is by far its gravest danger. But at the same time, and for the same reason, it is also its greatest challenge and clearest opportunity. The threat manifests, as never before, that the world in which we live is, in fact, a world of our own making, the co-construction of generations upon generations of socially-related people. If the acceptance of personal and social responsibility for the nuclear situation is a first precondition toward a constructive solution, a closer analysis of the nature of human knowledge, and its evolutionary history, may make a significant contribution in reaching this acceptance.

Our personal freedom and responsibility as rational persons has been severely undermined by the fallacious perspective of treating the world as nothing but a totality of objective facts and knowledge—especially scientific knowledge—as a faithful representation of these facts. The nuclear threat may persuade us to recognize that, on the contrary, so-called facts are *shaped* by our knowledge and our know-how. Therefore, we, as individuals and as a group, are to a large extent responsible for the facts. Remember that nuclear power did not exist, as a fact, for thousands of human generations, until today's scientists discovered it, and together with people acting within given political, military and economic systems, applied it to various uses.

It is now widely accepted that the human brain, and its knowledge capacity, have evolved primarily in the service of personal and social relations, and that the milieu to which humans are biologically adapted is the world of socially-related people. If, then, the quality of interpersonal relations has been selected for its survival value, people, in relation to each other, must be considered the proper object of human knowledge. Consequently, to treat knowledge as an impersonal representation of objective facts is a biological perversion and abdication of reason. The notion of value-free knowledge was helpful and perhaps even necessary in the past, in order to overcome the social fetters that hindered the autonomous use of human reason. But today's crisis is the opposite, and in the false name of an impersonal, emotion-free knowledge, we are now in the position of being able to destroy the world which true knowledge, in the form of personal relating, has created.

That emotions should be considered an integral part of all knowledge, particularly also objective knowledge, must sound strange to our customary way of thinking. We like to believe that emotions can only distort and interfere with, but in no way contribute positively to, knowledge improvement. More adequate evolutionary and psychological considerations, however, could readily convince us that socially-positive emotions are at the base of all cultural achievements and progress. Just as new forms of social-relation characterized the first emergence of humans, so the individual development of an infant, into a thinking and feeling adult, is linked to a world of positive, interpersonal emotions, without which there would be no person and no knowledge. Moreover, knowledge, like any other cultural achievement, is not something that belongs to me as an isolated individual, but is a social co-construction that is shared by the group. Consequently, it implies and requires a positive, emotional attachment to, and respect for, other people.

None of these statements denies the presence of negative emotions, or distorted knowledge, in the history of individuals or groups. But the argument hinges on the biological and psychological primacy of positive, interpersonal relations, and on the necessary connection between socially-positive emotions, and truly objective knowledge and its developmental improvement. Emotions motivate actions, and all actions relate the agent, in one way or another, to other people. Ultimately then, I argue against a static, mechanical model of knowledge that would reflect a static world of fact. Instead, I propose—in line with leading biological, psychological and philosophical scholars—a dynamic, personal theory of knowledge, which both reflects and, more importantly, shapes an open-ended world of interpersonal actions.

To put the relation of emotion and knowledge succinctly: positive emotions impel individuals to relate and engage in communicative actions; knowledge provides the rational coordination and content of these actions. Emotional openness to others is the basis of developmentally becoming a person; it is also the obligatory human context for knowledge development, and the constructive solving of problems. In contrast, emotional closure, in the form of self-defensiveness and aggressiveness, is the context for knowledge rigidity, and ultimately leads to personally-destructive resolutions of problems.

Consider the paradox: we labor to discover a reasonable solution to the nuclear dilemma, and we plan according to the best available, objective facts. But the negative, personal context militates against contructive reason and our best, conscious intention. The goal of security is ever elusive. We can as little 'discover' a correct solution to the nuclear threat as Beethoven 'discovered' the *Ninth Symphony*. We are working from the wrong end of the stick. The reasonable solution does not exist as an objective fact to be discovered, but consists, or rather will consist, in a reasonable co-construction of people relating to each other. In other words, what is missing is not factual knowledge, but positive emotions and relations.

Only humanity-as-a-whole can provide the rock-bottom, absolute basis for this positive morality. In fact, this new morality is nothing else but the positive, emotional prerequisite to a rational solution of the nuclear threat. This change toward emotional openness and a positive morality does not begin in political, economic or military circles, but only in ourselves. And we must show this change in our feeling, thinking, and everyday relations and communication with others.

Hans A. Nieper

"Too many people lack the education and information to really analyze the threatening problems of today. Further, the educational state of most people in power is, most often, far behind that which today's problems require."

THE NUCLEAR THREAT offers a yes-or-no chance to the people of this globe: either a more peaceful world, or complete annihilation. Therefore, all responsible governments must act accordingly (provided they are of sufficient responsibility). It is, however, my belief that the nuclear threat has protected us from wars in the last decades. This is especially true for Europe, and possibly, also the U.S.

Likewise, in forthcoming years and decades, the introduction of Tesla weapons—exploiting the extremely energetic, gravity-field energy in space—will confront us with new aspects of the problem, but possibly, also with new, hopeful horizons, since this kind of defense technology will be useful to suppress even bush-level warfare. This would mean that in the future, it will be largely impossible to impose despotic dictatorship upon a people which does not want it. So Tesla weapons, in the long run, will ensure the dominance of people's free will.

The nuclear threat, then, is frightening. But is has certainly helped us to conserve peace in certain areas of the world (which is not at all flattering to humankind), until it will, eventually, be partly dissolved

HANS A. NIEPER, *West German research physician, Silbersee Clinic, Hanover; president, German Society of Oncology, and of the German Association of Gravity-Field Energy;* Conversion of Gravity-Field Energy: Revolution in Technology, Medicine and Society *(1984, U.S. edition) is among his published works.*

and followed by Tesla defense technology.

I am very optimistic about our future. The reason for this, however, is not that people 'mature' by themselves. Rather, it is technological progress which eventually urges people to 'behave more prudently'. Even the very positive reaction for environmental conservation is, after all, a positive result of the silly use of technology.

Nuclear technology—and even more so, Tesla technology—will make large-scale wars impossible to rational people, just as a present war between England and Germany, or France and Germany (which I experienced when I was 14 years old) is unimaginable today... first for technical reasons, then also for reasons of mentality. For example, German-English and German-French relations are now drastically better than ever before in history. We have, however, to concede that it was the technical revolution which urged the English, French and Germans to 'mature' this highly, not the other way around.

The American and Russian people will certainly experience the same development, for the same reason, and for the same causative connection. For the exploding progress of technology works on humankind like the beating stick of the teacher of old on the undisciplined pupil.

Too many people lack the education and information to really analyze the threatening problems of today. And very often, orthodox ideology in people of power weighs more than realistic insight. So the Catholic Church refuses to accept the second-most-dangerous threat: from an exploding, world population. And the Marxists refuse to accept that their ideology is hopelessly outdated. And still, the collectivists, as well as the shrewd capitalists, refuse to accept that humankind is made for individualism, and not for collectivism. Further, the educational state of most people in power is, most often, far behind that which today's problems require.

Most of the problems on Earth carrying an imminent danger find their roots in poor, lacking, or even worse, distorted education. Too much emphasis is given the fields of applied knowledge (e.g., mathematics), and too little the fields of fundamental, broad education, including history, Latin, foreign languages, geography and basal commercial knowledge (which includes foreign mentality).

It is an open secret that the quality of education along the aforementioned categories, in the average U.S. school, is poor. And in the average school of communist and socialist countries, it is distorted. This even applies to Germany, where after the socialists came to power in 1969, the school system became heavily corroded. What has to be done is that in all countries, a committee of educated people should set the standards of what school education should accomplish, free from ideology, perhaps using the present school standard of Switzerland as an example.

Finally, what has to be done is the introduction of gravity-field energy conversion, which will end the 30,000-year era of 'fireplace technology,' and will offer us an extremely inexpensive, individualistic kind of energy, free from environmental challenge. This will automatically lead to higher standards of wealth everywhere, facilitate more individualistic independence, and thus blow the squeezing jackets of despotic dictatorship from the inside—with the help of their own people.

CHAPTER IV

The Solution

WE have grasped the mystery of the atom and rejected the Sermon on the Mount. The world has achieved brilliance without wisdom, power without conscience. Ours is a world of nuclear giants and ethical infants. We know more about war than we know about peace, more about killing than we know about living.

> —OMAR BRADLEY, *former chairperson, U.S. Joint Chiefs of Staff*

Edward Teller

"Replacing deterrence based exclusively on mutually-assured destruction with deterrence that assures survival is both scientifically feasible and our best hope for better relations with the Soviets."

THE MOST URGENT need of our time is to establish peace. This is particularly true because the one major nation whose military power surpasses that of the rest of the world combined—the U.S.S.R.—is led by a group of people who, in contrast to the rest of the world, can be seen by their actions to emphasize power, at least as much as peace.

Many thoroughly feasible, rational solutions are present. My first proposal is to eliminate long-term secrecy, at least as it relates to ideas, rather than details or blueprints. Our present policy of exaggerated secrecy helps to create hopeless and helpless confusion in our democracy.

My second proposal is to work on defensive weapons. Replacing deterrence based exclusively on mutually-assured destruction with deterrence that assures survival, is both scientifically feasible and our best hope for better relations with the Soviets. A number of years ago, the Soviets deployed powerful defenses around Moscow; they were later powerfully upgraded. Much evidence suggests they are emphasizing many forms of ingenious, active defense, as well as civil defense. Any success in protective defense on our part will

EDWARD TELLER, *U.S. physicist; senior research fellow, Hoover Institution on War, Revolution and Peace; professor of physics emeritus, University of California (UC); director emeritus, UC Lawrence Livermore Radiation Laboratory; Manhattan Project physicist generally known as the creator of the H-bomb; Albert Einstein Award, 1958; Enrico Fermi Award, 1962;* The Pursuit of Simplicity *(1980),* Energy From Heaven and Earth *(1979),* General Theory of Electron Structure *(1970) and* Legacy of Hiroshima *(with A. Brown, 1962) are among his published works.*

increase the uncertainty of results of an attack. The leaders of the Soviet Union are not less power hungry than Hitler, but they are incredibly more circumspect. Believing in their ultimate triumph, they are not apt to take deadly risks unless they are certain of success.

President Reagan, in a speech on Mar. 23, 1983, proposed to emphasize protective defense. He asked, "Would it not be better to save lives than to avenge them?" He never mentioned the word 'space,' nor identified any specific measures. Under our exaggerated secrecy laws, the only defensive systems that are publicized are those that deserve ridicule. Reasonable and effective defensive measures are kept secret. Research on them is being pursued at a very modest rate. Cooperative work on this vital project needs to be organized among the people of the free world.

My third proposal is that the democratic nations resume work on biological warfare, emphasizing the development of countermeasures. The present danger from lack of preparedness seems greatest in this area. During the Second World War, superior research and results on our side deterred Hitler from using biological and chemical weapons. The same result can be obtained at this time. Successful deterrence is most promising because biochemistry has undergone an incredible period of development in the free world, while at the same time, the Soviet Union is still paying for a terrible mistake. Urged on by Lysenko (who denied the validity of Mendelian theory), Stalin tried to grow wheat in the Arctic, and sent a generation of excellent Soviet biologists who disagreed to labor camps. Neither Soviet agriculture nor biosciences have yet recovered in full.

My fourth and last proposal is to pursue peace (which is more than the absence of war). Instead of meaningless, unenforceable arms negotiations, we should pursue cooperation throughout the world on constructive progress. Such cooperation can and should include the Soviet Union. Such agreements are violated only by nonperformance, an easily-identified event. Thus, they cannot add to distrust or suspiciousness, and they would add to the well-being of all the world's people, a concrete basis for peace. Examples of possible joint projects include development of ocean-food resources, and work on weather prediction and modification.

Implementing such agreements would certainly be difficult, but at least our efforts would not lead to self-delusion. Furthermore, any positive results will produce mutual benefits, which are inducements to avoid war. Joint work forges the human links that lead to mutual understanding and some form of order, while avoiding the great dangers inherent in any form of super-government. The unavoidable technical progress of our era can be made to serve humankind at peace.

Nicolaas Bloembergen

*"The current leadership of the two great
nuclear powers needs to be persuaded that a
higher degree of national security is obtained
by fewer nuclear weapons on both sides.
They need education on the fact that the
concepts of limited nuclear war, and a
complete defense against nuclear attack,
only exist in hypothetical war-game
scenarios."*

I AM NOT very optimistic right now, but I hold on to the belief that the present nuclear confrontation will abate, and that a nuclear holocaust will be avoided.

I believe the large majority of human beings is in favor of de-escalation. The current leadership of the two great nuclear powers needs to be persuaded that a higher degree of national security is obtained by *fewer* nuclear weapons on both sides. They need education on the fact that the concepts of limited nuclear war, and a complete defense against nuclear attack, only exist in hypothetical war-game scenarios.

The two superpowers should continuously negotiate about verifiable, strategic arms reductions. In this country, the public should be alerted about the consequences of the current arms race. It should be made an issue in every political campaign at the national level.

NICOLAAS BLOEMBERGEN, *U.S. physicist; 1981 Nobel Prize in Physics for contribution to development of laser spectroscopy; professor of applied physics, Harvard University;* Nonlinear Optics *(1965)* and Nuclear Magnetic Relaxation *(1961) are among his published works.*

Robert J. Lifton

*"If we can imagine our own death, we can
not only imagine an act of mass suicide and
murder, the nuclear holocaust—which we
must imagine in order to prevent—but we
can imagine alternatives to that act."*

Human existence itself may be absurd, as many have claimed,
but we live now in a special realm of absurdity; we are haunted by
something we can neither see nor imagine. We are afraid of something we call "nuclear holocaust," and at the same time, are removed
from, and have little awareness of, that threat.

There is a structural layer to our absurdity. The obvious one has
the two superpowers poised to exterminate each other, and in the
process, the rest of the world. Then there is a second layer that is
more or less existential: it is the way we all live—with the sense that
we can be annihilated in a moment, along with everything we've
known, loved and experienced in our existence, while we carry on
our everyday activities, business as usual. The third layer involves
the mind's relationship to the things we can't locate in our images,
this thing called "nuclear holocaust". In a way, our task is what
Martin Buber called "imagining the real".

To characterize our predicament with regard to nuclear weapons,
I would identify three present dangers. First, the danger of war is
greater than ever; that's the terrible truth, and there is a lot of evidence that is beyond the scope of this reply.

Second, there are manifest and important psychological contributions to that danger, which have to do with the expansion of nuclear-
weapons systems, bureaucratically and technologically, to the extent
that they are no longer controllable by individuals or groups. On the

ROBERT J. LIFTON, U.S. psychiatrist; professor of psychiatry and psychology,
City University of New York; Indefensible Weapons (with R. Falk, 1982),
Boundaries: Psychological Man in Revolution (1970), History and Human Sur-
vival (1970), and Death in Life: Survivors of Hiroshima (1968, National Book
Award) are among his published works.

one hand, there's a certain psychological stance that moves toward resignation. But a more hopeful, second psychological tendency is the increasing disquiet with the rationalizations or justifications given by our leaders for continuing the arms race. People don't quite believe them anymore, and that's a starting point for us.

The third element here is the call for more numbing. As the numbing, or diminished feeling, breaks down, our leaders, along with various leaders in different parts of the world, tell us: "Numb yourselves some more, don't feel. Above all, don't question." And that is the situation we have to confront.

My own perception of these dangers has been intensified, and perhaps rendered even more grotesque, by work I've done on the psychology of Nazi doctors. I've interviewed both ordinary men, who were not inherently demonic and could yet engage in demonic pursuits, and professionals who took pride in their profession, and could lend themselves to mass murder. Mass murder was not impossible for others, and it's not impossible in our society.

Colin Gray and Keith Payne have said that if American nuclear power is to support U.S. foreign-policy objectives, the United States must possess the ability to wage nuclear war *rationally*. We are dealing not with personal madness here, but with social madness; these are clinically-sane people advocating this, and that makes it hard. It's the normal people who are always the dangerous ones.

Strictly speaking, national security is simply impossible, as is individual security, because everybody is vulnerable. Therefore, the insistence upon more and better nuclear devices is partly an effort, on the part of our leaders, to deny this unacceptable truth; partly a residium of pre-nuclear thinking, and partly an effort to reestablish a psychological sense of security, in themselves and in all Americans.

Each new bomb system that is developed destabilizes our sense of psychological security; with every attempt to regain it, we're exposed to an ever-greater danger of massive annihilation. It's like a thermostat in reverse: the thermostat manipulators keep the temperature reading low, and keep on putting up the heat. People tend to get a false assurance, because in part, it works, in that you are 'more secure' in a psychological sense if you have more and bigger weapons. That's why I call it the "ultimate psychologism," and urge that we keep addressing it as that, in the hope that one of these days, our political leaders will have the courage to say exactly that.

Secrecy is very much a part of this process. Even though we now know other countries can indeed make the weapons, the myth of the secret helps maintain illusions about security. It also helps a very small group of bomb managers assume priest-like stances as exclusive possessors of secrets, too arcane and sacred to be made available to the rest of us. The assumption holds that if they can protect this secret again, if they can maintain vigilance, they can retain security. But in actuality, what they do is increase danger, and stifle opposition.

There seems, then, to be a vicious psycho-political circle: the sense of loss of security, the onset of fear, the loss of credibility and of stability, and the desperate but impossible quest to regain these by stockpiling nuclear weapons. Then the existence of a nuclear armamentarium provokes a sense of still greater loss and insecurity, and the embrace of more and more weapons. It is this vicious circle that we must interrupt.

Our situation is desperate and, at the same time, hopeful. Desperate, because of the danger of war, nuclear war; hopeful, because something is really happening in America, and elsewhere. The need now is to move from the fragmemtary awareness that's beginning to take shape, toward more formed awareness, toward awareness that informs, that becomes part of our world view, that influences our actions, our behavior, our commitments, our lives.

Part of becoming human is developing the capacity to imagine the future, to symbolize, to create culture. Imagining the future includes being able to imagine one's own death, and we perceive this capacity to be in danger. If we can imagine our own death, we can not only imagine an act of mass suicide and murder, the nuclear holocaust—which we *must* imagine in order to prevent—but we can imagine alternatives to that act. That is what's beginning to happen, not only in the movement of doctors, represented by groups such as Physicians for Social Responsibility and International Physicians for the Prevention of Nuclear War, but in similar movements forming among the clergy, lawyers, students, teachers, and others.

Everyone, people from all professions and all areas, should be urged to take part in these movements. Strangely enough, when one addresses these issues—and, of course, they *are* grim, and one *has* to immerse one's imagination in this grimness to imagine the real— there is personal value to be realized. One puts oneself more in touch with actuality, with things as they are, with our world, for better or worse, and, indeed, with things that matter to us, such as love, sensuality, creative realization, and life goals that have significance. These are concomitants of commitment to this issue.

The issue is deadly serious, but our call is not a grim one. It is a call to life.

Andrei D. Sakharov

*"It is possible that for a
limited period of time, the
mutual, nuclear terror had a
certain restraining effect on
the course of world events.
But at present, the balance
of nuclear terror is a dangerous remnant of the past!*

ALL-OUT NUCLEAR WAR would mean the destruction of contemporary civilization, hurl humanity back centuries, cause the deaths
of hundreds of millions or billions of people, and, with a certain
degree of probability, cause humankind to be destroyed as a biological species, and could even cause the annihilation of life on Earth.

Clearly, it is meaningless to speak of victory in a large nuclear
war, which is collective suicide. I think that basically, my point of
view coincides with the opinion of a great many people on Earth.

If the 'nuclear threshold' is crossed (i.e., if any country uses a
nuclear weapon, even on a limited scale) the further course of events
would be difficult to control. The most probable result would be
swift escalation, leading from a nuclear war initially limited in scale
or by region, to an all-out nuclear war (i.e., to general suicide).

It is relatively unimportant how the 'nuclear threshold' is crossed
—as a result of a preventive nuclear strike; or in the course of a war
fought with conventional weapons, when a country is threatened
with defeat, or simply as a result of an accident (technical or
organizational).

ANDREI D. SAKHAROV, *Soviet physicist; 1975 Nobel Peace Prize; principal
designer of Soviet H-bomb; since January, 1980, has been exiled to the city of
Gorky; co-founder, Moscow Human Rights Committee; member, U.S.S.R.
Academy of Sciences; foreign associate, U.S. National Academy of Sciences;
Alarm and Hope (1979), My Country and the World (1975), Sakharov Speaks
(1974), and Peaceful Co-existence and Intellectual Freedom (1968) are among
his published works.*

In view of the above, I am convinced that the following basic tenet is true: *Nuclear weapons only make sense as a means of deterring nuclear aggression by a potential enemy;* i.e., a nuclear war cannot be planned with the aim of winning it. Nuclear weapons cannot be viewed as a means of restraining aggression carried out by means of conventional weapons.

This statement is, of course, in contradiction to the West's actual strategy of the last few decades. For a long time, beginning as far back as the end of the 1940s, the West has *not* been relying on its 'conventional' armed forces as a means sufficient for repelling a potential aggressor, and for restraining expansion. There are many reasons for this: the West's lack of political, military and economic unity; the striving to avoid a peacetime militarization of the economy, society, technology and science, and the low numerical levels of the Western nations' armies. All that at a time when the U.S.S.R. and the other countries of the socialist camp have armies with great numerical strength, and are rearming them intensively, sparing no resources.

It is possible that for a limited period of time, the mutual, nuclear terror had a certain restraining effect of the course of world events. But at present, the balance of nuclear terror is a dangerous remnant of the past! In order to avoid aggression with conventional weapons, one cannot threaten to use nuclear weapons if their use is inadmissible. One of the conclusions that follows here is that it is necessary to restore strategic parity in the field of conventional weapons.

The restoration of strategic parity is only possible by investing large resources, and by an essential change in the psychological atmosphere in the West. There must be a readiness to make certain limited, economic sacrifices and, most importantly, an understanding of the seriousness of the situation, and of the necessity for some restructuring. In the final analysis, this is necessary to prevent nuclear war, and war in general.

Will the West's politicians be able to carry out such a restructuring? Will the press, the public, and fellow scientists help them (and not hinder them, as is frequently now the case)? Can they succeed in convincing those who doubt the necessity of such restructuring? A great deal depends on it—the opportunity for the West to conduct a nuclear-arms policy that will be conducive to the lessening of the danger of nuclear disaster.

I should especially stress that a restructuring of strategy could, of course, only be carried out gradually and very carefully, in order to prevent a loss of parity in some of the intermediate phases. Therefore, I hope that some criterion for assessing nuclear strength will be accepted as the basis for negotiations both on intercontinental missiles and (independently) on medium-range missiles. Thereafter, in both cases, it will be much more difficult than it now is to insist on unfair conditions in the agreements, and possible to move from word to deed more swiftly. Most likely, the very acceptance of such criterion will require a diplomatic and propaganda struggle—but it's worth it.

Of course it would be wiser to agree now to reduce nuclear and conventional weapons, and to eliminate nuclear weapons entirely. But is that now possible in a world poisoned with fear and mistrust, a world where the West fears aggression from the U.S.S.R., and the U.S.S.R. fears aggression from the West and from China, and where China fears it from the U.S.S.R., and no verbal assurances and treaties can eliminate those dangers entirely?

I know that pacifist sentiments are very strong in the West. I deeply sympathize with people's yearning for peace, for a solution to world problems by peaceful means; I share those aspirations fully. But, at the same time, I am certain that it is absolutely necessary to be mindful of the specific political, military and strategic realities of the present day, and to do so objectively, without making any sort of allowances for either side. This also means that one should not proceed from an *a priori* assumption of any special peace-loving nature in the socialist countries, due to their supposed progressiveness or the horrors and losses they have experienced in war. Objective reality is much more complicated, and far from anything so simple. People both in the socialist and the Western countries have a passionate, inward aspiration for peace. This is an extremely important factor, but, I repeat, itself alone does not exclude the possibility of a tragic outcome.

What is necessary now, I believe, is the enormous, practical task of education, so that specific, exact, and historically and politically meaningful, objective information can be made available to all people... information that will enjoy their trust and not be veiled with dogma and propaganda. Here, one must take into account that in the countries of the West, pro-Soviet propaganda has been conducted for quite a long time, and is very goal-oriented and clever, and that pro-Soviet elements have penetrated many key positions, particularly in the mass media.

The history of the pacifist campaigns against the deployment of missiles in Europe is telling in many respects. After all, many of those participating in those campaigns entirely ignore the initial cause of NATO's 'dual decision'—the change in strategic parity in the 1970s in favor of the U.S.S.R.—and, when protesting NATO's plans, they have not advanced any demands on the U.S.S.R. Another example: President Carter's attempt to take a minimal step toward achieving balance in the area of conventional arms; i.e., to introduce draft registration, met with stiff resistance. Meanwhile, balance in the area of conventional arms is a necessary prerequisite for reducing nuclear arsenals. For public opinion in the West to assess global problems correctly—in particular the problems of strategic parity, both in conventional and in nuclear weapons—a more objective approach, one which takes the real, world strategic situation into account, is vitally needed.

A second group of problems in the field of nuclear weapons, about which I should make a few supplementary remarks here, concerns the talks on nuclear disarmament. For these talks to be successful, the West should have something that it can give up! The case of the 'Euromissiles,' once again, demonstrates how difficult it is to negotiate from a position of weakness. Only very recently has the U.S.S.R. apparently ceased to insist on its unsubstantiated thesis that a rough parity now exists, and therefore everything should be left as it is.

Now, the next welcome step would be the reduction of the number of missiles—which must include a fair assessment of the *quality* of missiles and other means of delivery. And what is absolutely at issue here is not moving the missiles beyond the Urals, but *destroying* them. After all, rebasing is too 'reversible'. Of course, one also must not consider powerful Soviet missiles, with mobile launchers and several warheads, as being equal to the now-existing Pershing I, the British and French missiles, or the bombs on short-range bombers—as the Soviet side sometimes attempts to do for purposes of propaganda.

No less important a problem is that of the powerful, silo-based missiles. At present, the U.S.S.R. has a great advantage in this area. (Seventy percent of the Soviet arsenal, according to TASS, consists of gigantic land-based missiles and somewhat smaller intermediate-range missiles, on mobile launchers. Eighty percent of the U.S. arsenal consists of submarine-based nuclear missiles, much smaller but less vulnerable than silo-based missiles, and also of strategic bombers carrying nuclear bombs.) Perhaps talks about the limitation and reduction of these most destructive missiles could become easier if the United States were to have MX missiles, albeit only potentially (indeed, that would be best of all).

A few words about the military capabilities of powerful missiles: they can be used to deliver the largest thermonuclear charges for destroying cities and other major enemy targets—while for exhausting the enemy's ABM systems, such as the planned U.S. Strategic Defense Initiative, or 'Star Wars' system, there will most likely be a simultaneous use of a 'rain' of smaller missiles, false targets, and so on. (Much is written about the possibility of developing ABM systems using super-powerful lasers, accelerated particle beams, and so forth. But the creation of an effective defense against missiles, along these lines, seems highly doubtful to me.)

A specific danger associated with silo-based missiles is that they can be destroyed relatively easily as a reult of enemy attack. At the same time, they can be used to destroy enemy launch sites in an amount four to five times larger than the numbers of missiles used for the attack. A country with large numbers of silo-based missiles (at the present time, this is primarily the U.S.S.R., but if the U.S. carries out a major MX program, then it, too) could be 'tempted' to use such missiles first, before the enemy destroys them. In such circumstances, the presence of silo-based missiles constitutes a de-stabilizing factor.

In view of the above, it seems very important to me to strive for the abolition of powerful, silo-based missiles at the talks on nuclear disarmament. While the U.S.S.R. is the leader in this field, there is very little chance of its easily relinquishing that lead. If it is necessary to spend a few billion dollars on MX missiles to alter this situation, then perhaps this is what the West must do. But at the same time, if the Soviets, in deed and not just in word, take significant, verifiable measures for reducing the number of land-based missiles (more precisely, for destroying them), then the West should not only abol-ish MX missiles (or not build them!), but carry out other significant disarmament programs as well.

On the whole, I am convinced that nuclear disarmament talks are of enormous importance and of the highest priority. They must be continuously conducted—in the brightest periods of international relations, but also in the periods when relations are strained—and conducted with persistence, foresight, firmness and, at the same time, with flexibility and initiative. In so doing, political figures should not think of exploiting those talks and the nuclear problem in general for their own immediate political gains, but only for the long-term interests of their country and the world. And the planning of the talks should be included in one's general, nuclear strategy as its most important part!

The third group of problems which should be discussed here is political and social in nature. A nuclear war could result from a conventional war, while a conventional war is, as is well known, a result of politics. We all know that the world is not at peace. There are a variety of reasons for this—national, economic and social rea-son, as well as the tyranny of dictators.

Many of the tragic events now occurring have their roots in the distant past. It would be absolutely wrong to see only Moscow's hand everywhere. Still, when examining the general trend of events since 1945, their has been a relentless expansion of the Soviet sphere of influence. Objectively, this is nothing but Soviet expansion on a world scale. This process has spread as the U.S.S.R. has grown stronger economically (though that strength is one-sided) and in scientific, technological and military terms, and has today assumed proportions dangerously harmful to international equilibrium. The West has grounds to worry that the world's sea routes, Arab oil, and the uranium, diamonds and other resources of South Africa are now threatened.

One of the basic problems of this age is the fate of the developing countries—the greater part of humankind. But, in fact, for the U.S.S.R., and to some degree for the West as well, this problem has become exploitable and expendable in the struggle for dominance and strategic interest. Millions of people are dying of hunger every year; hundreds of millions suffer from malnutrition and hopeless poverty. The West provides the developing countries with economic and technological aid, but this remains entirely insufficient, due largely to the price of crude oil. Aid from the U.S.S.R. and the socialist countries is smaller in scale and, to a greater degree than the West's aid, military in nature and bloc-oriented. And, very important-ly, that aid is in no way coordinated with world efforts.

The hot spots of local conflicts are not dying, but are rather threatening to grow into global wars. All this is greatly alarming.

The most acutely negative manifestation of Soviet policies was the invasion of Afghanistan, which began in December, 1979, with the murder of the head of state. Years of appallingly cruel, anti-guerrilla war have brought incalculable suffering to the Afghan people, as attested by the more than four million refugees in Pakistan and Iran. It was precisely the general upsetting of world equilibrium caused by this invasion, and by other concurrent events, which was the fundamental reason that the SALT II agreement was not ratified.

Yet another subject closely connected to the problem of peace is the openness of society and human rights. In 1948, the U.N.'s member states adopted the Universal Declaration of Human Rights and stressed its significance for maintaining peace. In 1975, the rela-tionship of human rights and international security was proclaimed by the Helsinki Final Act, which was signed by 35 countries, includ-ing the U.S.S.R. and the U.S. Among those rights are: the right to freedom of conscience; the right to receive and impart information within a country and across frontiers; the right to a free choice of one's country of residence, and domicile within a country; freedom of religion, and freedom from psychiatric persecution.

Finally, citizens have the right to control their national leaders' decision-making in matters on which the fate of the world depends. But we don't even know how, or by whom, the decision to invade Afghanistan was made! People in our country do not have even a fraction of the information about events in the world, and in their own country, which the citizens of the West have at their disposal.

The opportunity to criticize the policy of one's national leaders in matters of war and peace, as you in the West do freely, is in our country entirely absent. Not only critical statements, but those merely factual in nature, made on even much less important question, often entail arrest and a long sentence of confinement or psychiatric prison.

In December, 1982, there was an amnesty to honor the U.S.S.R.'s 60th anniversary. But just as in 1977, and in the preceding amnesties, there was a point made of excluding prisoners of conscience, so distant is the U.S.S.R. from the principles it proclaims . . . a country which bears such great responsibility for the fate of the world!

In conclusion, I again stress how important it is that the world realize the absolute inadmissibility of nuclear war—the collective suicide of humankind. It is impossible to win a nuclear war. What is necessary is to strive, systematically though carefully, for complete nuclear disarmament, based on strategic parity in conventional weapons. As long as there are nuclear weapons in the world, there must be a strategic parity of nuclear forces so that neither side will venture to embark on a limited or regional nuclear war.

Genuine security is possible only when based on a stabilization of international relations; a repudiation of expansionist policies; the strengthening of international trust, openness and pluralization in the socialist societies; the observance of human rights throughout the world; the rapprochement—convergence—of the socialist and capitalist systems, and worldwide, coordinated efforts to solve global problems.

Thor Heyerdahl

"Innumerable civilizations have preceded ours on this planet, and none has survived. For ours to become the only exception, we must lose faith in arms as the only means of security, for this time, the risks are total."

THE FACT THAT we can seriously speak of a nuclear threat and still consider ourselves the builders of a civilized society, shows that we are lulled away into an unrealistic dream world, unable to grasp the madness in the present situation.

Innumerable civilizations have preceded ours on this planet, and none has survived. For ours to become the only exception, we must lose the faith in arms as the only means of security, for this time, the risks are total. Humankind has survived the collapse of previous civilizations because women and children were normally spared in warfare, and defeated tribes and nations could flee to another land. In a nuclear holocaust, no sex or age will be spared, and no astronauts can find us another abode for our descendants.

What can and must be done is to wake up the dormant public, and join them into unions for peace; make it known that 'arms balance' has been man's illusive goal from the days of the club and the spear, to the era of gunpowder and dynamite. The founder of the Nobel Peace Prize rejoiced at his own invention of dynamite, because it would end all wars. So did we, when we tested the Hiroshima bomb ... until we found that others began to produce them, too, and thus

THOR HEYERDAHL, *Norwegian anthropologist and explorer; vice-president, World Association of World Federalists;* The Tigris Expedition *(1979),* Early Man and the Ocean *(1978),* The Ra Expedition *(1971) and* The Kon-Tiki Expedition *(1948, translated into 64 languages) are among his published works.*

the arms race had to go on.

Why does it have to go on? Because most industrialized nations survive today, due to an industry resting heavily on the arms race. Stop the armament industry, and the world economy will collapse and cause a global chaos almost as disastrous for humankind as a major war. Let us first find means of alternative employment, allowing survival for the millions now nourished by the arms race. Only then may we see future generations building a smiling society on this fabulous planet.

Sidney D. Drell

"There is no technology known today, or on the technological horizon reaching into the future to the end of this century, that is capable of repelling an attack against our nation by thousands of nuclear warheads, in their intercontinental missile paths that span distances of 6000 miles in less than a 30-minute time . . . no prospect whatsoever of deploying—on the ground or in space, with missiles or lasers—an effective defense of the nation's people and cities."

THE UNPRECEDENTED SCALE of destruction and devastation of which nuclear weapons are capable presents us with fundamental issues—moral as well as practical. As a scientist, it is natural for me to approach the issues of war and peace with a technical orientation. That is my strength and experience, as I work to understand the physical realities of nuclear weapons, and I study how these physical realities impose limitations on the available alternatives for national policy. These are important issues. But I am also a human being, and I understand that the challenge of nuclear weapons is ultimately a moral challenge, for these are weapons of mass destruction.

Today, we recognize that the vast arsenals of these weapons of mass destruction that we have already accumulated could shatter the civilization created by human genius and inspiration over our entire, recorded history of some 30 centuries. What right has man to cause—or even threaten—such a devastating insult to the Earth, the

SIDNEY D. DRELL, *U.S. physicist; professor, deputy director, and executive head of theoretical physics, Linear Accelerator Center, Stanford University; adviser for more than 20 years to U.S. government on national security and arms-control issues; currently advises Executive agencies and Congress on defense and intelligence issues; Leo Szilard Award, 1980;* Facing the Threat of Nuclear Weapons *(1983),* Relativistic Quantum Mechanics and Relativistic Quantum Fields *(both with J. Bjorken) are among his published works.*

ecosphere, the very condition of human existence? If modern civilization is to improve its chances for avoiding nuclear holocaust in the long run, I believe it is absolutely necessary to return the nuclear debate to such fundamental issues.

Simply, it is a fact that any nation initiating a nuclear war may be literally committing suicide. This fact is based on a technical reality that is almost universally recognized: there is no effective defense against nuclear retaliation. There is no technology known today, or on the technological horizon reaching into the future to the end of this century, that is capable of repelling an attack against our nation by thousands of nuclear warheads, in their intercontinental missile paths that span distances of 6000 miles in less than a 30-minute flight time... no prospect whatsoever of deploying—on the ground or in space, with missiles or lasers—an effective defense of the nation's people and cities.

Owing to the very great destructive power of nuclear weapons, the offense has—and can maintain—a predominance over the defense. No matter how effective the defense, if it is less than perfect, it fails, for it takes but one medium-size bomb on target to extinguish Seattle. If only one out of 20—or five percent—of the Soviet missiles were to arrive at American cities, our *immediate* casualties would very likely number in the many tens of millions, or more, and our industry and major cities would be reduced to radioactive rubble.

The basic, technical realities of nuclear weapons present a stark picture for us all to recognize. Defenseless against these nuclear weapons of mass destruction, we live in a balance of terror, as mutual hostages in today's world. This is a situation unprecedented in history. There will, indeed, be no winners in a nuclear war. I conclude, therefore, that the sole purpose of nuclear weapons is, and must remain for as long as they are deployed, to deter nuclear war.

U.S. and Soviet forces are very different, having developed out of different technological and bureaucratic styles and geographic needs. In particular, the Soviets emphasized the strength of their land-based force of large ICBMs, while America wisely focused its best technology on the mobile and quiet, and therefore untargetable, submarine-based systems and on long-range, strategic bombers, that can take off and fly out on warning of attack.

But both countries have deployed far more forces than are required for deterrence. When one starts counting and comparing numbers, it is easy to forget that a very small fraction of these nuclear bombs would cause greater damage than humankind has ever conceived of. That fact—and *not* small numerical differences—is the important message.

I think it is time—and the need has never been more urgent—for us to return to the basics and to common sense in facing the nuclear challenge. We have to stop being prisoners of numbers and 'Who's ahead?' thinking. At today's levels of nuclear weapons, the question of 'Who's ahead?' has lost meaning. We have to keep in mind what these weapons do. We have to realize that nuclear weapons are so destructive, and their danger so great, that we cannot buy security by greater nuclear strength. Quite the contrary! With growing nuclear arsenals—and particularly with growing numbers of nuclear-armed nations—it is our *insecurity* that is increasing. We need not the MX, but effective arms control to *improve* our national security.

It has often been said that war is too important to be left to the generals, and that peace is too vital to be left to the politicians. So are matters of nuclear weapons and policy too important to be left to the 'experts'. Nuclear weapons and policies are matters of life and death, for our entire planet; there is, therefore, no excuse for us not to constitute an *informed and an effective public constituency* insisting on the imperative of arms control.

I wish to be clear that as a technician, I find difficulty with a comprehensive freeze as literal policy. I also reject the suggestion that a freeze offers a realistic escape from serious, detailed negotiations. I have, however, supported the freeze campaign, and I continue to support it as a mandate for arms control. I reject the claim by some of our leaders that the freeze movement weakens the U.S. position at the arms-control negotiations by showing us as a divided country. Not so. Our strength as a democracy rests on the involvement and constructive efforts of an informed citizenry. I also reject the claim that there is a window of vulnerability that we must close by building more weapons, before we can negotiate reductions.

To me, the primary importance of the freeze is that it has served as the first step in building a constituency, by uniting many who found cause to reject both the record of the past, and the rhetoric of the present, in arms control.

It is a welcome and important development that the citizenry has finally concluded, that in this vital issue of life and death, it is unacceptable to abdicate responsibility to the 'experts' alone. We all have a personal stake in it; it is our own lives. We must continue to insist that our elected officials, in meeting their obligations for our security, give arms control at least as high a priority as arms.

We must never forget what these weapons do, and that what is at stake is the survival of civilization, as we know it. Avoiding a nuclear holocaust is our sacred, moral obligation to generations yet unborn.

We should begin by removing all battlefield nuclear weapons— and along with them, the dangerous fantasy of current NATO doctrine. In 1982, the Soviet Union officially affirmed a change in its policy and announced a doctrine of "no first use" of nuclear weapons. In addition, the Soviet military has rewritten army manuals to reflect that change. Such declarations and words are welcome—and not without value, as a signal of Soviet thinking and intentions. Of course, actions and evidence of actual military preparations are of considerably greater value.

For NATO, the first step of a real nuclear disengagement must be the maintenance of a conventionally-armed force, by the Alliance nations, that is adequate for the defense of Western Europe. This does not require a big military buildup, although some have attempted to portray the requirements for a conventional defense of Europe in such terms. We could pay for our share with a modest reprogramming of existing defense dollars—from our gold-plated nuclear programs, such as MX, B-1B, and new nuclear, aircraft carriers—to the conventional forces, with appropriate emphasis given to the newest technology of precision-guided munitions.

Progress in the MBFR (mutual and balanced force reduction) talks in Vienna, that have dragged on for more than a decade, could decrease these costs. An agreement there to redeploy battlefield nuclear weapons farther back from the front lines, and to create a nuclear-free zone in Europe, would also be an important step toward nuclear disengagement. But we shouldn't wait for those developments. Here, if anywhere, is a prime area for bold, unilateral action by the United States. We should simply begin removing some of these dangerous weapons. There is a precedent for such action. We reduced this arsenal from 7,000 to 6,000 in 1979, and the same year, the Soviets withdrew 20,000 troops and 1,000 tanks. It matters not that these were not weapons or troops of top quality. It was a constructive action. We need more bold, unilateral actions of that sort.

In order to expedite such actions, we should also engage in discussions leading to improved cooperation at the military level, including more communication between staff, and the presence of observers, especially during maneuvers. These are actions that come under the heading of confidence-building and crisis-avoidance measures, and are, I believe, practical. They are often advocated by both sides in discussions with colleagues from Moscow, but they need implementation.

I consider them the necessary prelude if we are to effectively back off from current doctrines that imply early first use, and to take, instead, a position of no early first use of nuclear weapons. Our eventual goal should be a policy of no use—first, second, or third, or at any level. When dealing with weapons of suicide, there are no sensible way stations. Sanity is synonymous with no use whatever.

There are also no sensible way stations—or comfort stops—along the negotiating route, short of the goal endorsed by President

Reagan when he said he would "negotiate as long as necessary to reduce the numbers of nuclear weapons to a point where neither side threatens the survival of the other." His emphasis on negotiating our way out from the nuclear threat is well placed, but I would welcome more convincing evidence of *actions* by his Administration.

On Mar. 23, 1983, President Reagan also proposed that we turn to space-age technology in order to counter the nuclear threat to our survival, with a defensive umbrella. I believe there is more 'pie in the sky' than realism in that proposal. In search of security, I know of no technological alternative to the imperative of arms control. George Kennan stated it elegantly and forcefully in his book, *The Nuclear Delusion*, in words that summarize this statement:

> *Whoever does not understand that when it comes to nuclear weapons, the whole concept of relative advantage is illusory; whoever does not understand that when you are talking about absurd and preposterous quantities of overkill, the relative sizes of arsenals have no serious meaning; whoever does not understand that the danger lies, not in the possibility that someone else might have more missiles and warheads than we do, but in the very existence of these unconscionable quantities of highly-poisonous explosives, with their existence, above all, in hands as weak and shaky and undependable as those of ourselves or our adversaries, or any other mere human beings . . . whoever does not understand these things is never going to guide us out of this increasingly dark and menacing forest of bewilderments, into which we have all wandered.*
>
> *I can see no way out of this dilemma other than by a bold and sweeping departure, a departure that would cut surgically through the exaggerated anxieties, the self-engendered nightmares, and the sophisticated mathematics of destruction in which we have all been entangled over these recent years, and would permit us to move, with courage and decision, to the heart of the problem.* °

°George F. Kennan, *The Nuclear Delusion: Soviet-American Relations in the Atomic Age* (New York: Pantheon Books, 1982).

Laura Huxley

"Who can imagine that this species has built, methodically, year after year, a death instrument with which it could kill itself, not once, but 40 times over?"

ONLY AFTER IT touches the flame does the baby KNOW that it burns. In relation to the unspeakable folly of nuclear fire, most of us are babies.

In my imagination, I view the nuclear threat as if I were standing on another planet. I see that what is considered the most advanced species on Earth has built a death instrument that could, in the shortest time, kill each of its members.

It is difficult, but may be possible, to view such a folly. But who can imagine that this species has built, methodically, year after year, a death instrument with which it could kill itself, not once, but 40 times over? Where, when, has any creature methodically planned to kill its victim THIRTY-NINE times after it was dead?

Nevertheless, if the death instrument is the outer expression of our inner consciousness, so is the fact that we have not used it. The same intelligence, money, and fervor that have been used to make total destruction possible can be used to make peace possible.

However, just as important as survival is the quality of life. Even if we avoid destruction now, its possibility will face the children of the future—unless we address ourselves to the roots of the matter... where health and disease begin, where love and fear begin, where war and peace begin: IN THE WOMB.

LAURA HUXLEY, U.S.author; founder, Our Ultimate Investment, a nonprofit organization for the nurturing of the possible human; Between Heaven and Earth, This Timeless Moment: A Personal View of Aldous Huxley (1968) and You Are Not the Target (1963) are among her published works.

Tom Hayden

"I believe that the people who stopped the Vietnam War can stop the growing cancer of nuclear madness. Those who stopped Richard Nixon can stop our present collision course with the Soviet Union."

A FEW YEARS ago, I was looking through a book of photographs of the victims of the atomic bombing of Hiroshima and Nagasaki, given me by a Japanese friend, and I hardly noticed when my son, then seven, climbed onto my lap to read along.

As he stared at the scenes of disfiguration and destruction, I felt his small body tighten. "Did this happen, or is this made up? Will this happen here?" he asked. "No," I replied, "because your mother and I, and many of our friends, will stop it from happening." He then started to cry, the kind of uncontrollable sobbing that breaks your heart. After awhile, he pulled himself together and demanded to know: "What if you don't stop it?"

That's the ultimate question each generation has to ask its predecessor. And the greatest tyranny imaginable is for one generation to make decisions which threaten not only its own children, but all of humanity. The generation of political leaders since the 1940s has done just that. They've imposed on *all* generations a radioactive future in which hundreds of innocent millions are threatened by the continuously escalating specter of nuclear war.

We Americans still live under an Administration whose dream of the future lies in restoring the past, the days of the American frontier. They believe that American strength and prosperity depend on

TOM HAYDEN, *U.S. member, California Legislature; chairperson, Campaign for Economic Democracy.*

unlimited access to resources, that we must maintain our present control of 40 percent of the world's resources, in particular the oil in regions like the Persian Gulf. They believe the U.S. has become weaker, and the Soviet Union stronger in the past generation. They believe this must be reversed rapidly, before Soviet influence reaches the Persian Gulf, Southern Africa and other key areas. They believe the U.S. must show an immediate determination to be militarily aggressive, and even prepare for war, even a nuclear showdown, with the Soviet Union in the next few years.

Therefore, they are talking tough, they are invading Central America, meeting with generals from South Africa to Chile, increasing the military budget, and expanding the supply of nuclear weapons . . . all as a signal to the Soviets of a new American toughness, a signal that the Pentagon can override a few million protestors, a signal that the days of anti-war feeling in America are over. What this means for you is that you are not only fighting for yourselves and your loved ones, but you are part of a larger struggle for the direction of America. You are pawns in the Administration's game plan. But if you refuse to be pawns, if you become responsible and effective citizens, if you show that Americans refuse to live in the darkening shadow of nuclear war, then you will be a key force in upsetting the Administration's grand design. You will be helping democracy prevail over the tyranny of Reagan's Pentagon.

So it is important that you speak not only of nuclear weapons, but also of peace. Across America, citizens must begin to demand that the U.S. and the U.S.S.R. immediately and jointly freeze the nuclear-arms race. Every forum, every civic organization, every campus, every city council should see a debate and resolution to freeze the arms race. If the governments of America and the Soviet Union cannot achieve a SALT agreement on their own, it is up to the people of this country, and others around our world, to make it a political necessity.

It also means that peace cannot be separated from broader judgment about Soviet behavior, global trends, and especially the crisis of energy and inflation. The '80s are not the '60s. In those days, the U.S. had clear nuclear supremacy; now, the Soviet Union has strategic parity. In those days, America was the aggressor in Vietnam, and American citizens watched in horror as we bombed the villages of innocent people. Today, Americans watch the Soviets invade and brutalize Afghanistan, and threaten Poland. They watch the madness in the Middle East and in Asia. They worry about the Soviet Union, about American strength, and about security. And they are right to worry.

It is time to join the debate about security, before it is completely dominated by the false prophets of "peace through strength". First, we must emphasize that there are factors more important than military stockpiles in determining the destiny of nations. Moral factors, religious ideals, the desire for national independence—these have proven more important than weapons in Vietnam, Iran, Afghanistan, El Salvador, Poland, Nicaragua, Haiti, the Philippines and South Africa. It is time we apply this understanding to our relationship with the Soviet Union. We have to carry out our conflicts with the Soviets on a moral and political basis, not just militarily . . . except for the necessity of deterrence.

Secondly, we should stand for economic security. The military and foreign policy of our government does not protect and stimulate economic health. Instead, we are like an armored giant, protected on the outside, but deeply ailing within. We have a fetish about military security, but no government commitment to economic security. Only a conversion process, a retooling of industry—the dying industries of yesterday such as steel and autos, and the new industries of tomorrow such as electronics and solar—can bring us real economic strength in the modern world.

Third, we must stand for energy security. We are becoming more insecure every day, because of our government's outmoded energy policies. All experts agree that one of the most likely flashpoints for igniting a superpower confrontation is the Middle East. Yet by sending sophisticated aircraft and weapons to Saudi Arabia, for example, we only intensify that nation's problems, and provoke Israel. The answer is conservation, rather than conscription. For the path of energy efficiency, conservation, and investment in renewable resources is the only way to avoid oil blackmail, reduce our addiction to imports, attack inflation, and have a consistent domestic and foreign policy.

It can be done. We can construct a positive, alternative vision going beyond protest, with answers to our combined problems of the nuclear threat, world tension, energy, inflation, unemployment, centralized power, environmental damage and cancer. The only question is whether we have to go through another Vietnam War or Chernobyl before America decides to make the change.

I believe that the people who stopped the Vietnam War can stop the growing cancer of nuclear madness. Those who stopped Richard Nixon can stop our present collision course with the Soviet Union. The issue is simply one of democracy: we still have the right to choose whether or not we wish to be sacrificed in this old men's game with nuclear toys.

We will win this battle. But it will be hard, and there will be setbacks. We have to think harder, work harder, and move our protest ever more into the mainstream of life. But this is the only way to keep faith with our children, and not repeat the self-serving errors of past generations.

We must live by a new American ethic. The old ethic was that we deserved what we had, and could take. We were entitled to use it as we wished, even if we soiled our own nest, and those of others. A Native American leader once said of the majority of Americans: "The love of possession is a disease with them."

Now, at the end of the open frontier, the end of an age of cheap energy, the end of the technological fix (witness the Challenger, Chernobyl and U.S.A.F. rocket failures), we must begin to realize that we need less love of possession, and more possession of love.

Paul Ehrlich

"I'm very optimistic about what could be done; I'm very pessimistic about what will be done."

THE NUCLEAR THREAT is the most serious threat facing humanity today, and must therefore occupy at least part of the time of all people who are concerned with the other problems of society. There is no point, for instance, in worrying about the population-resources-environment-equity problems if we're all going to be blown to hell anyway.

Tragically, our leaders are still acting as if the world were the pre-1945 one in which they matured, and they try as hard as possible to indoctrinate younger people with pre-nuclear, pre-limits-to-growth notions of how the world works. It's not a death wish; rather, it's a natural result of the belief that growth is progress, and that science and technology can solve all problems. Unfortunately, the most powerful forces in our society have a great, vested interest in promoting such ideas. And even those who see through the nonsense often feel helpless in the face of the overwhelming forces moving us towards catastrophe.

Humanity seems determined to discover whether nuclear holocaust will mean the demise of *Homo sapiens*, the destruction of civilization in the Northern Hemisphere, or the loss of 'only' some 60 million people in a limited nuclear exchange between the Soviet

PAUL R. EHRLICH, *U.S. biologist; professor of population studies, Stanford University;* The Machinery of Nature *(1986),* Extinction: The Causes and Consequences of the Disappearance of Species *(1981),* Race Bomb *(1977),* Biology and Society *(1976) and* Population Bomb *(1968) are among his published works.*

Union and the United States. The Soviets keep building missiles as if socialism will be secure only when Russia has a warhead available for every living capitalist. The United States threatens to blow up the entire world to preserve its access to the last few decades of Arab oil production. Other nuclear powers and soon-to-be nuclear powers also continue to play the game of international politics as if ignorant of the complete change of rules.

Why? Fear. Fear that any step back from the nuclear arms race will lead not away from, but toward war. Fear that the other side will cheat or take advantage if disarmament is attempted. Fear that if wars are fought only with conventional weapons, the enemy will win. Fear of living under the yoke of imperialists or commissars. Fear of the cold, if Arab oil is cut off. Fear of starvation, if U.S. grain is withheld or access to fishing grounds restricted. Fear of having to share with have-nots; fear of remaining a have-not. Fear of being unable to defend against waves of immigrants or pollutants.

In short, on an ever-more-crowded, resource-depleted, environmentally-degraded, inequitable planet, human beings are not ready to abandon a system of nation-states and military security—especially when there appears to be no practical alternative. Jonathan Schell, at the end of his in-depth analysis of doomsday (*The Fate of the Earth*, 1982), could recommend only that we "lay down our arms, relinquish sovereignty, and found a political system for the peaceful settlement of international disputes".

These steps are certainly necessary. To take just one example, the global nature of many ecological problems makes at least partial surrender of sovereignty to international bodies essential. But a restructuring of the political system will take unprecedented effort and considerable time. The problem now is how to get started and how to buy the time. Presently, I'm very optimistic about what *could* be done; I'm very pessimistic about what *will* be done.

If the job *is* to be done, the United States, as the only superpower with an open society, must lead the way. It must face a fundamental asymmetry. At present, the risks of a thermonuclear-arms race are considered by most Americans as ones that must be accepted—even though a likely end to the race is the permanent destruction of America. In contrast, no risks are considered acceptable in the direction of disarmament—only a completely fail-safe system will do.

Yet, continuous risk-taking in the nuclear-arms race buys only the opportunity of continuing to take the risks, while risk-taking in the direction of disarmament could, in theory, lead to a world with no risk of nuclear war. So far, humanity has insanely preferred the arms race; now may be the last chance to try the other route.

As a first step, President Ronald Reagan could indicate the willingness of the United States to accept the bilateral, nuclear-freeze proposal. Additionally, he could announce the immediate and unilateral dismantling of all 52 Titan missiles and their thermonuclear warheads, under U.N. supervision. The Soviets would be challenged to match us or raise us.

These would be small steps toward meeting U.S. obligations under the Non-Proliferation Treaty. They would increase U.S. security, since the nation has no need of more nuclear weapons and the obsolete Titans are at least as great a threat to us as to the Soviets. If the Soviets failed to join the freeze and to start dismantling some of their arsenal, the United States would win a great propaganda victory.

President Reagan could also greatly increase the visibility of the Arms Control and Disarmament Agency by raising that office's niggardly budget and giving its chief well-publicized, direct access to the Oval Office. The President could request that other nuclear powers take similar steps. Many ingenious systems for virtually cheat-proof nuclear disarmament have already been invented. These could be perfected and the political climate for implementing them created. And implementation could buy the time needed for the enormous task of dealing with the broader, human predicament.

Ronald Reagan is in a better position, politically, to take such steps than any other recent President. By so doing, he could go down in history as one of the greatest; if he fails to do so, there may not be much further history for him *or* humanity.

Léon Van Hove

"In short, I see only one way of avoiding widespread and devastating wars; to wit, the existence of a credible and balanced nuclear deterrent— i.e., of a nuclear threat."

I SHARE WITH MANY the view that the consequences of a nuclear war would be disastrous and horrible beyond imagination. But this terrible threat can no longer be erased, and it has an important consequence which I regard to be positive: the threat of all-out nuclear war is the first and only effective deterrent against a new, worldwide military conflict, the effectiveness of the deterrent being guaranteed only to the degree that the consequences of nuclear warfare would be unbearably devastating.

I believe that the possibility of total nuclear disarmament is a dangerous illusion. It could not be reliably controlled over any length of time, especially during conventional wars, and would soon lead to the extension of local conflicts into World War III. In short, I see only one way of avoiding widespread and devastating wars; to wit, the existence of a credible and balanced nuclear deterrent—i.e., of a nuclear threat.

A maximum number of people should be made and kept aware of the extreme gravity of this threat. The necessary nuclear arsenals need not be very large, but a reduction from present sizes can only be realistically expected if it's coupled with further technological developments.

LÉON VAN HOVE, *Belgian physicist at CERN, the European Organization for Nuclear Research, in Geneva; foreign associate, U.S. National Academy of Sciences.*

Many of today's pacifists and antinuclear activists use arguments and evoke feelings which, in my opinion, are superficial and unrealistic. I believe we need fewer of these, not more. But we do need more people acting for a policy of credible, balanced deterrence, at a minimum level of the nuclear arsenals. Further, continued dissemination of honest information on the disastrous consequences of nuclear warfare is also very important.

Regarding our future, I am rather optimistic, because with balanced deterrence, we have one way of avoiding nuclear war (I do not know of any other), and because many people (mostly in the silent majority) are courageous enough to live under this threat for a long time.

An important cause of my optimism lies in a feature of nuclear deterrence which makes it uniquely effective—namely, the fact that *nobody* would escape the war, not even heads of state, governments, chiefs of staff, politicians, leaders of industry and financiers. Thus, destructive decisions are less likely to be taken when the decision-makers know themselves to be among those *most* exposed to destruction. Furthermore, learning to live with this threat may well provide the *only* effective way to stop nuclear proliferation among even more nations.

Bernard Lown &
James E. Muller

"We must not resign ourselves to a future in which security on both sides depends on threatening the lives of millions of innocent men, women and children."
—PRESIDENT RONALD REAGAN,
address to World Affairs Council, March 31, 1983

"We cannot consider it [nuclear deterrence] adequate as a long-term basis for peace."
—AMERICAN CATHOLIC BISHOPS,
Pastoral Letter on War and Peace, May 3, 1983

BOTH PRESIDENT REAGAN and the American Catholic Bishops have challenged the conventional wisdom that nuclear deterrence is an acceptable policy. As physicians, we share their concern. Examination of the medical realities compels the conclusion that nuclear deterrence is a dangerous, costly, and doomed policy.

The pertinent medical facts are these. Detonation of even a single-megaton warhead over a metropolitan area would cause a blast four million times that of the bomb which destroyed the American Embassy in Lebanon. Hundreds of thousands of innocent men, women and children would be killed instantly. Burns would claim 50 times more individuals than could be cared for in all the specialized burn facilities of either the Soviet Union or the United States. Most hospitals in the city would be destroyed, most health personnel would be killed, and most of the burned, irradiated and crushed victims would not receive even minimal pain-relief before their death.

BERNARD LOWN & JAMES E. MULLER, *of the 150,000-member (in 38 nations) International Physicians for the Prevention of Nuclear War, recipient of the 1985 Nobel Peace Prize. Lown is IPPNW co-president and professor of cardiology at Harvard School of Public Health. Muller, an IPPNW co-founder and former secretary, is assistant professor of medicine at Harvard Medical School.*

Debate about nuclear deterrence has drifted far from these stark realities. The following illusions must be addressed:

The first illusion is that nuclear deterrence is an ethical policy. The essence of nuclear deterrence is the threat to use instruments of indiscriminate, destructive power against an adversary. On the basis of this policy, responsible governments are prepared to kill hundreds of millions of innocents, who are being held hostage. The moral depravity of such a policy can best be appreciated by reducing its scale, removing the high technology, and abandoning sanitized words. Would people accept a policy which forced their national leaders to threaten to pour gasoline on ten young children of an adversary nation, and burn them to death?

The second illusion is that thousands of nuclear warheads are needed to deter a nuclear attack. We believe that neither President Reagan nor General Secretary Gorbachev would, with a clear knowledge of the medical effects of a nuclear weapon, take any action that would lead to the explosion of a single-megaton warhead over one of their major cities. Others might contend that threats to destroy Moscow, Leningrad and Kiev, or Washington, New York and Chicago, are needed to deter. This would require the delivery of three warheads. Three-hundred warheads from only two modern submarines could destroy all major cities of either country. But each side has indulged in a blatant exercise in redundancy, and now can deliver more that 7000.

The third illusion is that nuclear weapons have conventional, military or political value. It is claimed that imbalance of certain types of nuclear weapons can be used for "nuclear blackmail"—an extension of deterrence. But all such claims rest on the hidden promise of "limited nuclear war"—an event as likely as an explosion restricted to the top third of a dynamite keg. These are not weapons, in the conventional sense, but instruments of genocide.

The fourth illusion is that nuclear deterrence has been a successful policy. It is commonly asserted that the absence of direct military hostilities between the US and the USSR demonstrates that deterrence works. This assertion cannot be proven scientifically—it is impossible to know if conflict has been avoided because of, or in spite of, nuclear deterrence. In the period before the US and the USSR began to threaten each other with incineration, they not only avoided military conflict, but were military allies against Hitler.

Although the purported benefits of deterrence are debatable, its harmful effects are not. After a period of nearly three decades, the deadly by-products of deterrence are now apparent. Under the guise of deterrence, and stimulated by the fear and dehumanization of the enemy inherent in such a policy, we have embarked on an arms race of historic proportions. The world is now spending over one million dollars per minute on weapons needed for "deterrence," while over 40,000 children die each day of starvation-related illnesses. Nuclear weapons are now proliferating to other countries, while jeopardized populations—and in particular the threatened children—are afflicted with inordinant, psychologic stress.

The risk of an accidental nuclear war continues with computer errors, and the identification, each year by physicians, of more than 4,000 U.S. military personnel who must be removed from access to nuclear weapons, because of psychological problems, alcoholism, or drug abuse. In any given year, the risk might be slight, but because of the principle of cumulative probability, even a one-percent annual risk becomes a 40 percent risk when projected over the expected life span of today's young people. It is an *accident* that nuclear war has not yet occurred with this policy. We may not be as lucky over the ensuing decades.

Even more sinister is the fact that, out of the seemingly innocuous cocoon of deterrence policy, have emerged first-strike weapons more suitable for provoking, than for preventing, nuclear war. In fact, deterrence itself is inherently unstable, and has set in motion forces over which the people will have increasingly less and less control. Ultimately, the computer and the bomb will take command.

Escape from this doomed policy requires a change in the social order, similar to that which occurred with the abolition of slavery. How will such a change come about? Although governmental leaders and strategists may believe that nuclear deterrence is not an acceptable, long-term policy, they are trapped by habitual modes of thinking . . . in response to revolutionary developments in destructive technology.

If we are to survive, the people of the world must perceive—and act on—the warning signs that the policy of deterrence has failed. Let us hope and pray that the intelligence and foresight which are characteristic of our species, will enable us to alter our potential, tragic destiny.

Louis Néel

"It is evident that any reasonable person, no matter where in the world, is convinced that the armament race is a ruinous folly which should be stopped, and be followed by a progressive disarmament."

IT IS EVIDENT that any reasonable person, no matter where in the world, is convinced that the armament race is a ruinous folly which should be stopped, and be followed by progressive disarmament. Not only nuclear arms, but all armament must be reduced.

Actually, though the U.S., on its soil, has nothing to fear but nuclear arms—because there is no great risk from conventional arms deployed by neighboring states—this is not the same for other countries; because, even if they were delivered from the nuclear threat, they would, nonetheless, be exposed to the conventional threats, of which we have unfortunately had several examples during the last 35 years.

Since a progressive disarmament, on a world scale, bearing on all categories of arms, is a terribly difficult, geopolitical problem, it does not seem to me that scientists — even Nobel Prize scientists — are better prepared than any other citizens to imagine and propose valid solutions.

LOUIS NÉEL, *French physicist; 1970 Nobel Prize in Physics; president, Conseil Supèrieur Sûreté Nucléaire; Scientific Advisor to French Navy; French Representative to Scientific Committee of NATO; foreign member, U.S.S.R. Academy of Sciences, American Academy of Arts and Sciences.*

Richard Pryor

*"What can be done?
Stop."*

W<small>HY ARE MORE</small> not acting to save our world? Because they're acting to destroy it.

What can be done? Stop.

R<small>ICHARD</small> P<small>RYOR</small>, *U.S. actor;* Jo Jo Dancer, Here and Now, Superman III, The Toy, Live on Sunset Strip, *and* Some Kind of Hero *are among his films.*

Emilio Rosenblueth

I ASSIGN A PROBABILITY of 2 percent per year to the actual or virtual destruction of the human race, as a consequence of a nuclear war. This is unacceptable.

What can be done? I refer to Bertrand Russell: We need first state whether we prefer to be red than dead, or dead than red. If only *our* lives were at stake, or even those of half the world, there might be room for argument. Nay, one plate of the balance holds the complete, future existence of the human species, until the end of time; the other contains the life style of perhaps several generations of humans.

Some experts tell us otherwise, but their assessments are uncertain as to the probability of nuclear war, and about its consequences. And however small the uncertainty, the balance tilts overwhelmingly in one direction. Clearly, one thing can and must be done: unilateral disarmament, no matter how painful to those who regard themselves as possessors of the Truth.

EMILIO ROSENBLUETH, *Mexican professor of engineering, National University of Mexico; foreign associate, U.S. National Academy of Sciences; former Mexican Vice-Minister for Educational Planning.*

John Cameron Swayze

LIKE EVERYONE ELSE who considers it, I recognize the terrible potential of nuclear war. But I think our strength will help prevent it.

So much has been said on this subject, pro and con, that I don't believe I can add anything constructive that has not already been spoken or written. I believe we must remain strong, being one who thinks the best defense is a strong offensive power, at the ready. If we were not strong, I think Russia would move more aggressively than ever, to the detriment of the free world.

JOHN CAMERON SWAYZE, *U.S. former TV and radio news commentator;* The Art of Living *(1979) is among his published works.*

Franklin L. Gage

UNLIKE MANY OF my colleagues in the antinuclear movement, I feel the threat comes more from those who have the weapons, than from the weapons themselves, and that so long as manifestly-evil people have them, it is essential they not be allowed to gain an ability to use the weapons, for war or blackmail.

On the question of whether we shall avoid nuclear war/blackmail, the key is, I think, whether people will be educated in time to support a strong nuclear-weapons policy. History tells us they won't, as was the case when the world let Hitler gain great strength, without being prepared to defend itself against him. I think the case for a strong defense is so obvious that once the current hysteria passes, people will be supportive.

FRANKLIN L. GAGE, *coordinator, U.S. Task Force Against Nuclear Pollution.*

Maria Isabel Barreno

"The nuclear threat is, in fact, like a children's game...but too dangerous. And we adults should find a way to stop it."

THE NUCLEAR THREAT is, in fact, like a children's game...but too dangerous. And we adults should find a way to stop it.

It is not easy; before acting to save our world, we have to find out *how* to act. What can we do? Whatever it is, it has to be efficient, for to talk, and to express our opinion, is not enough—in fact, it is part of the same game.

We are living the consequences of the exclusive valorization of a way of knowledge: the so-called 'scientific' or 'rational' view of the world. The whole tragedy started centuries ago, had a climax with the 'scientific triumphalism' in the 19th century, and still goes on with the belief that 'science and technology' are equal to 'human progress'. Material comfort and laziness are the real causes for this spoiling and spoiled behaviour.

The nuclear threat is also *the* symptom of the entire political situation: we have to find another basis for the power (real knowledge, instead of force), other ways of sharing and structuring political power. The so-called 'democratic government' is an old institution—good for the last century; inefficient for this century.

I really don't know anymore if I am pessimistic or optimistic about our future. Human history would be too absurd if it is supposed to end in a few years, in a nuclear holocaust. We have too many potentialities, and so many dreams!! But I don't know if this feeling of absurdness is enough to save the world. Maybe...if it is really shared.

MARIA ISABEL BARRENO, *Portugese writer;* The Three Marias: New Portugese Letters *(with M. Horta and M. Da Costa, 1973) is among her published works...a classic on the feminine condition, for which all three were imprisoned for "abuse of press freedom," their book banned.*

Leonard Bernstein

"We need desperately to cultivate new fantasies, ones which can be enacted to make this Earth of ours a safe, sound, and morally well-functioning world, instead of a disparate collection of societies limping along from crisis to crisis, and ultimately to self-destruction."

THESE WORDS ARE addressed, in particular, to everyone born on Earth since 1945:

The gift of imagination is by no means an exclusive property of the artist; it is a gift we all share. To some degree, all of us are endowed with the power of fantasy. The dullest of dullards among us has the gift of dreams at night—visions and yearnings and hopes. Everyone can also think; it is the quality of thought that makes the difference—not just the quality of logical thinking, but of *imaginative* thinking. And our greatest thinkers, those who have radically changed our world, have always arrived at their truths by dreaming them; they are first fantasized, and only then subjected to proof. That is certainly true of Albert Einstein, who always insisted that imagination is more important than knowledge. How often he spoke of having *dreamed* his unified field theory, and his principle of relativity—intuiting them, and then, high on the inspiration, plunging into the perspiration of working them out to be provable, and therefore true.

Now, what has all this to do with you, or with the grim realities we face each day? It has everything to do with you because you are the

LEONARD BERNSTEIN, *U.S. conductor, composer and pianist; laureate conductor for life, New York Philharmonic.*

generation of hope. We are counting on you, on your imagination, to find new truths—true answers, not mere stopgaps, to the abounding stalemates that surround us. But why us, you ask? Why are you laying this very heavy burden on our generation? I'll try to tell you why.

The generation that preceded yours has been a pretty passive one, and no wonder. It was the first generation in all history to be born into a nuclear world, the first people ever to have had to accept the Bomb as an axiom of life. Behold the Hiroshima generation! You are the first generation since Hiroshima that can look back and say no—not for me. Thus you are, can be, a new and separate generation, with fresh minds, ready for new thinking—for *imaginative* thinking—if you allow yourselves to cultivate your fantasy. More specifically, do you have the imaginative strength to liberate yourselves from the cold-war ambience in which the '80s began? Far too many people speak of the Third World War as if it were not only conceivable, but a natural inevitability. I tell you it is not conceivable, not natural, not inevitable. And the more this useless talk goes on, the more we witness a steady proliferation of nuclear arms. The mind boggles.

What do we do with our minds when they boggle? We quickly put them to strenuous, imaginative work. Mind-boggling time is the perfect time for fantasy to take over; it's the only way to resolve a stalemate. And so I ask you again: are you ready to dare to free your minds from the constraints we, your elders, have imposed on you? Will you accept, as artists do, that the life of the spirit precedes and controls the life of exterior action, that the richer and more creative the life of the spirit, the healthier and more productive our society must necessarily be?

If you are ready to accept all that (and I am not saying that it's easy to do), then I must ask if you are ready to admit the ensuing corollaries, starting bravely with the toughest one of all: that war is obsolete. Our nuclear folly has rendered it obsolete.

Do you not find something reprehensible, even obscene, about the endless and useless stockpiling of nuclear missiles? Isn't there something radically wrong with nation-states squandering the major portion of their wealth on military strength, at the expense of schools, hospitals, libraries and vital research in medicine and energy, to say nothing of preserving the sheer livability of our planetary environment?

Why are we behaving in this suicidal fashion? I am an artist, and my answer must necessarily be that we do not permit our imagination to bloom. The fantasies we do act out are still the old, tribalistic ones, arising from greed, lust for power, and superiority. We need desperately to cultivate new fantasies, ones which can be enacted to make this Earth of ours a safe, sound, and morally well-functioning world, instead of a disparate collection of societies limping along from crisis to crisis, and ultimately to self-destruction. We are told again and again that there is food enough on this planet to supply the human race 20 times over; that there is enough water to irrigate every desert. The world is rich, nature is bountiful, we have everything we need. Why is it then so hard to arrive at a minimal standard below which no human being is allowed to sink? Again, we need imagination, fantasy, *new* fantasies, with the passion and courage to carry them out. Only think: if all our imaginative resources currently employed in inventing new power games, and bigger and better weaponry, were reoriented toward disarmament, what miracles we could acheive, what new truths, what undiscovered realms of beauty!

Impossible, you say? Inconceivable to disarm without inviting annihilation? Okay. Let's invent a fantasy together, right now, and I mean a fantastic fantasy, no holds barred. Let's pretend that any one of us has become President of the United States, a very imaginative President, who has suddenly taken a firm decision to disarm, completely and unilaterally. I see alarm on your faces: this crazed artist is proposing sheer madness. It can't be done. A President is not a dictator; this is a democracy. Congress would never permit it; the people would howl with wounded national pride; our allies would scream betrayal. It can't be done. But of course it can't be done if everybody starts by saying it can't be done. Let's push our imagination; remember, we're only fantasizing. Let's dare to be simplistic. All right, someone would stand up in the Congress and demand that the President be impeached, declared certifiable, and locked away in a loony bin. Others would agree.

But suppose that one or two Senators or Congressmembers got the point, and recognized this mad idea as perhaps the most courageous single action in all history. And suppose that those few members of Congress happened to be hypnotically powerful orators. It might just become contagious—keep pushing that imagination button!—it just *might* get through to the people, who instead of howling, might well stand up tall, proud to be participating in this unprecedented act of strength and heroism. There might even be those who would feel it to be the noblest of sacrifices, far nobler, surely, than sacrificing one's children on the fields of Armageddon. And this pride and joyful courage could spread—keep pushing that button!—so that even our allies might applaud us. There is the barest possibility that it just might work.

All right, now what? Now is when we *really* have to push, let fantasy lead us where it will. What is your first thought? Naturally, that the Soviet Union would come ploughing in and take us over.

But would they really? What would they do with us; why would they want to assume responsibility for, and administration of, so huge, complex and problematical a society as ours? And in English, yet! Besides, who is the Soviet Union—its leaders, its army, or its people? The only reason for the army to fight is that their leaders would have commanded them to do so, but how can they fight when there is no enemy? The hypothetical enemy has been magically whisked away, and replaced by 200-odd-million smiling, strong, peaceful Americans. Now keep the fantasy going: the Russian *people* certainly don't want war; they have suffered far too much. And it is more likely that they would displace their warlike leaders, and transform their Union of Socialist Republics into a truly democratic union. And think of the example that would have been set up for the whole world; think of the relief at no longer having to bluster and sabre-rattle and save face; think of the vast new wealth, now available to make life rich, beautiful, clean, sexy, thoughtful, inventive, healthful, fun!

Well, maybe it won't work. But I don't give up. Something in all that fantasy-trip must have struck you as—well, just possible. And if one little seed or syllable of an idea may have entered one single ear, where it can grow among the fertile neurons of one imaginative brain, then I could pray for no more. And at the very least, you must admit that nothing I have fantasized, lunatic artist though I may be, is actually inconceivable. After all, we did imagine it together, from beginning to end, which is a hell of a lot better than trying to imagine Armageddon—the extinction of humankind—which is, for *this* artist at least, indeed inconceivable. And this artist challenges you to pursue the fantasy, *all* your fantasies, while there is still time.

Dudley Moore

"Perhaps only in the facing of the absurdity and insolubility of the situation will a solution of everybody, as it were, giving up this mad race, occur."

MY INCLINATION IS to join very strongly with the voices in the world that demand nuclear disarmament, either globally or unilaterally. But realistic caution makes me hesitate, as the prospect of tyrannical, fanatical, and not entirely stable leaders taking advantage of nuclear-armaments reduction looms dangerously. The passion for disarmament has to go hand-in-hand with the reeducation of anarchists! This issue is the one thing that makes me hesitate in the idea of nuclear disarmament.

A nuclear freeze, yes . . . a nuclear build-down, yes. But total disarmament? No weapons at all? If there were an absolute, foolproof way of detecting weapons in the world, then perhaps we could rest easy. But are all missiles that exist on the Earth's surface detectable by whatever means is chosen? I'm not at all sure of the scientific rules for all of this. Suppose mild-mannered Mr. Kaddafi had cruise missiles in either pocket. Could we establish that through surveillance? Because if we can't, then we have to think carefully about the efficacy of total disarmament.

I want to see a nuclear-free world as much as anybody, but nuclear technology seems to exist in the world now, and may be almost as uneradicable as the pain of living. I would say, in the flush

DUDLEY MOORE, *British actor, musician;* 10, Arthur, Six Weeks, Unfaithfully Yours *and* Micki and Maude *are among his films.*

of innocence, enthusiasm, and perhaps misplaced zeal, that I would like to see everything stopped and everything dismantled. The only mitigating circumstance is created by the permanent existence of madmen in the world, who might feel that this is an opportune moment for them to step forward with a nuclear right-arm.

The people who advocate nuclear armament are not stupid, unpragmatic, inhuman beings. Nor, on the other hand, are people who advocate disarmament (or freeze, at least) gentle, wise, insightful, or totally right.

Ideally, I'm a pacifist. I advocate nonintervention. But reality steps in and demands *adult ambivalence!* As Kissinger said: "Stability is all-important, but with 44 wars going on for whatever reason, getting people to back off is not easy." I am now rambling on, feeling very impotent about the whole thing. However, right now, discussion is everything...awareness, consciousness, clarity, pragmatism, and good old common sense. I think the horrible picture of postnuclear devastation painted by Carl Sagan, Paul Ehrlich, and others could be a very useful deterrent, even to the most psychotic leader.

I think what can be done is being done. Progress is bound to be slow. Education regarding the perils of the situation is scant, and it is hard to know how to accelerate it. To this question, I find myself particularly unable to respond with anything that could even marginally be called constructive. But perhaps to realize that there is no solution is a way to building a solution. Perhaps only in the facing of the absurdity and insolubility of the situation will a solution of everybody, as it were, giving up this mad race, occur.

Wolfgang K.H. Panofsky

"I consider the nuclear-war threat to be the most awesome problem humanity has ever faced. As long as the probability of nuclear war is significant, then if you wait long enough, it will happen, and this the world cannot afford."

I CONSIDER THE nuclear-war threat (not the nuclear-power threat) to be the most awesome problem humanity has ever faced. I do not believe the likelihood of nuclear conflagration is any more likely today than it was, say, ten years ago; but that is small comfort. As long as the probability of nuclear war is significant, then if you wait long enough, it will happen, and this the world cannot afford. We must work hard to decrease that likelihood.

Some people give grudging credit for the absence of all-out war during the last 40 years to the effectiveness of nuclear deterrence between the superpowers. Most people simply avoid worrying about the problem. The media have done a poor job representing the nuclear-war issues in their totality. The daily news stories—dealing with nuclear war out of context—simply are not understandable to the lay reader who does not continuously follow negotiations, military authorization bills, or technical developments.

Most citizens are suffering from the 'leave-it-to-the-experts' syndrome, not recognizing that the experts can only make limited contributions in their respective fields of expertise. I do not have any

WOLFGANG K.H. PANOFSKY, *U.S. physicist; professor and director, Linear Accelerator Center, Stanford University; consultant for more than 20 years to U.S. government on strategic weapons, arms control, etc. (former member, General Advisory Committee, U.S. Arms Control and Disarmament Agency, 1968-81); Enrico Fermi Award, 1979; National Medal of Science, 1969; California Scientist of Year Award, 1967.*

prescription which is unique, or which promises success, but the following steps are urgently needed:

A. Expand the campaign to inform the public and the political decision-makers about the physical nature and potential effects of nuclear weapons. Persuade the body politic that nuclear weapons are much too serious—in their physical reality—to use as bargaining chips, symbols of political power, or means to apply political leverage in any sphere. In other words, when dealing with nuclear weapons, persuade political decision-makers to substitute reality for perception.

B. Use the political process to persuade decision-makers that nuclear weapons have only one mission, and that is to deter the use of nuclear weapons. Persuade political decision-makers that any other military use of nuclear weapons is both unproductive for military goals, and also extremely dangerous.

C. Work towards a 'no-first-use' policy in Europe, through establishment of an approximate balance of conventional weapons.

D. Make arms control the highest priority on the political agenda in Congress and the Executive Branch, and make it a major issue in political campaigns.

E. Make it clear that a policy which refuses to take risks in arms control, but which, in fact, involves enormous risks in any military confrontation, is unacceptable.

F. Exert pressure on the U.S. government to resume negotiations which the Reagan Administration discontinued— negotiations towards discontinuance of all nuclear testing, negotiations toward banning anti-satellite warfare, etc. Accept the request of the Soviet Union to negotiate the issues of discontinuing testing, and of banning all weapons from outer space.

I believe that all-out nuclear war can be avoided, and I am gratified about the increased preoccupation of people all over the world—and that includes the Russians—with the problem. I do believe that decision-makers behave rationally when faced with extremely grave situations. Nevertheless, I trust my own optimism will in no way decrease the efforts which are so badly needed to reduce nuclear inventories, and to put the relationship between potential adversaries on a more rational basis.

Thomas M. Powers

*"A growing body of scientific knowledge
about the consequences of nuclear war
suggests that American war plans provide
for nuclear attacks on the Soviet Union on a
planet-threatening scale—thereby
endangering American security and welfare
quite independently of any Soviet response."*

A GROWING BODY OF scientific knowledge about the consequences
of nuclear war suggests that American war plans provide for nuclear
attacks on the Soviet Union on a planet-threatening scale—thereby
endangering American security and welfare quite independently of
any Soviet response.

Recent scientific[1] studies suggest that a nuclear war involving as
few as 100 megaton-equivalents, detonated over as many major
urban centers, could produce ecological effects on a planet-threatening scale. These studies claim that smoke from as few as 100 burning
cities could cast a pall over the Northern Hemisphere, obscuring the
sun for up to a year, bringing sub-zero temperatures in July and
August, disrupting the food chain, and threatening many forms of
plant and animal life. In the case of large-scale nuclear wars, these
effects could extend to the Southern Hemisphere, with consequences for life on the planet difficult to calculate in advance.

The authors of the "Nuclear Winter" report conclude: "The mag-
nitudes of the first-order effects [of a nuclear war] are so large, and
the implications so serious, that we hope the scientific issues raised
will be vigorously and critically examined." An earlier study[2] by the
U.S. National Academy of Sciences, "Long-Term Biological Consequences of Nuclear War," concluded that immediate survivors of a
nuclear war in the Northern Hemisphere "would face extreme cold,

THOMAS M. POWERS, *U.S. freelance writer; contributing editor,* The Atlantic;
Pulitzer Prize, national reporting, 1971; Thinking About the Next War *(1982),*
The Man Who Kept the Secrets: Richard Helms and the CIA *(1979),* The War at
Home *(1973) and* Diana: The Making of a Terrorist *(1971) are among his
published works.*

water shortages, lack of food and fuel, heavy burdens of radiation and pollutants, disease, and severe psychological stress—all in twilight or darkness. The possibility exists that the darkened skies and low temperatures would spread over the entire planet. Should this occur, a severe extinction event could ensue, leaving a highly modified and biologically depauperate Earth. Species extinction could be expected for most terrestrial vertebrates of north-temperate regions, a large number of plants, and numerous freshwater and some marine organisms...the possibility of the extinction of *Homo sapiens* cannot be excluded."

Published accounts of American war plans[3] establish that attacks on a potentially planet-threatening scale have been contemplated since the early 1950s. The first Single Integrated Operational Plan (SIOP), issued in December, 1960, called for a full-scale attack on the Soviet Union with approximately 4,000 nuclear warheads[3]. As recently as 1974, the low option in the SIOP—the *smallest* pre-planned strike—called for 2,500 U.S. warheads targeted on Soviet nuclear war-fighting potential—air fields, submarine bases, nuclear-weapons storage depots, hardened missile and command-and-control sites, etc. Some of these strikes would have hit urban areas, and many would have involved ground bursts sucking up large quantities of dust and debris into the atmosphere.

Current American war plans envisage all-out strikes involving thousands of warheads on Soviet "recovery targets," many of them in urban areas[3]. The Joint Strategic Target Planning Staff (JSTPS), at Offut Air Force Base near Omaha, currently identifies primary and alternate targets for *all* the approximately 10,000 warheads on American strategic delivery vehicles. It is, therefore, clear that American war plans provide for nuclear attacks which competent scientific authorities believe could have planet-threatening effects.

The process of American war-planning has always been, and remains, haphazard in the extreme. The demands of secrecy have traditionally restricted knowledge of war plans to a small circle. The complexity of these plans has limited their oversight by the President and his Secretaries of Defense and State to a cursory level. The urgency of military requirements, in wartime, has taken precedence over the possible environmental dangers posed by execution of war plans. Thus full, detailed knowledge of American war plans has been restricted almost entirely to the operational level.

The current war-planning process provides for no general review of the SIOP at the White House, or even at the Joint Chiefs of Staff (JCS) level. At no stage in the process is scientific knowledge of the probable environmental effects of the execution of war plans factored into the consideration of targets or strategy. It is, therefore, fair to conclude that the President, the JCS and the JSTPS simply do not know, and have never known, whether our own war plans might have broad, planet-threatening effects endangering our own security and welfare.

Congress, therefore, has an obligation to (a) determine whether American war plans include planet-threatening strike-options which, if executed, would threaten our own welfare (by our own hand), and (b) to propose such remedies as it deems fit. Thus, Congress should immediately establish a Joint War Plans Oversight Committee to:

(1) Hear public testimony from competent authorities on the probable medical, economic, environmental and other effects of executing American war plans;

(2) Review in detail American war plans providing for the use of nuclear and other potentially planet-threatening weapons, with particular regard to the scale and type of attacks called for by these plans;

(3) Consider the possible danger posed to the United States and its allies by the execution of American war plans;

(4) Recommend changes in American war plans to ensure we do not threaten our own security with our own hand, and

(5) Report its findings to the public on an annual basis, in sufficient detail to make it clear the United States does not contemplate the execution of war plans on a planet-threatening scale, in ignorance of their probable effects.

1. R.P. Turco, et. al., "Nuclear Winter: Global Consequences of Multiple Nuclear Explosions," *Science*, Dec. 23, 1983.
   Paul R. Ehrlich, et. al., "Long-Term Biological Consequences of Nuclear War," Ibid.
   Carl Sagan, "Nuclear War and Climactic Catastrophe: Some Policy Implications," *Foreign Policy*, Winter 1983/4.
2. U.S. National Academy of Sciences, *Long-Term Worldwide Effects of Multiple Nuclear-Weapon Detonations*, Washington, D.C., 1975.
   Office of Technology Assessment, *The Effects of Nuclear War*, Washington, D.C., 1979.
3. Fred Kaplan, *The Wizards of Armageddon* (Simon & Shuster, 1983).
   Thomas Powers, "Choosing a Strategy for World War III," *The Atlantic*, Nov., 1982.
   William Pringle and William Arkin, *SIOP: The Secret U.S. Plan for Nuclear War* (Norton, 1983).
   Gregg Herken, *The Winning Weapon: The Atomic Bomb in the Cold War, 1945-1950* (Alfred A. Knopf, 1980).

Anne Seifert

"Our future literally is in our hands. If we press the wrong button, communicate the wrong message, life as we know it on this planet may come to an end. How intelligent are we? The future will tell us."

THE ISSUES ARE war and the devastation of our planet. In past wars, people have been able to resume their lives in the wake of war—to suffer their losses, and to continue. In a nuclear war, this possibility becomes remote.

There are two basic avenues to counteract nuclear devastation: (1) finding ways to allow planetary life to survive, and (2) preventing this catasprophe from occurring. If we could find a way to survive, assuredly the remaining quality of life would be abysmal. Perhaps the human species, as we know it, would be extinguished. To prevent war, history would suggest, is not within the nature of man. To prevent the use of nuclear weaponry, however, is within the realm of possibility.

What *can* be done *must* be done by *all* nations: universal agreement to the rules of war and weaponry. In every nation's self-interest is the survival of life on this planet. The only country that has ever dropped nuclear bombs is the United States. So perhaps we are the people the world fears. We showed the world what could happen. Can we now show the world that it will never happen again?

Our future literally is in our hands. If we press the wrong button, communicate the wrong message, life as we know it on this planet may come to an end. How intelligent are we? The future will tell us.

ANNE SEIFERT, *U.S. epidemiologist and psychologist; member, Advisory Board, California Concil on Wellness and Physical Fitness;* The Intelligent Woman's Diet *(1982)* and His, Mine, and Ours *(1979) are among her published works.*

Arthur C. Clarke

"Looming monstrously above all other evils is the ever-present threat of nuclear war."

LOOMING MONSTROUSLY ABOVE all other evils is the ever-present threat of nuclear war. I wish I could claim that improved communications would lead to peace, but the matter is not as simple as that. Excellent communications—even a common language!—have not brought peace to Northern Ireland, to give but one of many possible examples. Nevertheless, good communications of every type, and at all levels, are essential if we are ever to establish peace on this planet. As the mathematicians would say: they are necessary, but not sufficient.

Perhaps an additional necessity may be the International Monitoring Satellite System proposed by the French government in 1978, and the subject of a UN report reissued in May, 1983, at the request of the General Assembly. I refer you to this 123-page document (E.83.IX.3—"The Implications of Establishing an International Satellite-Monitoring Agency") for details; all I need say here is that it considers the potential benefits to humankind if *all* nations had access to the orbital-reconnaissance information now available only to the United States and the Soviet Union. Roughly speaking, these

ARTHUR C. CLARKE, *British author; chancellor, University of Moratuwa, Sri Lanka; founder, Arthur Clarke Centre for Modern Technologies, Sri Lanka;* The Songs of Distant Earth *(1986),* Ascent to Orbit *(1984),* 1984: Spring, 2010: Space Odyssey II *(1982), and* 2001: A Space Odyssey *(with S. Kubrick, 1968) are among his published works.*

powers now have the ability to observe any piece of military equipment larger than a rifle, in clear weather during daylight, and to track surface vessels at *any* time.

You will not be surprised to know that both the U.S. and the U.S.S.R. agree in opposing any scheme that will break their joint monopoly on strategic information, and one of their main criticisms of the Monitoring-Satellite System is all too valid. Even if it were established, could it *really* work during a period of international crisis, if more than 100 nations each had a finger on the ERASE button of the computer that stored the disputed information?

I have a modest proposal. The French, who suggested the IMS in the first place, have now launched an Earth Resources Satellite (SPOT) whose capabilities, in some respects, approach those of military reconnaissance satellites. Its images are available, on a purely commercial basis, to anyone who wants to buy them, at the rate of about 30 cents per square kilometer.

Suppose a small consortium of traditionally neutral countries set up an image-processing and intelligence-evaluating organisation. (Sweden, with its Stockholm International Peace Research Institute, is an obvious choice; one could add Switzerland and the Netherlands. Perhaps that would be enough!) It would contract with the SPOTimage comany for satellite information, and analyse it for any country which considered itself threatened, on condition that the results were made available to the whole world.

This would be only a beginning, of course. The next step would be to purchase a SUPERSPOT, with much higher resolution. I leave others to work out the details, but none of the problems seem insuperable. And with all respect to the distinguished United Nations, three or four nations could have the system running smoothly *years* before 155 could even agree on its desirability.

Such an institute could well adopt, without irony, the ambiguous slogan of the U.S. Strategic Air Command:"Peace is our profession".

Edward Lamb

I T'S NOT A question of our being optimistic that somehow we can gain nuclear control. Reality teaches us that human history reveals no parallel to the present nuclear threat. We have developed a weapon for mass suicide, and placed the trigger in the hands of many leaders of government around the world. Many there are who could destroy global life.

The forces pushing for disarmament and international controls *do* have the power to outlaw all weaponry, and accomplish planetary security. This happy achievement will come about through action within the international structure of the United Nations. We ask, "What are we to do?" We can act on a local, regional and international basis to support the United Nations, and all of its disarmament and peace-keeping efforts. International security will follow.

EDWARD LAMB, *U.S. lawyer, business executive (controls $600 million in assets); governor, U.N. Association-U.S.A.;* Planned Economy of Soviet Russia *is among his published works.*

Frank K. Kelly

"I view the nuclear threat as a challenge and
an opportunity for the human race to move
toward a world community."

I VIEW THE NUCLEAR threat as a challenge and an opportunity for the human race to move toward a world community. As a science fiction writer in the 1930s, I assumed that the release of nuclear energy would bring great benefits, as well as great dangers. I believed—and still believe—that human beings are created in the likeness of their Creator, with infinite possibilities. The unlocking of nuclear knowledge is part of the Creator's plan for the high development of the human species.

As an officer of the Nuclear Age Peace Foundation, I am circulating a statement headed "Parents and Grandparents Call to End the Nuclear Arms Race." This statement contains five points for action:

(a) Full implementation of the World Disarmament Campaign launched by the United Nations in 1982;

(b) Establishment of Peace Academies in all nations, to promote research, education and training in the peaceful resolution of conflicts;

(c) Serious disarmament proposals and actions by the most heavily-armed nations, to reduce all forms of weapons;

(d) Pledges of "No First Use" of nuclear weapons—under any circumstances—given by chief executives and legislatures of all nations with nuclear arms, and

(e) Formation of a joint U.S.-Soviet Crisis-Consultation Center in Geneva, to be operated 24 hours a day, to prevent any crisis from building into a nuclear war.

The late John F. Kennedy once said: "We must design and propose a program that combines disarmament with the strengthening of the United Nations, and with world development. We must propose the creation of new United Nations institutions of inspection and control, and of economic development." The time has come to wage peace, not war, using the strategy suggested by John Kennedy.

FRANK K. KELLY, U.S. *senior vice-president, Nuclear Age Peace Foundation;*
210 *board member, U.S. Academy of Peace.*

Josef Tal

"The encircling of the official-government atom bomb by unofficial terror organizations, possessing atomic weapons themselves, is already clearly written on the wall."

REGARDING WHAT CAN be done, it could be useful to first think: where would we be today without Hiroshima? The deterrent effect of the atomic armament is obvious, so far. The growing danger of world destruction does not come from merely technological development of this kind of weapon, but from the tremendous fear it produces while laying silent in waiting position.

Worldwide terror organizations are the first symptoms, demonstrating the attempt to transform the atom-bomb fear to the invisible-terror fear. This new, more and more growing fear is not less destructive than the atom bomb itself; only the time factor is different. This might not be in the interest of the rules of bomb manufacture, as atomic warfare, to a large degree, will not take place between human enemies, but between industrialized enemies. The encircling of the official-government atom bomb by unofficial terror organizations, possessing atomic weapons themselves, is already clearly written on the wall.

The fear produced by this combination is unbearable, no matter if the explosion occurs or not. The body of the UN is already fear-reacting narcoticized, as can be seen by UNESCO's convulsions. For all these reasons, optimistic or pessimistic outlook into the future

JOSEF TAL, *Israeli composer; director, Israel Centre for Electronic Music; honorary member, U.S. Academy of Arts and Letters; Israel State Prize, 1970; besides full and short operas, concertos, cantatas, quintets and music for ballet, several books on music theory are among his compositions.*

is irrelevant. But to raise the question of mental illness is predominant.

The cure can only be a thorough renewal of educational activities at all levels, and for all ages. What we commonly call 'abstract thinking' must be trained right from the educational beginning. The prevailing subjects must be the arts, according to the spontaneous inclination of the pupils.

The arts will be the bridge between science and the humanities, as far as those terms are still used as counteractors. Politicians, arising from this educational background, for which great educators like L. Nelson have already construed the fundaments, are the only hope for a turn towards a healthy and positive life for humankind.

M. Cameron Pollock

"Nuclear weapons are in the possession of a very small minority of the world's nations, yet threaten all nations; so this weapon-possession is nothing less than an act of international terrorism."

F REEDOM'S FIRST DEFENCE is in the mind, not the early-warning systems of Alaska, or the Kamchatka peninsula. If we can clear our minds—for a moment—of political prejudices and national identities, how can we answer the question: What right has man to make and deploy weapons of indiscriminate, mass destruction?

In contemplating this question, we should consider the victims, who in the human field include those we normally protect, from babes in arms to the aged, the sick, and the afflicted, to those victims beyond—the silent majority . . . every living animal, insect, bird or plant. Anyone who can justify such destruction must be arrogant to the point of paranoia.

There are national and international laws to protect endangered species; the nuclear threat makes every living creature an endangered species; so, what *can* be done? Nuclear weapons are in the possession of a very small minority of the world's nations, yet threaten all nations; so this weapon-possession is nothing less than an act of international terrorism. While the superpowers go through the verbal motions of arms limitation, they extend their armouries, and smaller powers try to join the club.

M. CAMERON POLLOCK, *British chartered mechanical and civil engineer; managed construction projects in the ceramic industry in the U.K., Nigeria and Algeria; sugar cane processing in Kenya; construction in Arabia; edible oil refining and electrical plant manufacture in Pakistan, and dairy plant manufacture in New Zealand.*

So the majority of nations must now unite to protect themselves against the increasing nuclear threat. Through either a new, international confederation, or the United Nations (hitherto a toothless organization, whereas fangs and claws are now required), a demand must be made—and forced into effect—to stop the manufacture of any more nuclear weapons, and establish an international inspectorate to ensure that this happens. From this point, a phased elimination of all nuclear weapons must follow. For as long as one nation has one bomb, innocent people are at risk.

The nuclear arms race is a race without a winner. Proliferation of weaponry in East and West, and an extending number of nations with the bomb, increases the risk of nuclear disaster. Human error in missile manufacture or manning; material failure in service; misinterpretation of events; or, an act of terrorism, might result in a trigger action. Or, fear of being the first victim may make first use seem a rational option. Never has such mass destruction—controlled by so few—threatened so many.

Theodore M. Hesburgh

"All other moral questions pale into insignificance when compared to this one. If this problem is not solved, we can forget about the others, because there will not be human beings around to have problems."

I BELIEVE THAT THE nuclear threat to humanity is the greatest moral problem that has faced humankind since our appearance on Earth. Never before was there, in our hands, the power to reverse the work of God's creation—at worst, the elimination of all of humankind and, at best, a return to the Stone Age.

All other moral questions pale into insignificance when compared to this one. If this problem is not solved, we can forget about the others, because there will not be human beings around to have problems.

I believe that everyone must do what she or he can, wherever one happens to be, and with whatever power one happens to have. By power, I don't just mean physical power, but rather talent, ideas, access to networks, and all the other things that can change the world.

For myself, I am trying to bring together the top world scientists and religious leaders. So far, we have 36 Academies of Sciences throughout the world—mainly the nuclear powers and those capable of becoming nuclear powers—signing a statement which they all

THEODORE M. HESBURGH, *U.S. priest; president, University of Notre Dame; chairperson, Academic Council, Ecumenical Institute for Advanced Theological Studies, Jerusalem; former director, American Council on Education;* The Hesburgh Paper: Higher Values in Higher Education *(1979) and* The Humane Imperative: A Challenge for the Year 2000 *(1974) are among his published works.*

helped draft. The statement not only calls for the total elimination of nuclear weapons everywhere in the world, in a mutually-verifiable fashion, but also indicates steps that might be taken to move in that direction, towards that ultimate goal.

We are now having this scientific statement examined by religious leaders of the world's religions. We have already had a meeting with the Holy Father at the Vatican, and with the religious leaders from East and West, in Vienna. We are proposing, under the aegis of a newly-created Academy of Peace, in Jerusalem, three more meetings: one with the Buddhists in Japan, one with the Hindus in India, and one with the Jews and Muslims in Cairo.

The reason for getting these two groups together is that they have not made common cause on anything since Galileo. When scientists now speak against nuclear war, they are said to speak with poor grace, since they created nuclear weapons. When religious leaders speak, they are told that they do not know what they are talking about.

Having religious and scientific leaders speak together undercuts both criticisms, and could create a potent force for raising the consciousness of people everywhere, to insist that their governments work more realistically towards the elimination of nuclear weapons by a series of smaller, yet ever-growing steps.

I have always been optimistic, not because I don't know the facts, the danger, and the probability of ultimate destruction, but because I have faith that with God's grace and a lot of hard work, we may be able to avert it in our time.

Jan Kostrzewski

*"The international tension which has led to a
crisis of confidence and lack of faith in the
possibility of attaining effective, peaceful
solutions creates a vision of catastrophe."*

As president of the Polish Academy of Sciences, I call on all
individuals and organizations responsible for the fate of science,
throughout the world, to intensify efforts to make both their peoples
and policy-makers aware of the present, dramatic course of world
peace, and to stress the necessity for a genuine action to counter all
forces, attempts, and moods that employ the uncontrolled arms race
to drive humankind into regional conflicts, and ultimately, a global
confrontation.

New kinds of nuclear weapons increase the danger of military
confrontation. Also, the international tension which has led to a crisis
of confidence and lack of faith in the possibility of attaining effective, peaceful solutions, creates a vision of catastrophe. Such catastrophe may be the consequence of deliberate aggression, of reck-
lessness, or of a fatal error that could activate forces of unprecedented and heretofore unknown destructive power, capable of
bringing about an instantaneous annihilation of humankind, together
with the intellectual, moral and material heritage humanity has
accumulated for thousands of years.

Scientists and scholars should be particularly aware of both the
growing threat to peace, and the developing methods of warfare,
for it is in this latter field that the intensely-accelerated developments
of science and technology presently find their application.

Thus, scientists and scholars have a duty—through personal contact, and in their research—to alleviate and smooth out differences,
to call for mutual concessions now essential for maintaining peace,
and to analyze the sources of the present crisis, in order to find
realistic and effective ways out. These should lead to a lasting peace

JAN KOSTRZEWSKI, *president, Polish Academy of Sciences, Warsaw.*

that will make it *possible* to solve the basic social and economic problems confronting humankind today.

The voices of scientists and scholars should also be heard in the struggle against the psychosis of war, against passiveness towards the persisting danger, and against ill will and fundamental miscalculations about the assumed profits to be derived, or the losses to be sustained, during a small or large-scale war.

They should speak out to sound a warning, as well as to proclaim their belief in averting the danger of nuclear holocaust, and trust that we *shall* manage to construct and maintain the necessary conditions for a creative co-existence between the nations.

Roger W. Sperry

"One sees little hope for a permanent, truly satisfactory control of nuclear armaments in the absence of some kind of international World Security Force . . . which presumably would proceed to systematically dismantle existing nuclear weaponry."

I VIEW THE nuclear threat with hope—that the nations of the world will perceive, in this, a compelling example of the need to control certain national activities by higher laws, based on principles and ideals that transcend national interests, for the common good and welfare of the biosphere as a whole.

One sees little hope for a permanent, truly satisfactory control of nuclear armaments in the absence of some kind of international World Security Force, with both the power and know-how to keep nuclear developments under strict surveillance and control, and which presumably would proceed to systematically dismantle existing nuclear weaponry. The problems of setting up and administering an effective, international force of this kind—involving a first step toward World Government—can hardly be more grave, formidable or insoluble than those we are destined to encounter on any alternative course.

Instead of accepting prevailing impressions that such a solution is hopeless and impossible, we can start thinking *positively* about ways

ROGER W. SPERRY, *U.S. neurobiologist and humanist; 1981 Nobel Prize in Physiology for his famous split-brain research, which galvanized neuropsychology; professor of psychobiology, California Institute of Technology; Lasker Award, 1979; Lashley Prize, 1976; California Scientist of Year, 1972;* Science and Moral Priority *(1983) and* Changed Concepts of Brain and Consciousness: Some Value Implications *(1982) are among his published works.*

to best achieve it. One would expect to build from existing organizations, especially the United Nations; but new thinking and creative strategies are now needed to an extent that suggestions from high school and college students might be as helpful as those from venerable politicians. With the aid of the media, we can extend the search for an acceptable plan to the grass-roots level, making it a prominent part of the ambient, public concern.

A starting precondition—for the kind of cooperation needed to organize a World Security Force—is a formula for determining representation and voting strength that will assure participant nations they will not suffer an unfair loss in relative power, living standards, prestige, etc. This will mean that factors other than population numbers should be taken into account, such as indicators of various economic, educational, military and cultural strengths, reflecting the quality as well as quantity of life, and which collectively might give a realistic measure of each nation's present status and relative rights. The countries of the world are today sufficiently interrelated and interdependent that, working together through a properly constituted, World governing body, they could bring any recalcitrant nation—even the U.S. or U.S.S.R.—into compliance, through united economic and other nonmilitary pressures. But again, instead of dwelling on the complexities and difficulties, we can get busy ironing out the issues and looking for creative solutions.

Another prime requisite will be a set of founding guidelines and principles that justify a higher world order, and which would transcend, but not conflict, with national interests. Principles for law and justice will be needed which all countries can respect, support, and agree to be ruled by, regardless of differing ideologies, religious beliefs, cultural values, political biases, and so on. Some concensus on what is right and wrong, and of what ought to be, is essential when it comes to ordering priorities, making decisions, formulating rules and regulations, etc. Thus far, no such concensus exists at the international level. Even a limited World Security System—of the sort envisioned for nuclear controls—will be much more successful if founded on principles and ideals that command common allegiance and a commitment above and beyond those at the national level, just as allegiance to a nation supersedes that to constituent states or provinces.

Just as in the United States, states' rights are respected and protected against Federal intervention, one presumes a World Security System would not usurp the rights of nations to govern their own internal affairs much as they always have, with the exception of a few things such as nuclear armaments, pollution of the oceans and atmosphere, etc., that are more reasonably and effectively dealt with at a global level, rather than at national levels.

Peoples of differing faiths and cultures understandably tend to recoil at the thought of being governed by the values and beliefs of opposing ideologies. Capitalist countries don't want to submit to Communist values, or vice versa; the same applies to Christians and Muslims, and all the rest. Historically, these ideological and religious differences have always been a main source of world conflict. There seems little chance, in the foreseeable future, that all the different countries are going to be persuaded to give up their beliefs, so as to unite under the ethical principles and values of any ideology currently existing. One can, however, see a reasonable possibility that enough countries might be willing—for purposes of nuclear control —to compromise on a new, relatively neutral, moral and legal code, founded in the truth and worldview of science.

Science, here, is not to be taken in the usual, traditional sense of referring to things that can be handled by numbers and measurements alone, and according to which everything in principle— including the human psyche—reduces to quantum mechanics. The reference, rather, is to the latest views in science, which bring a new philosophy, and a new worldview.

The feature that is new—and what offers new promise at this time—is the recent revisions that have emerged in science since the late '60s, as a result of the so-called consciousness or mentalist revolution in the behavioral and neurosciences. These bring changed views of Nature, of the human psyche, of the relation of mind to matter, of the relation of science to values, and related developments now transforming the scientific outlook, and its moral and value implications. Nature and all reality are no longer conceived to be determined solely from below upward, but also from above downward. The higher mental, vital and social forces, including the full spectrum of human needs and values, are now given their due, along with physics and chemistry.

In the past, the choice has been between materialist explanations of natural science, on the one hand, or various mystical, supernatural schemes of religious faith, on the other. The *new* stance of science rejects both of these, in favor of a newly-perceived third choice—a middle-of-the-road position which I have tried to outline in a book on *Science and Moral Priority.*

The time has passed when nations should be allowed to do as they individually wish with regard to global matters, each striving solely in its own interests, with the more powerful now able to destroy all humanity and more. For the common good, we need to frame and abide by a higher system of law and justice, designed with less national, more godlike, perspectives for the preservation and welfare of the biosphere as a whole. The intellectual, scientific and moral foundations are already in sight. Control of nuclear armaments is a logical place to start their implementation.

Joseph B. Glaser

"While I agree with the Catholic Bishops that the policy of deterrence is temporarily logical, my fear arises out of the possibility of accident, error, mischief, or madness, even drunkenness. Murphy's Law hangs heavily over us."

I CANNOT SAY that I am optimistic about our future. I am worried. I am scared. While I agree with the Catholic Bishops that the policy of deterrence is temporarily logical, my fear arises out of the possibility of accident, error, mischief or madness, even drunkenness. Murphy's Law hangs heavily over us. Also, I *do* believe that the logic of deterrence is only temporary, and since the deployment of the Pershing missiles in Europe and the Soviets' predictable but dismaying response, I think it safe to say that the timetable has been moved up.

What can be done? Every way I turn this thing, one answer keeps coming out: there is a lack of trust between the superpowers, and in spite of the bluster, or perhaps because of it, the stench of fear hangs heavily over the White House and the Kremlin. Some third agency— certainly not the utterly corrupt and inept United Nations—must make some fast and dramatic moves to start building some trust between the superpowers. Concomitantly, this third agency must establish a joint monitoring system with respect to the other nuclear powers, as well as the potential possessors of nuclear weapons, such as the madman Kaddafi, the apocalyptic Khomeini and terrorist groups. What that third agency is, I am not sure, but I am searching around for it, and maybe your collection of respondents is an answer. May God strengthen our hands as we seek to preserve Divine Creation.

JOSEPH B. GLASER, *U.S. executive vice-president, Central Conference of American Rabbis; chairperson, Religion in American Life.*

Louis N. M. Duysens

"I estimate that the probability for such a disaster is of the order of 10 percent per 10-year period, which is equivalent to a probability of about 60 percent in a century."

I ESTIMATE THAT THE probability for such a disaster is of the order of 10 percent per 10-year period, which is equivalent to a probability of about 60 percent in a century. In view of this extreme danger, humankind's highest priority should be the lowering of this probability to a negligible value—the prevention of nuclear destruction.

Reduction of nuclear weapons, of course, reduces tension and lowers the probability for a disaster. However, even complete removal of nuclear weapons by mutual agreement would, by itself, only take away the *immediate* threat. The probability for nuclear destruction over a period of one or two decades would not be diminished, in my opinion, since one or more nations would sooner or later start rebuilding a nuclear arsenal, and would be followed by other nations. During these transitions, the probability for a nuclear war would be larger than at the moment.

Nuclear rearmament can, in my view, only be prevented by an independent, state-like power, which I will call "The Peace-Keeping Power." This organization should consist of a relatively small number of people (less than a million) of vaious backgrounds, care-

LOUIS N.M. DUYSENS, *Dutch biophysicist; professor of biophysics, State University of Leiden, The Netherlands; foreign associate, U.S. National Academy of Sciences; Kettering Award for Excellence in Photosynthesis for discovering solutions to several, seemingly intractable problems regarding the mechanisms of photosynthesis.*

fully selected from expert people of various nationalities, all of whom are deeply dedicated to carrying out the extremely important task of preventing nuclear rearmament.

The peace-keeping power should be organized in such a way that it cannot—under any circumstances—interfere with internal matters of the states, except those related to nuclear armament. Additional criteria for selection, especially for the higher offices of the peace-keeping power, would be tolerance, plus a virtual absence of hunger for power. Such officers should also have little missionary zeal for propagating their own political, cultural or religious beliefs.

Of course, many things are badly in need of improvement in our world. But because there is little agreement about what should be changed and how, it would probably be impossible to initiate the organization of a peace-keeping power with *extended* tasks, within a time short enough to prevent nuclear disaster. However, in order to make aggression between states unprofitable, it appears unavoidable to also prohibit certain conventional weapons.

In order to make execution of its task possible with a limited number of people, it also seems unavoidable, at least initially, that the peace-keeping power possess a limited number of certain nuclear weapons. This power should also direct and guard the nuclear *dis*arming of all nations. Some of the bases of the peace-keeping power may be located on islands scattered all over the world. The supervision, especially of nuclear arms, should be distributed in such a way—in the executive branch of the organization—that the use of power for purposes other than peace-keeping will be virtually impossible.

The organization of this power, in such a way that nations are convinced it will perform its task effectively, but will not interfere with their internal affairs, is not easy. But this task *is* easier than organizing an existing nuclear state in such a way that it becomes virtually impossible that nuclear weapons are used within this state, for example, in a civil war. History shows that in the major nations, civil wars occurred a few times per thousand years. So the organization of the peace-keeping power can be more stable than that of a state, since its members will be specifically selected for their suitability and dedication to the task of maintaining nuclear disarmament. On the other hand, different criteria obtain for leading functions in a nation. Additionally, the peace-keeping power is organized solely for the purpose stated, while a nation is not. Thus, a nation would be safer from nuclear destruction under the peace-keeping power, than when possessing a nuclear monopoly.

The setting up of a constitution for the peace-keeping power, and of plans for the organization, will be a difficult task, requiring perhaps a decade or more after the major nuclear powers have agreed to proceed with it. However, the main barrier to a plan for prevention of nuclear war is that many influential people are reluctant to follow untraditional paths in their thinking, even if these paths would be the only possible ones for achieving the desired result.

People would be even more reluctant to support such plans if they would fear negative effects on their influence or income. So, although all people are morally obliged to assist in diminishing the daily threat of nuclear destruction, the acceptance of the new state of affairs would be made easier if a compensation would be promised to groups which would be negatively affected, when the plan is being carried out.

If, indeed, the establishment of a peace-keeping power, as indicated, is practically the only way to sufficiently reduce the probability for nuclear destruction, the major powers—in the first place, the United States and the U.S.S.R.—should initiate a study of this question.

Jerome D. Frank

"Perhaps the best hope—and one hates to think of it— would be afforded by an accidental nuclear explosion on the territory of one of the nuclear powers over a populated area, under circumstances that would not trigger a full-scale holocaust. Such a catastrophe might bring people to their senses."

VERY FEW PEOPLE have achieved world-consciousness. The vast majority think only in terms of protecting their own country against perceived enemies, or increasing its power at the enemy's expense. They fail to recognize that in a nuclear world, such activities endanger the whole globe, including themselves.

Since humans will never forget how to make nuclear weapons, any future war can become nuclear, so humanity will be in constant danger until successful ways are devised for outlawing war as a means for resolving international disputes.

Except for the dwindling band of survivors of Hiroshima and Nagasaki, no living humans have experienced the destructiveness of nuclear weapons; and the destructive power of the Hiroshima and Nagasaki atom bombs was tiny, compared with that of today's nuclear bombs and missiles. Moreover, nuclear explosions differ fundamentally from all previous ones. These explosions are hotter and brighter than the sun, create more violent winds than earthly hurricanes, and leave behind radiation that can be lethal for long

JEROME D. FRANK, *U.S. professor emeritus of psychiatry, Johns Hopkins University School of Medicine;* Sanity and Survival in the Nuclear Age *(1982) is among his published works.*

periods of time.

The basic psychological problem, then, is not an assumed death wish, but a failure of imagination; as Martin Buber put it, an inability to imagine the real.

As long as nations race to acquire more and 'better' nuclear weapons than their rivals, the outlook is bleak, and there is no sign yet that any have had a change of heart. So-called arms-control agreements simply determine the direction and form of the nuclear arms race; they do not reduce its dangers.

As the probability of a nuclear explosion in any given time interval is greater than zero, the longer the arms race lasts, the closer this probability approaches to certainty.

Perhaps the best hope—and one hates to think of it—would be afforded by an accidental nuclear explosion on the territory of one of the nuclear powers over a populated area, under circumstances that would not trigger a full-scale holocaust. Such a catastrophe might bring people to their senses.

The first and most difficult task for each of us is to reorder our priorities, and those of the organizations to which we belong, so that efforts to halt, and then reverse, the nuclear-arms race take precedence over regular activities and interests. Ask yourself, what could I or my organization do that we are not doing now?

Use every means accessible to you and your organization to convince your friends, colleagues, the public and political leaders that, to quote Admiral Noel Gayler (who was in charge of targeting U.S. nuclear missiles for several years): "There is no sensible, military use for nuclear weapons...there is no conceivable, military objective worth the risk of nuclear war."

Means for spreading this message include casual conversations with friends and colleagues; letters to the editors of local newspapers and to legislators; call-ins on talk shows; formal talks and informal discussions at meetings of organizations, and persuading these organizations to pass antinuclear resolutions.

Join and actively support those organizations working for nuclear disarmament that are in accord with your views, such as the Council for a Livable World, Federation of American Scientists, SANE, United World Federalists, and many others. As an individual and through these organizations, support specific measures for halting the nuclear arms race, such as the nuclear Freeze Campaign, No First Use, "Deep Cuts," and further funding of the National Peace Academy.

Promote programs that make use of new technologies for enhancing mutual understanding among the world's people; for example, worldwide television and radio programs sponsored internationally and transmitted by satellite, and vast expansion of existing programs for face-to-face meetings of citizens of different nations, such as the Institute for International Living, and the Forum for U.S.-Soviet Dialogue. Join organizations for which you are eligible that arrange periodic, international meetings to promote nuclear disarmament, such as the "Pugwash" movement and International Physicians for the Prevention of Nuclear War.

Encourage international programs for achievement of goals that require international cooperation. Successful examples are: the International Geophysical Year, the Barcelona Conference on Cleaning up the Mediterranean, the WHO program to eliminate smallpox, and cooperative U.S.-U.S.S.R. programs in outer space. All such international, cooperative activities, and others that are needed for survival but haven't yet been activated—such as reduction of worldwide pollution of the atmosphere and the oceans—are the best means of reducing international mistrust and fostering awareness of common interests. These are the first, small steps toward the creation of world institutions for outlawing war, that are essential for human survival.

Massive, persistent efforts along the lines here indicated would provide the best hope that humanity can move past the danger of nuclear destruction, into a world in which the peaceful applications of new scientific discoveries, and technological advances, can create levels of human health, cultural richness, and opportunities for self-fulfillment that previous generations couldn't even imagine.

Gregory Peck

"I believe that we Americans have nothing to lose by testing unilateral cutbacks in the nuclear buildup, and that we ought to do it."

CALL IT WHAT you like, total annihilation is almost upon us. Listen to William Butler Yeats:

> *Turning and turning in the widening gyre*
> *The falcon cannot hear the falconer;*
> *Things fall apart; the center cannot hold;*
> *Mere anarchy is loosed upon the world,*
> *The blood-dimmed tide is loosed, and everywhere*
> *The ceremony of innocence is drowned;*
> *The best lack all conviction, while the worst*
> *Are full of passionate intensity.*

We are relying on systems of government and institutions that probably cannot solve the problem. National sovereignty should gradually be cast aside. We must share the resources of the planet, and preserve it, as brothers and sisters under the skin, members of one world.

I believe that we Americans have nothing to lose by testing unilateral cutbacks in the nuclear buildup, and that we ought to do it. Let us rely on, as our nuclear deterrent, a few hundred assorted missiles, instead of thousands. Do we really need more than we now have to deter the Soviets from a first strike?

If we don't try it, we may never comprehend the true nature of

GREGORY PECK, *U.S. Academy Award-winning actor, producer.*

their fear of "capitalist imperialism," nor will we put to the test the validity of our fear of "Communist, world domination". I am saying, in plain terms, that with the world watching, we should back off a little, in order to find out if they wouldn't, in turn, elect to back off a little. That could be a start down the long road toward acceptance of the concept of one world, and the continuation of our journey.

I dare to be optimistic, because I believe that the human race is haltingly, but inexorably, driven toward a higher destiny. I believe that good will prevail over evil, that powerful people's movements can and will force gradual nuclear disarmament and a coming together of the U.S. and the Soviets, comparable to the renewal of friendship between the U.S. and China.

Carl R. Rogers

"We have very little time. This is a life-and-death issue for all of us. Can we stop the drift toward destruction? We all have a responsibility in answering this question."

THIS IS AN awesome time in the history of the world. It is entirely possible that we are approaching our doom. Admiral Hyman Rickover, the father of nuclear submarines and an expert on nuclear warfare, was asked in a Senate hearing on Jan. 28, 1982, what he thought of the prospects of nuclear war. His reply was essentially, "I think we will destroy ourselves, and then perhaps a better, wiser species will emerge."

I believe that the prospect of this incredible holocaust is so horrendous that we often tend to trivialize it, or to deny its seriousness, or blot it completely out of our thinking. We refuse to grasp the *meaning* of it consequences. I believe that it is dynamics of this sort that help to account for the statements of Reagan and Bush about 'surviving' and 'winning' nuclear war, and the horrifying course upon which they have set our nation and our military might. The utmost of this socially-suicidal mentality was achieved in a 1982 speech by the then-advisor to the President, Edwin Meese, when he referred to nuclear war as "something less than desirable"!!

CARL R. ROGERS, *U.S. psychologist; resident fellow, Center for Studies of the Person, La Jolla, California; former president, American Psychological Association, American Association of Applied Psychology, and the American Academy of Psychotherapists; Humanist of the Year, American Humanist Association, 1964;* A Way of Being *(1980),* Carl Rogers on Personal Power *(1977),* Freedom to Learn *(1969), and* On Becoming a Person *are among his published works.*

Several years ago, my granddaughter taught in a training program for adolescents who had been rejected by their schools. These were obviously not ordinary young people. Yet what she found is significant. Early in the term, she asked them to write some paragraphs describing what they envisioned for themselves in five to ten years. The majority of them saw themselves dead in a thermonuclear holocaust, or living desperate lives in a harsh, polluted, overcrowded world.

Here are a few quotes: "In five years, I will either be dead, or in the Army, or playing lead guitar in a band. I do think the war will come before five years, and that most of us will be dead." "I believe in five years, if Reagan hasn't gotten us blown up, that our natural resources will either disappear, or they will be very difficult to get hold of. I really think that in five years, I will be dead, or really, really bad off."

The prospect of nuclear war hangs as a black cloud over all of us, but the young are especially sensitive and aware, and especially hopeless. But are these young people too gloomy? What is the view of those scientists, physicists and engineers who understand the technology of the situation? According to theoretical physicist Fritjof Capra, many of them have two blind spots: (1) they are employed by the military-industrial complex, and (2) they often see only a narrow, or fragmented view of their own task, and have no conception of how it all fits together.

Consequently, the only experts who can provide an unbiased and comprehensive assessment of the situation are those who are independent of nuclear development and, not surprisingly, they all tend to be in the antinuclear movement. Those who know the most are the most strongly opposed to the steps we are taking toward nuclear war, as the work and publications of the Union of Concerned Scientists clearly show.

And what about military men who know the plans and strategies for nuclear war? The Center for Defense Information strongly opposes nuclear war, the senseless arms race, and the escalating military budget. And who are its leaders? Two rear admirals of the Navy, and a major general of the Marines. They have all been deeply involved in planning nuclear war. Now retired, they are devoting full time to try to stop our self-destructive military policies. So it is clear: those who really know nuclear possibilities are most deeply committed to *stopping* the arms race, and stopping it *now!*

What can we do to prevent the possibility of a nuclear war? Psychologists have made valuable proposals as to steps that might be taken. Perhaps the most exciting is Charles Osgood's plan for "Graduated and Reciprocated Initiatives in Tension-reduction" (GRIT). Osgood's book, *An Alternative to War and Surrender,* should be carefully restudied by all of us, especially by those in government.

One of the greatest difficulties in any dispute is to recognize, and even more difficult, to *accept* that the certitude we feel about our own rightness and goodness is equaled by the certitude of the opposing group about its rightness and goodness. If tension is to be reduced, it is this pattern that must somehow be dissolved. Here is where a facilitative approach has *often* been successful.

One example involving a deep feud was a group I worked with from Belfast, Northern Ireland. There were five Protestants, including one Englishman, and four Catholics in the group. The nine were chosen to include extremists and moderates on both sides, men and women, older and younger. Our group wanted to facilitate straightforward communication and to film this interaction. We only had funds enough to finance one long and intensive weekend.

In the early sessions, the bitterness, horror, and despair of everyday life in Belfast was abundantly clear in the experience of the members: a sister blown to bits by a bomb; a family hiding behind mattresses as bullets struck their home; carrying away torn bodies, living and dead, from bomb explosions. The whole mixed stream of hatred and violence, of fear and despair, seemed so powerful that to think one weekend could possibly make any difference seemed incredibly visionary.

Yet changes did occur. There were only 16 hours of group interaction, yet during that very short period, the centuries-old hatreds were not only softened, but in some instances, deeply changed. So rapid was the progress, so significant the changes, that some of the statements made in the group had to be deleted from the film. To show such understanding of the opposition would have endangered the lives of the speakers when the film was later shown in Belfast.

This is evidence that facilitative attitudes can create an atmosphere in which open expression can occur. Open expression in this kind of a climate leads to communication. Better communication very often leads to understanding, and understanding washes away many of the ancient barriers. You may feel such a process could not possibly help with international issues where we are dealing with large political entities. In this connection, I would like to call your attention to the Camp David experience involving Sadat, Begin and Carter.

There were two notable outcomes. First, these two world leaders, starting from very divergent points of view, were able to come to a major agreement on constructive next steps. The second outcome is astonishing. Begin and Sadat were almost violently hostile toward each other at the outset. At the end of the 12 days, they felt sufficiently warm toward each other that they embraced on public television.

To be sure, there were deficiencies, but Camp David marks a new step in international negotiation. It affirms the potentialities of the intensive group experience. It is a model that should be utilized and improved.

In the people, there appears to be a will toward peace. In Europe, millions are making known their desire to stop further deployment of nuclear missiles. In the United States, the millions are just beginning to move. As early as June, 1981, a Gallup poll showed that 72 percent of the American public wanted the US and USSR to stop building nuclear weapons. There is great support for a bilateral nuclear-weapons freeze—a proposal that both nations "halt the testing, production and further deployment of all nuclear weapons . . . in a way that can be checked and verified by both sides."

And in Russia? Our information is scanty, but 20 million Russians died, and an equal number were injured, in World War II. The dread of war is even greater among the Russian people than in ours. Two Russian dissidents give us a current picture of the attitudes of their countrymen (*Medvedev & Medvedev*, 1982). According to these writers, the people live in great and understandable fear of the United States. They are especially fearful of an American nuclear first-strike.

There is, then, every reason to believe that many millions of people, in many countries, desire peace. If that desire is strongly voiced by massive numbers, it can stop the two governments in their disastrous course. We have evidence of this in my country. It was public protests that eventually stopped the Vietnam War.

What is needed is a great popular uprising to bring a halt to the step-by-step escalation toward nuclear war. President Dwight Eisenhower, not a flaming radical, said it well many years ago:

> *Some day the demand for disarmament by hundreds of millions will, I hope, become so universal and so insistent, that no man, no men, can withstand it. We have to mobilize the hundreds of millions; we have to make them understand the choice is theirs. We have to make the young people see to it, that they need not be the victims of the Third World War.*

Those millions are beginning to move, to be heard. The goal of this movement must be twofold: to stop the nuclear buildup and nuclear threats, and to substitute a process making for peace. The need for this positive program cannot be overstated.

The first step is to change the policy of the U.S. government. At the present time, the top officials show not the slightest intention of wishing to have *real* peace with Russia, or of wishing to understand the Russians. They make phony proposals, knowing in advance that they cannot be accepted by Russia. Threat seems to be almost their only diplomatic tool. We excoriate Russia for its invasion of Afghanistan, and its part in the military dictatorship in Poland. Yet, deplorable as those actions are, we should view them with some humility, in view of our own conduct in Vietnam, Chile, El Salvador and Nicaragua.

We need to bring pressure on the government of the United States to embark on a serious, vigorous program of communication with the USSR and the Russian people. We pour billions into creating redundant nuclear weapons sufficient to destroy the planet many times over. We need to put some of that money and energy to work in pursuing, developing and expanding the communicative process that leads toward peaceful reconciliation.

With a minute fraction of the dollars we spend for war, we could, as we know from experience and research, make definitive progress toward peaceful interaction that would prevent the holocaust from overwhelming us. We have very little time. This is a life-and-death issue for all of us. Can we stop the drift toward destruction? We *all* have a responsibility in answering this question. It is to carry out my personal share of this responsibility that I have spoken out so strongly. I intend to continue. I hope you will join me—and millions of others—in working for a stop to our terrible insanity—the trend toward nuclear war.

Charles E. Osgood

*"The assumption behind
mutual, nuclear deterrence—
that we can go spinning forever into eternity, poised for
mutual annihilation, kept
from it by only the fragile
bonds of mutual fear—is
untenable."*

W HAT HAPPENED IN the decade between the mid-Sixties and the
mid-Seventies, in the thinking of the U.S. military-industrial complex, was a subtle shift from the goal of disarmament, to the concept
of arms control—a concept which puts no real ceiling on the arms
race, and promises very profitable competition and proliferation.

For example, SALTs I and II are agreements to *increase* nuclear
capabilities on both sides. And as yearly reports of the Stockholm
International Peace Research Institute only too clearly indicate, the
arms-control approach has failed to prevent, or even damp, the
proliferation of potential, nuclear-weapons capabilities, as well as
sophisticated, conventional weapons. Even as of 1977, no less than
15 countries—excluding the U.S., the U.S.S.R., the U.K., and
France—had nuclear-power capacities for theoretical, nuclear-bomb
productions.

We have a *very* rational basis for fear in the military use of nuclear
science and technology. Each superpower was already capable of
destroying, at least once-over, the other's civilization more than a
decade ago. Yet driven by psycho-logic (the noble 'we's' must

CHARLES E. OSGOOD, U.S. *professor of psychology and communications, University of Illinois at Urbana; fellow, Center for Advanced Study in Behavioral
Sciences, Palo Alto;* Social Psychology and Political Behavior *(1971),* Perspective in Foreign Policy *(1966),* An Alternative to War or Surrender *(1962) and*
Method and Theory in Experimental Psychology *(1953) are among his published works.*

always be stronger than the evil 'they's'), reassured by Pollyannaism (a nuclear holocaust could never really happen), and with the military-industrial complexes getting immense power and/or profits from it all, both superpowers continue spending billions of dollars/ rubles in a nuclear arms race that is piling overkill upon overkill capacity.

Paradoxically, the conviction by each 'ego' that the 'alter' would never *dare* to initiate a nuclear exchange provides a sort of 'umbrella' under which aggressive excursions can be made—like the U.S. pressure in late 1979 upon its NATO allies to accept more advanced, tactical nukes on their soils, capable of devastating much of Russia; then the subsequent Soviet encroachment in Afghanistan.

Needless to say, such excursions dangerously exacerbate mutual tensions. Of course, the rest of humanity cannot feel any real security, either. A major nuclear exchange between the U.S. and the U.S.S.R. would spread deadly, radioactive fallout over the globe, in addition to its nuclear-winter effects. And who is to say that gradual death is to be preferred to near-instantaneous?

The focus of my own long-term concern at the international level has been the rationalization of a stategy alternative whose technical name is Graduated and Reciprocated Initiatives in Tension-reduction. One of the aims of GRIT is to reduce and control international tension levels. Another is to create an atmosphere of mutual trust, within which negotiations on critical military and political issues can have a better chance of succeeding. In other words, GRIT is not a substitute for the more familiar process of negotiation, but rather a parallel process, designed to enable a nation to take the *initiative* in a situation where a dangerous 'balance' of mutual fear exists—and, to the degree successful, GRIT smooths the path of negotiation.

However, being unconventional in international affairs, the GRIT strategy is open to suspicion abroad, and resistance at home. Therefore, it is necessary to spell out the ground rules under which this particular 'game' should be played—to demonstrate how national security can be maintained during the process, how the likelihood of reciprocation can be maximized, and how the genuineness of initiations and reciprocations can be evaluated.

RULES FOR MAINTAINING SECURITY

RULE 1: *Unilateral initiatives must not reduce one's capacity to inflict unacceptable nuclear retaliation, should he be attacked at that level.* Nuclear capacity can serve rational foreign policy (a) if it is viewed not only as a deterrent, but also as a *security* base from which to take limited risks, in the direction of reducing tensions, (b) if the retaliatory, *second-strike* nature of the capacity is made explicit, and (c) if only the *minimum* capacity required for effective deterrence is maintained, and the arms race damped. Needless to say, *none* of these 'if' conditions have been met, to date, by the two nuclear superpowers. Not only are nuclear weapons ambiguous as to initiation or retaliation, but both strategic and tactical weapons are redundantly deployed and in oversupply, as far as capacity for graded response to aggression is concerned.

RULE 2: *Unilateral initiatives must not cripple one's capacity to meet conventional aggression with appropriately graded, conventional response.* Conventional forces are the front line of deterrence, and must be maintained at rough parity in regions of confrontation. But the *absolute* level at which the balance is maintained is variable. So the general rule would be to initiate unilateral moves in the regions of least tension, and gradually extend them to what were, originally, the most tense regions.

RULE 3: *Unilateral initiatives must be graduated in risk, according to the degree of reciprocation obtained from an opponent.* This is the self-regulating characteristic of GRIT that keeps the process within reasonable limits of security. If bona fide reciprocations of appropriate magnitude are obtained, the magnitude and significance of subsequent steps can be increased; if not, then the process continues, with steps of about the same magnitude of risk. The *relative* risk thus remains roughly constant throughout the process.

RULE 4: *Unilateral initiatives should be diversified in nature, both as to sphere of action, and as to geographical locus of application.* The reason for diversification is two-fold: first, in maintaining security, diversification minimizes weakening one's position in any one sphere (e.g., combat troops), or any one geographical locus (e.g., Berlin); second, in inducing reciprocation, diversification keeps applying the pressure of initiatives *having a common, tension-reducing intent* (and, hopefully, effect), but does not 'threaten' the opponent by pushing steadily in the same sphere or locus, and thereby limiting his options in reciprocating.

RULES FOR INDUCING RECIPROCATION

RULE 5: *Unilateral initiatives must be designed and communicated so as to emphasize a sincere intent to reduce tensions.* Escalation and de-escalation strategies cannot be 'mixed'—in the sense that military men talk about the "optimum mix" of weapon systems. The reason is psychological: reactions to *threats* (aggressive impulses) are incompatible with reactions to *promises* (conciliatory impulses); *each strategy thus destroys the credibility of the other.* It is , therefore, essential that a complete shift in basic policy be clearly signaled at the beginning. The top leadership of the initiating power must establish the right atmosphere by stating the overall nature of the new policy, and by emphasizing its tension-reducing intent. To avoid 'self-sabotage,' it must be kept in mind that *all* of one government's actions with respect to another, have the function of communicating intent. Therefore, control over de-escalation strategies must be just as tight and pervasive as control over war-waging strategies, if actions implying incompatible intents are not to intrude and disrupt the process.

Rule 6: *Unilateral initiatives should be publicly announced at some reasonable interval prior to their execution, and identified as part of a deliberate policy of reducing tensions.* Prior announcements minimize the potentially unstabilizing effect of unilateral acts, and their identification with total GRIT strategy helps shape the opponent's interpretation of them. However, the GRIT process cannot *begin* with a large, precipitate, and potentially unstabilizing, unilateral action. It is this characteristic of then-Senator Mansfield's proposal (in May, 1971), for example—to cut by about half the U.S. forces permanently stationed in Europe, in one fell swoop—that would have been most likely to destabilize NATO-Warsaw Pact relations, be threatening to our allies, and possibly encourage Soviet politico-military probes.

RULE 7: *Unilateral initiatives should include, in their announcement, explicit invitation to reciprocation in some form.* The purpose of this 'rule' is to increase pressure on an opponent—by making it clear that reciprocation, of appropriate form and magnitude, is essential to the momentum of GRIT—and to bring to bear pressures of world opinion. However, *exactly* specifying the form or magnitude of reciprocation has several drawbacks: having the tone of a demand, rather than an invitation, it carries an implied threat of retaliation if the demand is not met; furthermore, the specific reciprocation requested may be based on faulty perceptions of the other's situation, and *this* may be the reason for failure to get reciprocation. It is the occurrence of reciprocation *in any form,* yet having the same tension-reducing intent, that is critical. Speaking psychologically, the greatest conciliatory impact upon an opponent, in a conflict situation, is produced *by his own, voluntary act* of reciprocating.

RULES FOR DEMONSTRATING THE GENUINENESS OF INITIATIVES AND RECIPROCATIONS

RULE 8: *Unilateral initiatives that have been announced must be executed on schedule, regardless of any prior commitments to reciprocate by the opponent.* This is the best indication of the firmness and bona fideness of one's own intent to reduce tensions. The control over what and how much is committed, is the graduated nature of the process; at the time-point when each initiative is announced, the calculation has been made, in terms of prior reciprocation history, that this step can be taken within reasonable limits of security. Failure to execute an announced step, however, would be a clear sign of ambivalence in intent. This is particularly important in the early stages, when announced initiatives are liable to the charge of 'propaganda'.

Rule 9: *Unilateral initiatives should be continued over a considerable period, regardless of the degree or even absence of reciprocation.* Like the steady pounding on a nail, pressure toward reciprocation builds as announced act follows announced act of a tension-reducing nature, even though the individual acts may be small in significance. It is *this* characteristic of GRIT which, at once, justifies the use of the acronym—*and* raises the hackles of most military men! But the essence of this strategy *is* the calculated manipulation of the *intent* component of the perceived-threat-equals-capability-times-intent equation. It is always difficult to 'read' the intentions of an opponent in a conflict situation, and they are usually very complex. In such a situation, GRIT can be applied to consistently encourage conciliatory intents and interpretations, at the expense of aggressive ones.

Rule 10: *Unilateral initiatives must be as unambiguous, and as susceptible to verification as possible.* Although actions do speak louder than words, even overt deeds are liable to misinterpretation. Inviting opponent verification via direct, on-the-spot observation, or via indirect media observation (e.g., televising the act in question), along with requested reciprocation in the verification of *his* actions, is ideal—and what little might be *lost* in the way of secrecy by both sides may be more than made up in a *reduced need* for secrecy on both sides. However, nations in conflict have intense, mutual suspicions and, therefore, place a heavy emphasis on mutual secrecy. The strategy of GRIT can be directly applied to this problem: particularly in the early stages, when the risk potentials are small, observers could be publicly invited to guarantee the verifiability of doing what was announced—and, although entirely *without* explicit insistence on reciprocation by the opponent, the implication would be strong, indeed. Initiatives whose face-validities are very high should be designed—for example, initial pullbacks of forces from border confrontations—and they can operate to gradually reduce suspicion and resistance to verification procedures. This should accelerate as the GRIT process continues.

SOME APPLICATIONS OF GRIT STRATEGY

Over the past 15 years or so, there has been considerable experimentation with the GRIT strategy—but mostly in the psychological laboratory. There have been sporadic GRIT-like moves in the real world—for example, in the early 1960s, the graduated and reciprocated pullback of U.S. and Soviet tanks, which were lined up practically snout-to-snout at the height of the Berlin Crisis—but for the most part in recent history, these have been one-shot affairs, always tentatively made, and never reflecting any genuine change in basic strategy.

The one exception to this dictum was "The Kennedy Experiment." This real-world test of a strategy of calculated de-escalation was conducted in the period from June to November, 1963. The first step was President Kennedy's speech at the American University on June 10, in which he outlined what he called "A Strategy of Peace," praised the Russians for their accomplishments, noted that "our problems are man-made...and can be solved by man," and then announced the first unilateral initiative—the United States was stopping all nuclear tests in the atmosphere, and would not resume them unless another country did. Kennedy's speech was published in full in both *Pravda* and *Izvestia*, with a combined circulation of ten million. On June 15, Premier Khrushchev reciprocated with a speech welcoming the U.S. initiative, and announcing that he had ordered production of strategic bombers to be halted. The next step was a symbolic reduction in the trade barriers between East and West: on October 9, President Kennedy approved the sale of $250 million worth of wheat to the Soviet Union. Although the U.S. had proposed a direct, American-Russian communication link (the "hot line") in 1962, it wasn't until June 20, 1963—after the Kennedy Experiment had begun—that the Soviets agreed to this measure. Conclusion of a test-ban treaty, long stalled, was apparently the main goal of the experiment: multilateral negotiations began in earnest in July, and on Aug. 5, 1963, the test-ban treaty was signed. The Kennedy Experiment slowed down with deepening involvement in Vietnam—and came to an abrupt end in Dallas, Texas.

Had this real-world experiment in calculated de-escalation been a success? To most of the initiaives taken by either side, the other reciprocated, and the reciprocations were roughly proportional in significance. What about psychological impact? I do not think that anyone who lived through that period will deny there was a definite warming of American attitudes toward Russians, and the same is reported for Russian attitudes toward Americans—they even coined their own name for the new strategy, "the policy of mutual example"!

Perhaps recalling the successful, 1963 "Kennedy Experiment," President Leonid Brezhnev, on Oct. 8, 1979, proposed a very GRIT-like reduction of the numbers of Soviet medium-range, nuclear carriers (threatening Western Europe), along with graduated withdrawal of Soviet troops and tanks in East Germany over a 12-month period—*provided that* the NATO medium-range, nuclear weapons (threatening Western Russia) were not increased in numbers or quality, and implied reciprocations were undertaken. Apparently following advice from Zbigniew Brzezinski (and, no doubt, our own military), President Carter 'cold-shouldered' this proposal—and, indeed, *initiated greater* range than the existing NATO weapons. Actually, several of our NATO allies favored this GRIT-like Soviet proposal, and all of us may live to die regretting this decision.

The question I am most often asked is: "Doesn't any novel approach like this involve too much risk?" Actually, *anything* we do in the nuclear age means taking risks. Escalating conflicts which involve another nuclear power unquestionably carries the greatest risk. Simply doing nothing—remaining frozen in a status quo already at much too high a level of force and tension—is certainly not without risk, over the long run. GRIT also involves risk. But the risking comes in small packages.

Looked at in broad perspective, the superpower confrontation has many positive elements in it, many motivations on both sides that favor detente, and it therefore offers itself as a potential proving ground for a strategy that is novel, but yet appropriate to the nuclear age in which we are trying to survive. *The assumption behind mutual, nuclear deterrence*—that we can go spinning forever into eternity, poised for mutual annihilation, kept from it by only the fragile bonds of mutual fear—*is untenable*. The ultimate goal must be to get out from under the nuclear Sword of Damocles, by eliminating such weapons from the human scene.

Jessica Mitford

*"I would rather see an unre-
lenting effort to boot out the
powerful and their policies,
via stepping up of myriad
policies aready tried."*

W<small>HEN</small> I <small>WAS</small> writing *The American Way of Death* in the early
1960s, I strongly advocated cremation as the main way to avoid the
expense and absurdity of what the American undertakers are
pleased to call "the standard American funeral"—*their* standard, that
is. Following publication of my book, the incidence of cremation
has risen from 3.5 percent to over 14 percent. BUT: Has my message
been taken too seriously by our rulers? I never meant to suggest 100
percent cremation of the living, as well as the dead. In my view, this
is what their policies may lead to, unless checked by overwhelming
popular demand.

It is my impression that a lot more is happening in peace movements around the world than ever gets reported in any one newspaper. For example, the English are, by and large, unaware of the
California Livermore protest; ditto, Californians don't read much
about Greenham Common.

Indira Gandhi called for "an unrelenting effort to convert the
hearts of the powerful"—which is assuming that the powerful have a
heart. I would rather see an unrelenting effort to boot out the powerful and their policies, via a stepping up of myriad methods already

J<small>ESSICA</small> M<small>ITFORD</small>, *U.S. author;* Poison Penmanship: The Gentle Art of Muck-
raking *(1979),* Kind and Unusual Punishment: The Prison Business *(1973),* The
Trial of Dr. Spock *(et. al., 1969) and* The American Way of Death *(1963) are
among her published works.*

tried; ballot propositions for nuclear-free zones in a given community; demonstrations like those in West Germany, England, and many parts of the United States; close attention to and publicizing of the stand of candidates for office—at all levels—on the nuclear question, and wide dissemination of pamphlets like E.P. Thompson's *The Defense of Britain* (an exceptionally cogent argument, published by the Campaign for Nuclear Disarmament, 11 Goodwin Street, London N4).

Richard L. Garwin

"I don't believe we should bet on the success of President Reagan's request to develop a 'space-age' defense to nullify ballistic missiles.... Cruise missiles and bombers are not affected by space weapons, and there are many ways to counter such systems; so in my opinion, that approach is fated to failure."

BASED UPON 30 years of involvement in U.S. public matters, my judgment now is that this nation has lost its way. It is not that Republicans are in office, and want to reduce the influence of government or to reverse so-called progressive taxation, nor that Democrats may have opposite goals. Rather, many public officials regard themselves as above the law, which they consider as a goal and not as a strict requirement. This behavior is condoned (or ignored) by the administrations for which they work, and by the members of Congress of both parties. The Code of Conduct for Government Employees is ignored, as are the remedies of recall and impeachment.

In effect, the system does not work. Time and again, the Armed Services and civilian officials have concealed alternatives, wrongly

RICHARD L. GARWIN, *U.S. physicist; principal designer of U.S. H-bomb; consultant, more than 20 years, to U.S. government on military technology, arms control, etc.; IBM fellow, Thomas J. Watson Research Center; adjunct professor of physics, Columbia University; adjunct research fellow, Kennedy School of Government, Harvard University; professor-at-large, Cornell University; Wright Prize, 1983; co-authored* Science Advice to the President *(1980),* The Dangers of Nuclear Wars *(1979) and* Nuclear Weapons and World Politics *(1977).*

criticized programs other than their chosen ones, and ignored their responsibility to present to their superiors in the Defense Department, the Administration and Congress, a full range of options and an analysis adequate to evaluate them.

To my knowledge, no military officer or government official has ever been recalled, impeached, fired or even rebuked for what Spiro Agnew might have called "zealous presentation of his organization's case." The result is a kind of Gresham's law of officialdom. Those with little regard for truth and law are more valuable to their organizations than are those bound by conscience, or by observation of an official code of conduct. The tragedy is that although we all know examples of real integrity in public office, we may not have thought seriously enough about the damage to the country which is caused by a general lack, in recent administrations, of such integrity.

Many Representatives and Senators squander their *own* integrity to support any contract or system which provides expenditures in their districts. And the bureaucracy responds by spreading programs, through subcontracting, to provide something in almost every state. So every Representative or Senator has to be for every program.

A couple of years ago, I participated in a daylong "Defense Forum for National Educators" at the National Defense University, sponsored by the Defense Department. In his prepared speech, Secretary of Defense Caspar Weinberger stated that the Soviets had five new types of ICBMs, and that their average missile was less than five years old; whereas *all* our land-based missiles (the 1,000 Minutemen and the 52 Titans) had been deployed in the 1950s, and had been improved since then only by some modifications to the warheads. Only two weeks later, President Reagan said that the Minuteman III (of which we have 550) was "introduced in 1969," which is, itself, far from the "1950s". But most of them were, in fact, deployed in the *1970s*. Our Minuteman IIIs, deployed in the 1970s, have nothing in common with the Minuteman I of the 1960s (*not* 1950s), except the name. I suggested to the Secretary that if you have wrong information, you're likely to reach wrong decisions.

It is incredible to me that a business executive would tolerate mechanisms or persons providing demonstrably-wrong information for his public speeches, and presumably for his program decisions. And so I conclude that our leaders continue to be insulated from the facts.

I could go on. And I do, not to criticize these individuals, but to point out how widespread this practice is of arrogating to oneself decisions which belong to the Congress, to the Secretary of Defense, or to the President. If you say that the President does know, or the Secretary does know, that's an even worse situation than the one I imagine, where they do *not* know.

I urge that national organizations like Common Cause, and internal government apparatus, as well, focus on holding public officials and military officers to their oaths of office and conduct. This will not be done without punishment and disgrace. But the absence of integrity has had dire effects on our national security and economic status. The restoration of effective government is in the best interests of all of us, even those who believe they benefit from the present system.

I close with a prescription for our defense programs, and for arms-control treaties to limit the Soviet threat to our security:

(A) First, we ought to cancel the MX program. The only appropriate basing system for a 100-ton missile with ten warheads is on small submarines. The Air Force is not in the least interested, and has not studied it at all. The Navy has studied it, says it's feasible, but would prefer to continue to build Tridents. So we ought to cancel the MX program.

(B) On the other hand, we ought to develop and deploy something which has the name now of Midgetman—one-tenth the size of the MX (ten tons), with a single MX-type warhead. The first 450 should be put into the Minuteman-II silos—and we would be ready to build a lot more in very small, specially adapted silos. Or if (as I hope, and as the President requests) we have a very drastic reduction in nuclear weapons (I hope from our 25,000 to 1,000, and from the Soviets' 20,000 to 1,000), we'll be far better off with our warheads individually housed in silos, rather than ten in a silo, subject to destruction by a single warhead.

(C) Third, we ought to cancel the B-1 bomber program. The arguments for the cruise missile are as valid now as they were ten years ago, and eight years ago. The cruise missile exists. The Stealth technology, which is proposed for a follow-on bomber to the B-1, is better adapted to the cruise missile, because the Soviets would still have to shoot down 20 of those to destroy all of them, instead of destroying one target if multiple bombs are being carried on a Stealth bomber.

(D) Next, we should begin to build small submarines. Eventually, the large Trident submarine (18,000 tons with 24 missiles) or the Poseidon submarine (with 16 missiles, each with 10 warheads) will be just too many eggs in one basket. Now that Admiral Hyman Rickover has retired, one can even consider not only smaller submarines, but nonnuclear ones. Rickover now says that we made a big mistake in going for either nuclear power or nuclear weapons, but I wish he had felt such reticence when he was attacking the President's Science Advisory Committee in the 1960s, for requesting that he or his staff come over and tell us about the competition between nuclear power and non-nuclear power for submarine propulsion.

(E) The highest urgency is to ban all weapons from space, the testing of weapons in space, and the damaging or destruction of satellites. If we don't do this, then one side or the other is going to develop, and try to deploy in space, defenses against ballistic missiles. The other side, which has worked so hard to threaten retaliation on the other country, if attacked, will not stand for this and will deploy space mines next to these defensive satellites. The first side will either accept the space mines, which then negates these defensive systems, or will attack them, and we will have all of our satellites destroyed, as well as all of the Soviet satellites. They are all very vulnerable in peacetime. We will have war in space, not instead of war on Earth, but as a prelude to war on Earth. The Soviet Union, in August, 1981, presented a draft treaty of this type to the U.N. Committee on Disarmament. We ought to mark up that treaty until it satisfies us, throw it back to the Soviets and say, "sign here," as the beginning of an urgent, aggressive negotiation.

(F) We ought to ratify the SALT II treaty. President Reagan originally promised that the United States would abide by the provisions of SALT II (signed by President Carter in 1979) so long as the Soviets do. And the Soviet Union has said the same. If we *ratify* the treaty, we can then hold the Soviets to account, complain to them about things which seem suspicious, and use that as a base from which to negotiate further. For instance, the next treaty or protocol I would like to have is one which allows us to turn in two of the warheads to which we are entitled under SALT II, as a price for building a little new silo for the Midgetman missile (we can't build any new silos under SALT II). The Soviet Union ought to favor our reducing our entitlement from 8,200 land-based warheads to 4,100, and they might even want to reduce the vulnerability of their own land-based force by doing the same. So I think the prospects for such a protocol, given the ratification of SALT II, are pretty good.

(G) We ought to finish the negotiation of the Comprehensive Test-Ban Treaty, so that we would have no more nuclear explosions, nor would the Soviet Union. If we did that, the nuclear weapons establishments, on both sides, would take a much more aggressive attitude against the testing of nuclear weapons by other nations, because the greatest hazard is not further testing of nuclear weapons by the United States or the Soviet Union, but the spread of nuclear weapons to nations which do not now have them.

One may worry about these treaties, but any decent treaty of indefinite duration (which is the best kind, in my opinion) has in it a clause which says that if the supreme national interest demands, then either side may abrogate the treaty after six months. And we should, of course, use such a clause when our supreme national interest is engaged.

I don't believe we should bet on the success of President Reagan's request to develop a 'space-age' defense to nullify ballistic missiles. First of all, it's not like building a fission weapon or a hydrogen bomb, where you fight against nature and nature doesn't fight back. The Soviet Union is very much interested in maintaining their ability to deter the United States by the threat of retaliation, and will watch carefully whatever we do. Cruise missiles and bombers are not affected by space weapons, and there are many ways to counter such sustems; so in my opinion, that approach is fated to failure.

If we're really interested in developing and deploying such a defense, we might consider doing it jointly with the Soviet Union so that each side can defend against the weapons of the other. But the very question makes one wonder why we don't agree to *eliminate* those weapons, which will keep us from having to build a defense in the first place*.

Gen. David C. Jones, who retired in 1982 as chairperson of the Joint Chiefs of Staff, wrote that: "The Defense Department has evolved into a grouping of large, rigid bureaucracies, which embrace the past and adapt new technology (only) to fit traditional missions and methods. The result of this rigidity has been an ever-widening gap between the need to adapt to changing conditions, and our ability to do so."

I agree with that. I really hope that the people in industry and in the Defense Department will take this criticism seriously and try to revise the bureaucracy. The first step, though, is to restore integrity to the officials—in their testimony to Congress, and in their public statements. If it can be proved that an official has made statements knew were wrong, that official should leave office.

In my writings and Congressional testimony, I've shown how time after time, our national security choices have been misdirected by false argument, concealed assumptions, and hidden agendas, and how some of the best options have been ruthlessly suppressed. We have all, so far, paid for that with our wealth and our well-being. If we don't restore integrity to our government, we may well pay for it with our lives.

----

*See Richard Garwin's 1986 article, "Space Defense: The Impossible Dream?", in the issue "Defense Through Space—The Strategic Defense Initiative," of *NATO's Sixteen Nations.*

Victor W. Sidel

"The arms race is not iself a 'disease,' but a 'symptom' of the world's racism, nationalism and unbridled, short-sighted greed."

NUCLEAR WAR CAN cause unprecedented and perhaps unimaginable destruction, including irreparable damage to the fabric of human society. Indeed, it has the potential for omnicide—ending the life of the human species, or of all life on our planet. Furthermore, even before their use, the development of these weapons has great psychological, economic and social consequences ... what has been called "destruction before detonation".

The arms race is not itself a 'disease,' but a 'symptom,' a symptom of the world's racism, nationalism and unbridled, shortsighted greed. Our efforts must, therefore, be directed not only at reversing the arms race, but also at its underlying causes.

These efforts must include: (1) development of a new international economic order which shifts resources from the wealthy to the poor; (2) massive new efforts by all nations, through international agencies, to bring adequate nutrition and better health to the poorest people of the Earth, and (3) widespread exchange of citizens among countries, to share knowledge and skills, and to reduce the stereotypic thinking and 'dehumanization' of others that divide the world's peoples.

If we but begin now, it is not too late.

VICTOR W. SIDEL, *U.S. professor and chairperson, Department of Social Medicine, Montefiore Medical Center-Albert Einstein College of Medicine; president-elect, American Public Health Association; member, board of directors, Physicians for Social Responsibility.*

David R. Brower

"The nuclear threat is the worst threat to the Earth since the asteroid headed our way 65 million years ago and hit."

THE NUCLEAR THREAT is the worst threat to the Earth since the asteroid headed our way 65 million years ago and hit. We were not here to do anything about that Act of God, but we are here to act swiftly to forestall the ultimate Atomic Act of Man. We probably have no equivalent of cave-protected Dead Sea scrolls to convey to a later intelligence that we were ever here.

Death is certain, but there is no need to hurry it. We will have plenty of time to be dead, and have too little to be alive, proud of it, and ready to make the most of our being here.

I urge that we realize that there can be no peace on the Earth until we make peace *with* the Earth. We fight the Earth with every technical and economic tool we can brandish. We are addicted to unreasonable growth in demands for nonrenewable resources, we obliterate renewable resources, and we insist upon exponential growth in our own numbers, despite having long ago passed the people limit. We speed euphorically on, borrowing irresponsibly from our children and theirs.

I should like to see a Global Fate of the Earth Week every year, as long as a sustainable society eludes us. For sustainable life styles, we could all take a day a week for renunciation, listing things we don't have to do for that week. We could take another day for creativity, thinking about how to add our modicum of joy to the Earth's passengers at least that often.

There are six crucial *Cons* that I'd like on the global agenda:

Conservation can get our numbers and demands back within the Earth's limits, and steer us away from the environmental causes and consequences of war. We were told how to treat each other, thanks

DAVID R. BROWER, *U.S. founder and chairperson of the environmentalist organization, Friends of the Earth (with sister organizations now in 27 countries); former executive director, Sierra Club.*

to the two tablets Moses brought down from the mountain. He must have overlooked the third tablet, however, informing us how to treat the Earth well enough not to have to fight over it.

Conversion is well worth a friendly, global contest. How ought people spend, on something worthwhile, the trillion dollars a year about to go to weapons, worldwide? How can we make jobs of trying to heal the Earth, instead of contriving to blow it and us up? How can we improve upon the conversion to peaceful enterprise we achieved at the close of World War II?

A *Constitution* has served our nation; why not the Earth? How do we move toward law and order, including an environmental Bill of Rights, for the only planet we know to have life on it? Tribes have coalesced into nations. Can nations now coalesce into humanity, since the alternative is oblivion?

Conscience is something to listen to once again. Let the older voice of the heart inform the freshly fact-sated mind. We know deep inside what we have to do now, besides being freaked out by 'the communist threat' (after all, there are far more communists on our side than on the Soviet's). Don't disdain facts—and don't perish while waiting for all of them.

Conviviality is the juice in which the other Cons can flow. There must be some joy in the effort, some music, too (it crosses borders without a visa), and appreciation of beauty (which often does the same). An extended hand can achieve what a clenched fist cannot. Problems can be superseded by opportunities. And let those too cynical to believe this be superseded, too . . . in their leadership.

Within recent years, we have had Fate of the Earth conferences nationally, internationally, and regionally. We are planning more of that scope, and would also like to see them in every precinct, so that people who think survival can be economically and politically feasible, can help it become so.

Heed Walter Cronkite: "We cannot do it by force of arms; we must do it by example." Let the 'it' be defined by George Dyson: "Find freedom without taking it from someone else."

Michael N. Nagler

"I view the nuclear threat as an inevitable condition of our failure to resolve the spiritual struggle within ourselves. It is simply a—horrible—technological magnifying lens held up to our own unresolved hatreds and alienation."

I VIEW THE NUCLEAR threat as an inevitable condition of our failure to resolve the spiritual struggle within ourselves. It is simply a—horrible—technological magnifying lens held up to our own unresolved hatreds and alienation.

Every one of us can undertake the bitterly difficult resolution of the unfinished spiritual struggle within us. Then peace can be (a) conceptualized (it has not been, to date; even antinuclear people have hardly a notion of what peace would look like, or how it would work) and (b) institutionalized. Here, each must, and can, find his or her proper role.

For convenience, we can consider what is to be done under three heads:

ALTERNATIVE DEFENSE — Every citizen, without exception, should know something about the general principles and some historic instances of societies which have successfully defended themselves against aggression by nonviolent (and, therefore, purely defensive, not counteroffensive) means. People who are in favor of peace should *never* advocate defense build-downs in any mode, without simultaneously offering a build-up of plausible and appropriate alternatives.

MICHAEL N. NAGLER, *U.S. professor of classics and comparative literature, University of California at Berkeley; founder, Berkeley Peace Studies Project; participant, Program in Peace & Conflict Studies;* America Without Violence (1982) *is among his published works.*

Alternative defense is often subdivided as civilian-based, nonviolent defense (or 'social defense,' as the Germans call it nowadays); third-party peacekeeping (typically by nonviolent, volunteer peace brigades, but to a limited extent, also by armed, nonpartisan intervention forces, such as UN peacekeeping missions), and international arbitration-mediation mechanisms. Information about this vital, undeveloped resource can be obtained from the Center for Nonviolent Sanctions in Conflict and Defense, Harvard University, Cambridge, MA 02138, USA, or from ISTNA, Box 515, Waltham, MA 02254, USA.

SOCIO-POLITICAL RECONSTRUCTION — We now live in a war system—that is, as Richard Barnet puts it, our society is "organized for war". We must plan and execute a reorganization toward stable peace, of all our social institutions. Decentralization, for example, on the economic level, must be part of this; the other parts are rather complex to discuss in short compass. In any case, both alternative-defense planning, and institutional reorganization depend upon:

VALUES REEDUCATION — We need a worldwide, individual rejection of present mass-media values. That is, the values of individual alienation and competition, usually summed up in the concept of what's called a 'zero sum' approach to life—in order for me to 'win,' somebody else has to lose—must be overcome by the commitment of strong individuals to a 'positive sum' worldview, in which reconciliation, not winning... cooperation, not competition ... unity, not separate advantage, are appreciated in their splendor and dignity. Since values spread rapidly through the human community, brave individuals can make the most difference here. But we cannot make a difference if we are not different—that is, if we do not live, breathe, represent, and gradually institute new values which sweep aside the prevailing, low image of the human being.

Martin Sheen

"Until we begin to fill the jails with protest, our governments will continue to fill the silos with weapons."

ALL OF US on Earth live from day to day, indeed from moment to moment, with the gravest risk of seeing it all end by design or accident.

It's far easier to put the responsibility for death in someone else's hand. On the other hand, we are here to accept the responsibility of life, totally and completely, ourselves. If we are to change the world, we must begin with our own personal life. How many people are willing to do that?

We have lost the name of action! Hence, we have lost the true right to survive. Until we begin to fill the jails with protest, our governments will continue to fill the silos with weapons. I speak in theory, of course. But I have not earned the right to suggest a way out, since I myself have not actually gone to jail in protest*. We need true leadership, people with great courage, who are willing to make a difference by going to *jail,* not Congress!

Oddly enough, I am very optimistic about the future.... I have given hostages to it in my children. I believe the weapons are the antichrist, and our biggest problem is not finding God—He is everywhere; our biggest problem is in trying to get rid of God.

---

*Editor's Note: As the degree of frustration increases, worldwide, toward political-military-industrial 'leaders' continuing this mad race toward nuclear self-annihilation, it's instructive to see the personal value to be realized when putting oneself more in *touch* with actuality, with things as they are, with our world, for better or worse. On June 20, 1986, Martin Sheen was finally arrested—during a Manhattan sit-in at the Riverside Research Institute, a company profiting from the arms race—along with *VOS* colleague Daniel Berrigan. Evaluating the experience, Sheen said: "This is the happiest day of my life!" Father Berrigan, of course, has long known that same feeling.

MARTIN SHEEN, *U.S. actor;* Samaritan, Choices of the Heart, Kennedy, In the King of Prussia, Gandhi *and* Apocalypse Now *are among his films.*

Gene Knudsen-Hoffman

"To heal our deranged selves, I believe we must learn to forgive, which means, to me, to wish for life for everyone on Earth, to wish for them happiness, fulfillment, and love, and then seek ways to bring this about."

I HAVE NO OPTIMISM, but I do have a faith in the mystery we call 'God,' and in the possibilities which continuously unfold for us as we seek them. Perhaps my faith lies in what Buddhists call "The Great Ball of Merit"—enough good people in the world, performing loving acts, to tip the scales toward humanity for all. I see much good around me: much love, much caring, and much new cherishing of the Earth, and of one another.

On the other hand, there is much fear: fear of loss of the status quo (which I see as fear of change), fear there isn't enough to go around, and fear of sharing. Fear sometimes paralyzes us. Sometimes, it propels us into psychotic behavior. I think that arming ourselves—seeking peace through threats and military means—is both unreal and psychotic.

To heal our deranged selves, I believe we must learn to forgive, which means, to me, to wish for life for everyone on Earth, to wish for them happiness, fulfillment, and love, and then seek ways to bring this about. If we begin radiating these new messages, we *will* reduce fear. And from these new messages—this paradigm shift—will come ways of behavior that will foster life. The late Milton Mayer, teacher and pacifist, wrote that no group should seek to save

GENE KNUDSEN-HOFFMAN, *U.S. program associate, U.S.-U.S.S.R. Reconciliation, American and International Fellowship of Reconciliation.*

or serve itself. Jews should serve the Chinese; Chinese, the Scandinavians; Scandinavians, the Blacks, and on and on. Our task should be to save lives not our own.

Secondly, we must learn how to love, and one way is through speaking our truths. Loving often means we must say *no* to what we consider antilife, so we can say *yes* to life. This may mean not cooperating with whatever is rushing us headlong into holocaust. How? Through acts of noncooperation, similar to those South African blacks are now using effectively. We can begin with one hour, refusing to use electricity, water and telephones—business *not* as usual. If there is no change after the hour's protest, we can lengthen it to a day; then another, and another. Another method is to boycott products of those corporations at the critical hub of the nuclear-weapons industry, such as the 1986 worldwide boycott of General Electric consumer appliances. This is now a time for dramatic risk-taking. And I have no doubt that our message—"We do *not* want military solutions to our problems."—will reach those in power, in a way no articles or letters or even demonstrations ever have.

Finally, I do not believe we can accomplish anything without opening ourselves to our own spiritual resources. This is different for each of us, for we are varied. For me, it means silence, listening to the Informing Presence (which, to me, is God). And I am sure of one thing, as A.J. Muste phrased it: "Our resources are in ourselves and in God, and they are *infinite!*"

Philip Berrigan

"We will prevent nuclear war, outlaw all war and will eradicate killing ... or we will embrace extinction."

SINCE OCTOBER, 1962 (the Cuban Missile debacle), I have regarded nuclear weapons as the most profound and urgent moral and political issue since the Crucifixion of Christ. According to my reckoning, therefore, we will prevent nuclear war, outlaw all war and will eradicate killing ... or we will embrace extinction.

We can choose life. The *Bible* matter-of-factly tells us (Deuteronomy 30:11) that choosing life is a "command," neither "mysterious" nor "remote". In the concrete, choosing life comes down to choosing laws—we cannot keep both God's law and the State's. God's law *is* life—raising an outcry for the victims, protecting the weak, loving enemies. The State's law is legalized disobedience (to God), legalized privilege, legalized nuclear cliffhanging, legalized threat of omnicide.

The choice of life (and law), of course, will make one an outlaw (outside the law), will acquaint one with the spartan furniture of a jail cell. But that is a trifling matter, making, as it does, the very point of life.

Optimism is an imperial attitude, having mostly to do with con-

PHILIP BERRIGAN, *U.S. priest, author, lecturer; Plowshares 8 activist (received three-to-twelve-year sentence for destruction of two Mark 12-A reentry vehicles —which carry W-78 nuclear warheads—at King of Prussia, Pennsylvania); co-founder, Catholic Peace Fellowship;* Of Beasts and Beastly Images *(1979),* Widen the Prison Gates *(1974),* Prison Journals of a Priest Revolutionary *(1970) and* Punishment for Peace *(1969) are among his published works.*

tinuance of the good life ... indefinitely. *Biblical* hope, however, is a radical difference, roughly equivalent to faith, and to faith-ful conduct. So I prefer to struggle on, putting one foot ahead of the other, trying not to sell out, not to 'join up' ... to give perhaps a little inspiration, a little hope to others, in jail and out.

Phillip L. Berman

THE NUCLEAR THREAT is real and frightening; the possibility of the destruction of this planet, and every life form that walks upon it, is at stake. This is easily understood if one contemplates the awesome power of just one three-megaton warhead—the area of fires from such a warhead is 150 times greater than from the Hiroshima bomb, and the area of destruction is 30 times greater. The detonation of such a warhead over a city would create a 40-square-mile area of total destruction. We have thousands of such weapons.

Wars can no longer be won, and as Clauswitz has said, can therefore serve no useful purpose—we can no longer speak of 'just' and 'unjust' wars, for there will be no more world left in which to consider the ramification of justice and the moral problematics attendant with such inquiry. The macrocosmic wave is moving in the wrong direction, and the wiser micros simply feel unempowered.

As strange as it may seem, I am optimistic about our future. I suspect this is simply the result of years of suffering, and a personal philosophy bent on survival. I see, also, a new and active mood in this country and abroad, which augers well for peace. The worse things get, the more people are impelled to act. So I still have faith that the ultimate war can be halted, and I still have faith in the goodness of humankind. However, a *true* spiritual revival seems essential at this time.

PHILLIP L. BERMAN, *U.S. author; president, Center for the Study of Contemporary Belief;* An Oral History of America *(forthcoming) and* The Courage of Conviction *(1985) are among his published works.*

Richard Alpert *(Ram Dass)*

"It is time for the individual human heart to stand up and be counted. As each heart comes forth in truth and love, it provides a resonance with other hearts, independent of cultural prejudices."

MOST PEOPLE CANNOT conceive of nuclear war. They approach this abstract concept with denial, in the same way as they deny thinking about their own mortality. They tend to focus on more immediate suffering, or they recognize ideological doctrines which they wish to protect with weapons, if necessary. Most people are confused.

We can develop credible and coherent strategies for non-nuclear defense, and simultaneously, support reciprocated initiatives in tension-reduction. We can recognize a global vision, and facilitate shared-consciousness through increasing global networking, through which truth is explored boldly, persistently and fearlessly.

We can recognize that nuclear war-threat is a symptom of a deeper malaise—the sickness of separation, without a simultaneous sense of unity. To see technology as the child of intellect, and to see the intellect as the power tool of the separate entity, is to begin to appreciate the source of the problem. We feel separate and we use our intellect to create security for us. But to the extent that that security is based on opposition to nature or to others, it can only be a

RICHARD ALPERT *(a.k.a. Ram Dass), U.S. lecturer, author; taught psychology at Stanford, UC Berkeley and Harvard Universities; founder, Prison-Ashram and Dying Projects;* How Can I Help? *(1985),* Miracle of Love *(1979),* Journey of Awakening *(1978),* Grist for the Mill *(1977),* The Only Dance There Is *(1974) and* Be Here Now *(1971) are among his published works.*

false sense of security that is shortsighted.

We can recognize that we have to use all methods, both internal and external, to re-connect with that which is unitive, rather than with that which is divisive. We must search our hearts for that place in which we love all manifest things. It is out of our deeper being— which knows its unitive nature with all things—that healing must come.

The individual human heart is a doorway to the source of energy, truth, peace and love. Through this door comes the energy which has increasingly been used by the intellect to protect our separateness, with increasingly devastating effect. It is time for the human heart to acknowledge its own power and responsibility to use its infinite energy in the service of God, in the service of the deeper harmony of all things.

It is time for the individual human heart to stand up and be counted. As each heart comes forth in truth and love, it provides a resonance with other hearts, independent of cultural prejudices. A heart knows heart. So we work on ourselves, we listen, we quiet, we act as purely as possible . . . in order that our heart may contribute to a resonance for peace, for compassion, for love.

Two simple rules:
1. Never underestimate the power of the human heart.
2. Never put another being out of your heart.

As Gandhi said, "Your life is your message."

Thubten Yeshe

Nuclear war is the product of the human mind. Without the creation capacity of the mind, there is no 'good' or 'bad'. If all of us control our own three poisonous minds of hatred, greed and ignorance, there is no danger. All of us do have the capacity to control our individual minds. I believe all human beings have loving kindness, so if we trust each other, there will be no nuclear catastrophe.

Thubten Yeshe, *Tibetan Buddhist Lama; late founder, Foundation for Preservation of the Mahayana Tradition, with centers in Nepal, India, Australia, New Zealand, Italy, Spain, England, the United States and other countries.*

Pope John Paul II

"Peace is not a utopia, nor an inaccessible ideal, nor an unrealizable dream.... War is not an inevitable calamity.... Peace is possible.... And because it is possible, peace is our duty: our grave duty, our supreme responsibility."

PERHAPS NO OTHER question of our day touches so many aspects of the human condition as that of armaments and disarmament. There are questions on the scientific and technical level. There are social and economic questions. There are deep problems of a political nature which touch the relations between states and among peoples. And our worldwide arms systems impinge, in great measure, on cultural developments. But at the heart of them all, there are present spiritual questions which concern the very identity of humankind, and its choices for the future and for generations yet to come. I am conscious of all the technical, scientific, social, economic and political aspects, but especially of the ethical, cultural and spiritual ones.

If human beings would bend to the task with goodwill, and with

---

HIS HOLINESS POPE JOHN PAUL II, *Polish leader of 800 million Catholics, worldwide.*

the goal of peace in their hearts and their plans, then adequate measures could be found, and appropriate structures erected to ensure the legitimate security of every people, in mutual respect and peace. Thus, the need for these grand arsenals of fear, and the threat of death, would become superfluous.

The teaching of the Catholic Church in this area has been clear and consistent. It has deplored the arms race, yet nonetheless called for mutual, progressive, and verifiable reduction of armaments, as well as greater safeguards against possible misuse of these weapons. It has done so while urging that the independence, freedom, and legitimate security of each and every nation be respected.

I wish to reassure you that the constant concern and consistent efforts of the Catholic Church will not cease, until there is a general, verifiable disarmament, and until the hearts of all are won over to those ethical choices which will guarantee a lasting peace.

In the current debate, we must recognize that no element in international affairs stands alone and isolated from the many-faceted interests of nations. However, it is one thing to recognize the interdependence of questions; it is another to exploit them in order to gain advantage. Armaments, nuclear weapons and disarmament are too important—in themselves and for our world—to ever be made part of a strategy which would exploit their intrinsic importance, in favor of politics of other interests.

Therefore, it is important and right that *every* serious proposal that would contribute to real disarmament—and that would create a better climate—be given the prudent and objective consideration it deserves. Even small steps can have a value which would go beyond their material or technical aspects. But whatever the area under consideration, we today need freshness of perspective and a capacity to listen—respectfully and carefully—to the honest suggestions of every responsible party in this matter.

In current conditions, 'deterrence' based on balance—certainly not as an end in itself, but as a step on the way toward a progressive disarmament—may still be judged morally acceptable. Nonetheless, in order to ensure peace, it is indispensable to *not* be satisfied with this minimum, which is always susceptible to the real danger of explosion.

What then *can* be done? In the absence of a supranational authority of the type Pope John XXIII sought in his Encyclical *Pacem in Terris*—one which one would have hoped to find in the United Nations organization—the only realistic response to the threat of war is still *negotiation*. As Saint Augustine expressed it: "Destroy war by the words of negotiations, but do not destroy men by the sword." Today, once again, I re-affirm my confidence in the power of true negotiations to arrive at just and equitable solutions. Such negotiations demand patience and diligence, and must notably lead to a reduction of armaments that is balanced, simultaneous, and internationally controlled.

To be even more precise: the development of armaments seems to lead to the increasing interdependence of kinds of armaments. In these conditions, how can one countenance a balanced reduction if negotiations do not include the whole gamut of arms? To that end, the continuation of the UN study of the "Complete Program of Disarmament" could facilitate the needed coordination of different forums, and bring to their results greater truth, equity and efficacy.

In fact, nuclear weapons are not the only means of war and destruction. The production and sale of conventional weapons throughout the world is a truly alarming and evidently growing phenomenon. No negotiations about armaments would be complete if they were to ignore the fact that 80 percent of the expenditures for weapons are devoted to conventional arms. Moreover, the traffic in these weapons seems to be developing at an increasing rate, and seems to be directed most of all toward developing countries. Every step taken to limit this production and traffic, and to bring them under an ever more effective control, will be an important contribution to the cause of peace.

Recent events have sadly confirmed the destructive capacities of conventional weapons, and the sad plight of nations tempted to use them to solve disputes. To focus, however, on the *quantitative* aspects of armaments—nuclear and conventional—is not enough. A very special attention must be paid to the *qualitative* improvement of these arms, because of new and more advanced technologies. Here one confronts one of the essential elements in the arms race. To overlook this would be to fool ourselves, and to deal dishonestly with those who desire peace.

Research and technology must always be at the service of humankind. In our day, however, the use and misuse of science and technology for other purposes is a too-well-known fact. May I be allowed at least to suggest that a significant percentage of the research that is currently being expended in the field of arms technology and science, be directed toward life and the welfare of humanity.

Pope Paul VI stated a profound truth when he said: "Peace, as you know, is not built up only by means of politics or the balance of forces and interests. It is constructed with the mind, with ideas, with works of peace." The products of the mind, ideas, the products of culture, and the creative forces of peoples are meant to be shared. Strategies of peace which remain on the scientific and technical level, which merely measure out balances and verify controls, will never be sufficient for real peace unless bonds that link peoples to one another are forged and strengthened. Build up the means that will enable peoples and nations to share their culture and values with one another. Put aside all the narrow interests that leave one nation at the mercy of another ... economically, socially, or politically.

The building of links among peoples means the rediscovery and reassertion of all the values that reinforce peace, and that join people together in harmony. This also means the renewal of what is best in the heart of humankind, the heart that seeks the good of the other in friendship and love.

May I close with one last consideration. The production and the possession of armaments are a consequence of an ethical crisis that is disrupting society in all its political, social and economic dimensions. Peace is the result of respect for ethical principles. True disarmament—that which will actually guarantee peace among peoples—will come about only with the resolution of this ethical crisis. To the extent that the efforts at arms reduction, and then of total disarmament, are not matched by parallel ethical renewal, they are doomed in advance to failure.

The attempts must be made to put our world aright, and to eliminate the spiritual confusion born from a narrow-minded search for interest or privilege, or by the defense of ideological claims. This is a task of first priority, if we wish to measure any progress in the struggle for disarmament. Otherwise, we are condemned to remain at face-saving activities. For the root cause of our insecurity can be found in this profound crisis of humanity. By means of creating consciences sensitive to the absurdity of war, we advance the value of creating the material and spiritual conditions which will lessen the glaring inequalities, and which will restore to everyone that minimum of space that is needed for the freedom of the spirit.

The great disparity between the rich and the poor—living together on this one planet—is no longer supportable in a world of rapid, universal communications, without giving birth to a justified resentment which can turn to violence. Moreover, the spirit has basic and inalienable rights. For it is with justice that these rights are demanded in countries where the space is denied them to live in tranquility, according to their own convictions. I invite all those struggling for peace to commit themselves to the effort to eliminate the *true* causes of the insecurity of humankind, of which the terrible arms race is only one effect.

To reverse the current trend in the arms race involves, therefore, a parallel struggle on two fronts: on the one side, an immediate and urgent struggle by governments to reduce—progressively and equally—their armaments; on the other hand, a more patient, but nonetheless necessary, struggle at the level of the consciences of people, to take their responsibility in regard to the ethical cause of the insecurity that breeds violence, by coming to grips with the material and spiritual inequalities of our world.

With no prejudice of any kind, let us unite all our intellectual and spiritual forces—those of statespersons, of citizens, of scientists, of religious leaders—to put an end to violence and hatred, and to seek out the paths of peace. Peace *must* become the goal of all men and women of goodwill. Unhappily still in our day, sad realities cast their shadows across the international horizon, causing the suffering of destruction, such that they *could* cause humanity to lose the hope of being able to master its own future, in harmony and in the collaboration of peoples.

Yet despite the suffering that invades my soul, I feel empowered, even obliged, to solemnly re-affirm before all the world what my predecessors and I myself have repeated so often in the name of conscience, in the name of morality, in the name of humanity, and in the name of God:

Peace is not a utopia, nor an inaccessible ideal, nor an unrealizable dream....War is not an inevitable calamity....Peace is possible.... And because it *is* possible, peace is our duty: our grave duty, our supreme responsibility.

Certainly, peace is difficult. Certainly, it demands much goodwill, wisdom and tenacity. But human beings can and must make the force of reason prevail over the reasons of force. That is why my last word is yet a word of encouragement, and of exhortation. And since peace, entrusted to the responsibility of women and men, remains even then a gift of God, it must also express itself in prayer to him who holds the destinies of all people in his hands.

May I thank you for the activity you undertake to make the cause of disarmament go forward: disarming the engines of death, and disarming spirits. May God bless your efforts, and may this project remain in history a sign of reassurance and hope.

H.H. the Dalai Lama

"The nuclear threat is unimaginably frightening. The horror and death that a nuclear holocaust is capable of bringing about can mean the total destruction of this world, and the extinction of the human race."

I SHOULD LIKE TO to speak to you about the importance of kindness and compassion, and their practical usefulness in our lives. When I address myself to this subject, I regard myself not as the Dalai Lama, not as a Tibetan, not even as a Buddhist, but rather as just one human being. And I hope that you who read my words will also think of yourselves as just human beings, rather than as Americans, or Westerners, or Easterners, or members of any other group, for all these things are secondary.

The main problems which humankind is facing today are basically created by ourselves—created by the divisions we make, based on the secondary factors of ideology, nationalism, economic systems, racial differences, and so on. These issues are hard to reconcile if we think of them as having primary importance. Therefore, I believe that the time has come when we should think on a deeper level—the level of actual, human being—and try to act, from that level of appreciation and respect, for all other human beings. We must build a closer relationship among ourselves, based on mutual trust, mutual understanding, mutual respect, and mutual help, irrespective of culture, philsophy, religion or faith.

After all, human beings are all fundamentally the same. We are made of human flesh, human bones, and human blood. What is

His Holiness Tenzin Gyatso, *the 14th Tibetan Dalai Lama, and the most well known Buddhist leader on Earth.*

more, our internal feelings—desires, hopes and ambitions—are the same: we all want to avoid suffering, and achieve happiness. And we all have an equal right to be happy. In other words, we belong to one big human family, which includes *all* of humankind on this planet.

This statement may sound very simple, but it's important to realize the truth: our quarrels with each other are all due to reasons which are only of secondary significance in our lives. In the long run, no real good results if we argue with each other, cheat each other, suppress or exploit each other. Anything we achieve by these means may last a few centuries, at most, and then it will pass away. But human beings remain. Among them, there are those who are bad as well as those who are good. Bad human beings think it is to their advantage to prevail over their fellow men...to use any method which seems expedient, no matter how cruel, in order to achieve this advantage. The advantage will not last; the methods used only create more problems, more suffering, more mistrust, more resentment, more division. The result is not good for anyone.

Today, the world is becoming smaller and smaller, not only economically, but from many other points of view. We are all much more closely interdependent. We cannot escape from one another. The global crisis we recognize today occurs, because although there is much more communication among nations, and even many summit meetings of leaders of state, everyone concentrates on the divisive problems of the secondary level, ignoring the primary truth that we are, first of all, human beings.

In ancient times, if there was war, the amount of destruction was limited. Today, the effects of war are beyond imagination. Although I had known something about the atomic explosion in Hiroshima, there was a big difference when I physically visited the place where the devastation took place, and met the people who actually suffered through that dreadful moment. Such an experience cannot but move us deeply.

Even though we may regard some people as potential enemies, we cannot want them to suffer so dreadfully. We must acknowledge openly that—on a level deeper than national ideology —they are human beings like ourselves, and that they, too, both want, and have the right, to be happy.

After thinking about that moment in Hiroshima, I am more and more convinced that anger and hatred can never solve our problems. Fire cannot be extinguished by fire, in the same way that internal fire, which is anger, can never be overcome by more anger. This only increases its disastrous power. If your opponent shows anger and you can control your feelings, and offer him the opposite —compassion and tolerance—then not only will you yourself maintain your peace and tranquility, but you will minimize the anger of your opponent. In the same way, world problems cannot be solved by anger and hatred, but only by compassion and loving kindness. This is our only protection. Arsenals of weapons cannot stop the destruction, for the buttons which will set them off are activated by human fingers. These move in response to human fear, hatred, and anger.

Many leaders of great nations are talking about arms limitation and nuclear disarmament. This is very good. But how are we to achieve such control? Not by compromises and limited agreements, which can so easily be disregarded. It is only when we can control ourselves that we will be able to control our weapons. Without the control of anger and hatred, no arms agreement—no matter how solemnly undertaken, no matter how widely supported—will last long. If somebody comes along who has the will to destroy, he can do it within a second.

If we look deeply into these matters, we see that the renunciation of violence must be born in the mind. Control of mind is something inborn. I am not talking here about the control of mind which is achieved in deep meditation. I am just talking about the kind of control which reduces anger, creates respect and concern for others, and allows a clearer realization that human beings are, basically, the same. From the Western viewpoint, it can be seen that the Eastern peoples are all our sisters and brothers. On the other side, the people of Russia should look upon the Westerners simply as their brothers and sisters. This attitude of mind may not solve problems immediately, but even the attempt to propagate that feeling, and that realization, will do a great deal.

Nobody wants to be angry, nobody wants mental anguish or depression, but because of ignorance about our power to dissipate these feelings, they arise in us involuntarily. With anger, we lose one of the best of human qualities: the power of judgment. Judging what is right and what is wrong is not only a benefit for today, but for the future good of all human beings. To achieve right judgment, moreover, we can use our normal common sense, for it will tell us whether this is the right method or the wrong method. But once our mind is influenced by anger, we lose the power to judge properly what may be the results of our actions. Having lost this power, we are no longer complete human beings.

We have to safeguard the power of judging—which is a precious, human good—and for this, the only security lies within ourselves: in our self-awareness, our ability to think deeply, our clear realization of the destructive effects of anger and hatred, and of the positive effects of kindness and love. Use of our power of judgment, of clear thinking, and of self-awareness, leads to self-control. Today, you may be the type of person who is easily irritated over small things. If you become aware of this, realizing the consequences of your irritation, self-control will result.

I do not deny that it will be very difficult to achieve a movement such as the search for peace of mind, on a global scale. Nevertheless, it must be attempted, because it is the only alternative to self-destruction. If any other means could be found that would be more practical and easier to achieve, I would of course support it, but I believe there is no other means.

If we could attain real, lasting peace through the production of more and more weapons, then all factories should be turned to their manufacture. No one would hesitate to spend all the national wealth in this way, if lasting peace could be gained thereby. But unfortunately, weapons are made to be used, if not now, then sooner or later, at some time in the future. If you do not use them, then millions of dollars will have been wasted on their manufacture—money which could have been used in more profitable ways. So spending on weapons is never profitable. A friend of mine told me about some businessmen in Lebanon who dealt in weapons purely for financial reasons. The result of their transactions is that many poor and innocent people have been killed in the streets, sacrificing their lives so that one or two human beings can make a profit!

All of these wrongs stem from our lack of human understanding, of mutual trust, and of mutual respect, based on kindness and love for all human beings. This is why I feel there is only one way to achieve lasting, world peace, and that it's worthwhile for us to make the effort, even if it may not be attained during our own lifetimes. Human life will go on, and surely in the next generation, or the next or the next, peace will come at last, if we persist in our efforts. Therefore, despite the practical difficulties, despite the fact that this view seems unrealistic to some people, I feel it is worthwhile for me to express these thoughts wherever I go.

My conclusion is that the time has come when we should begin to think of other people as brothers and sisters, whose welfare is important to us. This does not mean we should be required to sacrifice all our own benefits for others, for that would be unrealistic, but rather, that in our concern for our own welfare, we do not forget the welfare of others. In the long run, the two are the same. Therefore, in thinking about the future, think also what it may bring to all of us. If we try to subdue our anger, and develop more kindness and compassion for others, we will help them, but we, ourselves, will ultimately gain the greatest benefit.

The selfish man who is foolish thinks of nothing but himself, and therefore, the results are negative, for he arouses resentment, anger and mistrust in others. The selfish man who is wise, however, thinks of others, also, realizing that if he helps them, he is helping himself, for he will meet with a good response and achieve good results.

There is no need for us to agree philosophically, no need to share a temple or a belief. If we are full of good will, our own mind, our own heart, is the temple. Kindness, alone, is enough. This is my religion.

The nuclear threat is unimaginably frightening. The horror and death that a nuclear holocaust is capable of bringing about can mean the total destruction of this world, and the extinction of the human race.

I feel there is a great and urgent need to launch an educational campaign through the mass media. The press, radio, television, and the cinema must all be used for this purpose. People in the remote villages of Asia, Africa, Latin America and elsewhere must be made to see that the nuclear threat is not something which is far away, happening in some distant place. They must be made to see that the nuclear threat is at their very doorsteps, affecting their very lives, and endangering their personal happiness. I cannot imagine people failing to respond to such a campaign when they see that the threat is very personal.

Also, the scientists who are involved in the invention and manufacture of weapons of such destructive nature should bear a strong moral responsibility toward humankind. I strongly feel that either many are not concerned, or they fail to see the consequences, for the products of their scientific work are becoming the instruments of mass destruction.

It is human nature to have hope in the future. To lose hope means to abdicate our common, human destiny to chaos. But the uncertainty of the future is all too real. And to a large extent, our future is in the hands of the world leaders. It is, therefore, imperative that they have more frequent, person-to-person contact.

We cannot, of course, expect overnight changes in their differing standpoints and policies. But a greater opportunity to sit down and, honestly and frankly, discuss the problems confronted by the world, will increase the possibility of removing much of the mutual distrust and misunderstanding that exist at the present. Under an atmosphere of better understanding, there is hope for a general lessening of tensions, and a gradual cultivation of trust.

*Never doubt that a small group of thoughtful,
committed citizens can change the world. Indeed,
it's the only thing that ever has.*
                              —MARGARET MEADE,
                              U.S. anthropolgist

ALL OF HUMAN CULTURE—everything added to our magnificent planet for thousands of years—began as dreams in individual human minds. Now, for the first time in history, some of the best-trained minds on Earth have provided the means to destroy *all* dreams— past, present *and* future—with these hammers of hell that *can* break out world to bits.

This book is part of the dream to *prevent* such an aberrant misapplication of human intelligence. It began in Spring of 1982, off the eastern coast of Egypt in the middle of the Red Sea. There, I spent 30 days pondering how we might possibly part the insanity of this mad race to oblivion long enough to lead humanity to the new ways of thinking Einstein warned are now requisite for survival.

The dream continued that Summer as my two children took me on our annual pilgrimage into California's High Sierra backcountry above Yosemite. As we sat silently atop Half Dome, tuning our lowlander minds to the vast, calm, measureless inspiration the world's roof always offers, five-year-old Mallika, with no prompting whatsoever, mused, "It's *nice* you get a life before you die."

That statement triggered in me the emotional response necessary to finally drive me off my well-warmed seat on the fence of adult ambivalence. The intellectual exercise you now hold followed almost immediately. First, I decided that if Helen Caldicott, a deeply-concerned mother, could take a year off from teaching at Harvard to focus exclusively on this ultimate threat, I, a deeply-concerned father, could manage the same. I then spent two months in Santa Barbara's main library cross-referencing dozens of volumes, to discover 4000 of the most influential people on our planet.

Initially, I wanted to learn (1) why human society so quickly and fervently appropriates its scientific and technological skill for its own ghastly self-destruction; (2) what drives over half our world's scientists and engineers to work on military research and development; (3) what ideological differences among groupings of people could be so crucial and unresolvable as to justify devastation of whole social systems, and (4) why the intellectual communities on all sides appeared so complacent in the face of the steadily-mounting peril.

Additionally, I wanted to see what one ordinary person, living in the most open democracy on Earth, could do. In light of Alva Myrdal's Nobel Peace Prize acceptance remark—"Disarmament efforts have, for all practical purposes, come to nothing until now."—it was frighteningly clear that nothing we've tried, over 40 long years, has had much effect on those forces, East and West, preparing us so effectively for our own annihilation.

Also, realizing that my writer colleagues in the Soviet Union could not presently undertake such a project, it somehow seemed appropriate that we North Americans—the only ones to have atomized others... the ones most responsible for upleveling this suicidal game of nuclear leapfrog—now become the catalysts for planetary change, the avant garde through these uncharted waters, the pathfinders searching for a paradigm shift in our interdependent cause to stop this nuclear madness... before it stops us!

George Kistiakowsky, the Manhattan Project and Harvard chemist who had been science advisor to Presidents Eisenhower, Kennedy and Johnson, left us in 1981 with this paraphrased conclusion: "I spent 12 years trying to stop this insanity through the channels. Forget the channels! There's simply not time before the world explodes. Instead, build a massive movement of like-minded people in order to give politicians the *will* to stop this madness."

No one, of course, can say for sure how much time we have before our world explodes. But after four years of questioning over 4000 of our world's most influential people regarding this very question, I've come to agree with Harvard's renowned cardiologist, Bernard Lown, co-present of the 150,000-member International Physicians for the Prevention of Nuclear War (recipient of the 1985 Nobel Peace Prize), who warns in this book: "The brutal, most critical fact of our time can be simply stated: If the superpowers continue in their present course, none of us will see the year 2000, a mere 13 years away."

Translated into flesh and blood at the family level, this means my 10-year-old daughter, Mallika, and 11-year-old son, Atisha—who inspired this project—may reach middle age before becoming teenagers. With such awesome stakes, worldwide, *all* other issues become academic, should we fail to collectively solve this ultimate dillemma.

In the final analysis, we, along with our ultramodern technology, are embarrassingly fallible. Even a cursory glance at the Challenger explosion, the Chernobyl tragedy, and back-to-back failures of U.S. Titan and Delta rockets, reveals human inability to perfectly control complex, computerized systems. And in a world literally bristling with thermonuclear annihilators, superpower 007-machismo must now share the stage with suicidal terrorists, while most of the rest of us, as Harvard cardiologist James Muller laments, "drift passively toward that moment when chance brings together the critical mass of plutonium and drugs, alcohol, psychosis or computer error that will destroy us and all we value."

So as you sit there wondering what you—an equally responsible member of our human family—can do to help remove this Damoclean sword overhanging us all, before you consider slipping back behind the psychological barricades of numbing and denial—leaving your share of collective responsibility to either the so-called 'experts', or to what Germaine Greer describes as "tiny groups of dedicated agitators who are driven to crazy extremes by their isolation"—consider what French Nobel physicist Louis Néel wrote in these pages:

> *"Since a progressive disarmament, on a world scale, bearing on all categories of arms, is a terribly difficult geopolitical problem, it does not seem to me that scientists—even Nobel Prize scientists—are better prepared than any other citizen to imagine and propose valid solutions."*

Thus, it is planned that this critical first volume of VOICES OF SURVIVAL will be followed by sequels, until we've collectively stopped this mad race toward unparalleled disaster. Jacques Cousteau has been asked to write the Introduction for VOS-2, so if you're among our world's shapers and movers in *any* field, in any country, your contribution to this ultimate debate belongs in that, or subsequent, volumes.

I also hope to publish, internationally, several volumes each of a PEOPLE'S VOS and a CHILDREN'S VOS, to give voice to those presently given none in their planned annihilation—our world's children, who naively believe we adults are holding their future together, and 'common' householders like you and me, from throughout our severely-threatened global village.

In all planned volumes, because of obvious space limitations, the most cogent, poignant statements (as in VOS-1, from *all* fields and viewpoints in this ultimate debate) will be chosen. Each should be written around the following questions: How do *you* view the nuclear threat? Why are more not acting to save our world? Are you optimistic about our future? and What *can* be done?

Send it, along with a current photo (casual or formal; can't be returned), the words by which you'd prefer to be identified, and among the celebrated, titles of your most recent and forthcoming works, to: Dennis Paulson, Box 90222, Santa Barbara, CA 93190-0222, USA. Contributors to the PEOPLE'S VOS volumes should include: name, age, hometown and occupation. CHILDREN'S VOS contributors, kindly include your school's name and location, as well as your age, the grade you're in, and the career you'd like to pursue as an adult. All statements should be perfectly legible (typed, if possible), and again, please include a current photograph.

Finally, all VOS contributors should, if you will, include a signed statement reading: "I grant permission that my contribution to Dennis Paulson's VOICES OF SURVIVAL series may be edited and condensed in all editions throughout the world, including the book's serialization (excerpts published in magazines, etc.)."

Alone, we shall surely fail. But by now learning to work together more, as a global family, we *can* still avoid our own annihilation. And as Indira Gandhi warned in these pages: "Those who know the disastrous consequences of a nuclear war *must* make themselves heard. Silence at this juncture is treason against humankind." George Kennan, former U.S. Ambassador to Russian and emeritus professor at Princeton's Institute for Advanced Study, seconded that with his own plea that every one of us "neglect nothing—no effort, no unpleasantness, no controversy, no sacrifice—which could conceivably help to preserve us from committing this supreme and final folly."

In behalf of all 120 voices of survival in this visionary first volume, I thank you very much, indeed, for joining your energy with ours in whatever ways you can to help us *quickly* awaken the widest possible, worldwide audience...in order to finally build the unprecedented people's movement necessary for their (and our) survival. What we do will determine whether we have a history.

May we *all* enjoy long, healthy lives, in lasting peace. And may Earth's unborn generations one day smile on us for initiating the substantially new manner of thinking which allowed humankind to survive. Carry it on...with love.

DENNIS PAULSON,
Santa Barbara, California

Editor's Note

From a writer's perspective, organizing this initial volume of VOICES OF SURVIVAL has been a labor of love from the beginning. Not only are 120 of our world's most influential leaders standing heart-to-heart in an unprecedented, global polylogue on this ultimate issue, but each brings unique experience to bear in trying to answer the largest questions of our time...and probably of all time.

First and foremost, I'd like to acknowledge a special debt of gratitude to the 'critical mass' of early contributors—this volume's true visionaries—who not only saw the potential I'd imagined, but through their own commitment, allowed others to do the same... Carl Sagan, Bernard Lown, Indira Gandhi, Hannes Alfven, Michael York, Olaf Palme, Andrei Sakharov, Erich Honecker, His Holiness the Dalai Lama, Viktor Afanasyev, Niko Tinbergen, Maria Barreno, Willy Brandt, Roger Sperry, Dudley Moore, Paul Ehrlich, et al.

In conceiving this project for responding to the nuclear challenge in a psychologically-constructive manner, I've tried to prepare the emotional context for interpersonal openness by moving beyond the impersonal shortly after approaching those I'd chosen. And in nearly every case, my initiative has been welcomed and even rewarded.

Positive emotions and relations are now the *key* to preventing the world's destruction, and I've been humbled and overwhelmed by these 120 noble beings' generous outpourings. Beyond their statements, a number sent unsolicited financial support, recognizing the project's breadth. Viktor Afanasyev outlined the entire project to 2.5 million readers (mainly intellectuals) of Russia's *Literaturnaya Gazeta*, as well as in *Pravda*, which he edits. Arthur Clarke sent cover and other suggestions. Marilyn Ferguson, Michael Nagler, Linda Blitz, Scott Meredith, Michael York, Phillip Berman, Dudley Moore, Yvonne MacKenzie, Noel Young and Lynnette Pennings, in particular, gave helpful advice on content and style. Bernard Lown and Jules Masserman hand-carried invitations to driving forces in the Soviet Union, who promptly responded. Masserman even offered an opportunity to visit Russia, while His Holiness the Dalai Lama offered prayers for the project's success. And an impressive number moved through the editing process into friendship itself.

Two of these, Michael York and Dudley Moore, both premier, Oxford-trained performing artists, offered to help organize promoting VOS through the media, particularly TV talk shows such as *Tonight, Today, Merv Griffin, Donahue,* etc., guaranteeing that no book in America would receive greater national TV promotion. The list of metagestures is truly endless, as most contributors are now actively promoting this volume in every way they can. Such magnificent cooperation, internationally—usually reserved for dream states —is testament to what *can* be done.

Finally, I'm grateful to Scott Meredith, the world's number one literary agent, for guiding VOS (and its sequels) through the publishing dance; to Noel Young at Capra Press, for his prescient courage in launching this critical first volume, as well as for offering its final title, and to Lynnette Pennings, who became my left brain during a particularly important stage of the book's four-year preparation.

I thank each and every one of you, from the bottom of my soul, for your wisdom, skillful methods, and compassion for living beings everywhere, so beautifully reflected in the multicolored threads you've woven into this collective tapestry essaying our survival.

Awaiting Ratification
By the U.S. and S.U....

A Treaty Limiting
Anti-Satellite Weapons

ARTICLE I

Each Party undertakes not to destroy, damage, render inoperable or change the flight trajectory of space objects of other States.

ARTICLE II

1. Each Party undertakes not to place in orbit around the Earth weapons for destroying, damaging, rendering inoperable, or changing the flight trajectory of space objects, or for damaging objects in the atmosphere or on the ground.
2. Each Party undertakes not to install such weapons on celestial bodies, or station such weapons in outer space in any other manner.
3. Each Party undertakes not to test such weapons in space or against space objects.

ARTICLE III

1. For the purpose of providing assurance of compliance with the provisions of this treaty, each Party shall use national technical means of verification at its disposal, in a manner consistent with generally recognized principles of international law.
2. Verification by national technical means shall be supplemented, as appropriate, by such cooperative measures for contributing to the effectiveness of verification by national technical means as the Parties shall agree upon in the Standing Consultative Commission.
3. Each Party undertakes not to interfere with the national technical means of verification of the other Party operating in accordance with paragraph 1 of this Article.
4. Each Party undertakes not to use deliberate concealment measures which impede verification by national technical means of compliance with this treaty.

ARTICLE IV

1. To promote the objectives and implementation of the provisions of this treaty, the Parties shall use the Standing Consultative Commission, established by the Memorandum of Understanding Between the Government of the United States and the Government of the

Union of Soviet Socialist Republics regarding the Establishment of a Standing Consultative Commission of Dec. 21, 1972.

2. Within the framework of the Standing Consultative Commission, with respect to this treaty, the Parties will:

   a. consider questions concerning compliance with the obligations assumed, and related situations which may be considered ambiguous;

   b. provide, on a voluntary basis, such information as either Party considers necessary to assure confidence in compliance with the obligations assumed;

   c. consider questions involving interference with national technical means of verification, and questions involving unintended impeding of verification by national technical means of compliance with the provisions of this treaty;

   d. consider, as appropriate, cooperative measures contributing to the effectiveness of verification by national technical means;

   e. consider possible changes in the strategic situation which have a bearing on the provisions of this treaty, including the activities of other States, and

   f. consider, as appropriate, possible proposals for further increasing the viability of this treaty, including proposals for amendments in accordance with the provisions of this treaty.

ARTICLE V

The Parties undertake to begin, promptly after the entry into force of this treaty, active negotiations with the objective of achieving, as soon as possible, agreement on further measures for the limitation and reduction of weapons subject to limitation in Article II of this treaty.

ARTICLE VI

In order to ensure the viability and effectiveness of this treaty, each Party undertakes not to circumvent the provisions of this treaty, through any other State or States, in any other manner.

ARTICLE VII

Each party undertakes not to assume any international obligation which would conflict with this treaty.

ARTICLE VIII

1. Each Party may propose amendments to this treaty.

2. Agreed amendments shall enter into force, in accordance with the procedures governing the entry into force of this treaty.

ARTICLE IX

This treaty shall be of unlimited duration.

Each Party shall, in exercising its national sovereignty, have the right to withdraw from this treaty if it decides that extraordinary events related to the subject matter of this treaty have jeopardized its supreme interests. It shall give notice of its decisions to the other Party six months prior to withdrawal from the treaty. Such notice shall include a statement of the extraordinary events the notifying Party regards as having jeopardized its supreme interests.

ARTICLE XI

1. This treaty shall be subject to ratification in accordance with the constitutional procedures of each Party.
2. This treaty shall enter into force on the day of the exchange of instruments of ratification.

ARTICLE XII

1. Done in two copies, each in the English and Russian languages, both texts shall be equally authentic.
2. This treaty shall be registered pursuant to Article 102 of the Charter of the United Nations.

•

This document, presently awaiting ratification by the United States and the Soviet Union, was prepared by a panel organized under the auspices of the Union of Concerned Scientists. The participants, whose affiliations are listed for purposes of identification only, were:

KURT GOTTFRIED, Panel Chairperson and member, UCS Board of Directors; professor of physics, Cornell University; former chairperson, Division of Particles and Fields, American Physical Society.

HANS A. BETHE, professor of physics emertius, Cornell University; Nobel laureate in Physics; chief, Theoretical Division, Manhattan Project; member, President's Scientific Advisory Committee (1957-60); Strategic Military Panel (1957-69).

RICHARD L. GARWIN, fellow at IBM's Watson Research Center; member, President's Science Advisory Committee (1962-65 and 1969-72); member, Defense Science Board (1966-69).

NOEL GAYLER (Ret. Adm., USN), former director, National Security Agency; former commander-in-chief, U.S. Forces/Pacific; former deputy chief of Naval Operations (Research and Development).

HENRY W. KENDALL, chairperson, UCS Board of Directors; professor of physics, Massachusetts Institute of Technology.

FRANKLIN A. LONG, emeritus professor of chemistry, Cornell University; former associate director, U.S. Arms Control and Disarmament Agency.

LEONARD C. MEEKER, member, UCS Board of Directors; U.S. Ambassador to Romania (1969-73); Legal Advisor to U.S. State Department (1965-69).

CARL SAGAN, professor of astronomy and space sciences, and director, Laboratory for Planetary Studies, Cornell University.

HERBERT SCOVILLE, JR., deputy director, Research, Central Intelligence Agency (1955-63); president, Arms Control Association.

JOHN STEINBRUNER, director of Foreign Policy Studies, Brookings Institution (1978-present); associate professor of organization and management, Yale University (1976-78).

About the Editor

DENNIS PAULSON, born into an Ohio newspaper-publishing family, first awakened to the true dimension of the nuclear threat in 1960 by visiting Hiroshima and Nagasaki, while serving in Asia as a U.S. paratrooper.

Resuming his formal education, he shortened a four-year journalism program at Ohio State University to four quarters, eventually becoming the youngest full-time newspaper editor in the nation at 21.

Paulson has spent most of the past 24 years working and writing to effect beneficial changes in peoples' attitudes about each other and about our future in the only world we know, writing books on such diverse subjects as: the worldwide consciousness revolution of the Sixties; the beauty and holiness of natural childbirth; the limited effectiveness of Orthodox Western Medicine's symptomatic approach to cancer therapy; how Tibet's wise ones train others to control these rogue elephant minds; a plea to save what is perhaps the most highly advanced spiritual culture on Earth—developed over a millennium atop the Himalaya—from further desecration by its Chinese 'guests'; a lifetime optimum-health diet, combining the newest nutritional biochemistry with the oldest wisdom from our world's healthiest cultures, as well as the obligatory utopian vision.

Further travel has taken him out of North American for over eight years, to 60 nations, engaging in pursuits as varied as resource engineering in the Middle East; designing English-teaching programs in Spain; studying (and later teaching) Tibetan mind-control meditation in Nepal, India, Australia, Switzerland, England and the U.S.; directing a 215-acre retreat and conference center next door to Reagan's California ranch, and voluntarily chairing a Congressional campaign.

While organizing VOICES OF SURVIVAL over the last four years, Paulson has also become founder/director of the Santa Barbara-based Fasting Center, supervising California's largest, non-residential fasting clientage. He is the father of two children.

PHOTO CREDITS

Grateful acknowledgments to the following photographers for portraits as they appeared on the following pages:

Marvin Lewiton, 20; Godfrey Argent, 27; Sio Photo, 30; Egan O'Connor, 39; Matthew Rolston, 46; Nico Naeff, 50; J.H. Darchinger, 56; Michael Ziegler, 67; Ellis J. Malashuk, 78; Pat York, 83; Kenneth S. Lane, 99; Gary Brothers Fotowest, 101; Blackstone-Shelburne, N.Y., 109; L.C. Shaffer, 128; Clemens Kalischer, 131; Bell Labs News, 138; Nick Crettier, 148; Efrem Yankelevich, 162; Walter Leonardi, 169; Rohan De Silva, 207; Alfred Bernheim, 211; A. Bruce Goldman, 222; Leonard L. Greif, Jr., 226; D.A. Land, 231; Richard Bermack, 243; Kevin Sidel, 250; Multiple Photos, 255; Toni, 258; Serviz Fotografico, Arturo Mari, 264; Gilbert Johnson, 284.

A Song of Peace

This is my song, O God of all the nations,
A song of Peace for lands afar and mine;
This is my home, The country where my heart is
Here are my hopes, My dreams, my holy shrine;
But other hearts in other lands are beating
With hopes and dreams as true and high as mine.

My country's skies are bluer than the ocean,
And sunlight beams on clover leaf and pine.
But other lands have sunlight too, and clover,
And skies are ev'ry where as blue as mine.
O, hear my song, thou God of all the nations,
A song of Peace for their land and for mine.

—JEAN SIBELIUS, *Finnish composer*

Add *your* voice for survival;
help educate those we now *must!*

This book is a tool . . . the single most comprehensive, up-to-date, effective teaching tool in four decades for finally building, internationally, the massive people's movement necessary to give politicians the *will* to stop this mad race toward oblivion.

As we're all *equally* threatened, we *all* must share this educational responsibility. These 120 noble men and women have provided all the wisdom and skillful methods necessary to prevent humankind's self-annihilation. *Spreading* their message is now up to *each* of us.

To send copies to those we *must* now educate—legislators at local, state and federal levels; future leaders at college, high school and even grade school levels; friends, relatives and our closest loved ones, as well as decision-makers at every level of the military-industrial complex . . . *all* of whom will incinerate as fast as you and I—please take a moment from your busy schedule.

The publisher has agreed to pay the mailing cost. Simply send the price of this book, for *each* intended recipient, to: Capra Press, VOS Order Dept., Box 2068, Santa Barbara, CA 93101 (805-966-4590).

In Europe, send to: Wisdom Publications, 23 Dering St., London WIR 9AA, England.

Enclosed, find money order or check for $_____, for _____ copies of VOICES OF SURVIVAL, to (please print):

To: _____   To: _____

_____   _____

_____   _____

To: _____   To: _____

_____   _____

_____   _____

To: _____   From: _____

_____   _____

_____   _____